oe

CHALLENGES TO THE
WESTERN
ALLIANCE

CHALLENGES TO THE
WESTERN
ALLIANCE

AN INTERNATIONAL SYMPOSIUM ON THE CHANGING POLITICAL, ECONOMIC AND MILITARY SETTING

Edited by Joseph Godson
for the Center for Strategic and International
Studies, Georgetown University, Washington, DC
and

TIMES BOOKS LIMITED, LONDON

First published by
Times Books Ltd.,
16 Golden Square,
London, W.1.

© Times Newspapers Limited, London 1984

Five additional essays are extracts from papers
to be included in a forthcoming Westview-CSIS
joint publication *The Future of NATO and Global Security*

British Library Cataloguing in Publication Data
Challenges to the western alliance
    1. North Atlantic Treaty Organization
    2. Godson, Joseph
    355'.031'091821   UA646.3
    ISBN   0-7230-0264-9

Typesetting by Nene Phototypesetters Ltd, Northampton
and Swanston Typesetting, Derby

Printed and bound in Great Britain

CONTENTS

PART 4
Public opinion and NATO

PART 5
Regional security problems outside the alliance

PART 6
Summit views on East-West and West-West relations

PART 7
Is Western civilization an obsolete concept?

PART 8
Appendices

PREFACE

This book reproduces, with later additions and substantial enlargements, the texts of a series of essays published between January and June, 1984, in *The Times*, London. It also contains major extracts from five lengthy papers (pages 6, 51, 80, 100, 125) commissioned by Georgetown University's Center for Strategic and International Studies (CSIS) in connection with its multinational conference convened in Brussels, Belgium, January 12-14 of this year. Also included are important excerpts from the keynote address delivered at that conference by former United States Secretary of State, Henry A. Kissinger.

The Times' series and the CSIS conference were both conceived in connection with the 35th anniversary of the Atlantic alliance and the political, economic and security problems which have arisen of late between the United States and Europe. Differing perceptions within the alliance about the nature of the Soviet threat are evident in a host of areas; the requirements of defence and arms control have become increasingly intertwined; economic issues and differing interests are impacting on Western security as rarely before; and the role of public opinion, both in financing needed defence increases and in managing complex issues of nuclear weapons and arms control, is becoming increasingly important.

The agenda of the CSIS Brussels conference and *The Times'* symposium, which ran over a five-month period, bore especially in mind that the survival of NATO as a viable alliance is increasingly being challenged by a shift in the strategic balance of power, as well as by global events and contingencies that extend far beyond NATO's boundaries, especially in the Middle East and Latin America.

Some of the issues facing NATO – and Western states, in general – are familiar, and on the whole, quite well managed; others are breaking new ground, or putting new strains on the capacities of existing processes and procedures. The need to review past assumptions has become obvious for some time, as has the need to project global trends to the future and to plan accordingly with NATO and in conjunction with other Western allies, like Japan.

The major purpose of the CSIS conference and *The Times'* series was to concentrate on identifying and analysing those issues most salient to NATO as it moves into the remainder of the twentieth century, and to explore ways of strengthening the network of transatlantic communication that might help the West meet future challenges.

Among those invited to contribute to *The Times'* series were some heads of governments, leading academic experts, parliamentarians and representatives of industry and labour. The participants were especially asked to think out loud – even the unthinkable – about the future, rather than recycle existing and well-known statements of position. In other words, the hope was expressed that the series of contributions would prove stimulating, provocative and forward-looking, in order to make the maximum impact on public opinion. We believe that this has proven to be the case and are glad to record that Lord Carrington, the new Secretary General of NATO, shares this view, as do many of the readers of *The Times*.

The editor of *The Times*, Mr. Charles Douglas-Home, and I are most grateful to the distinguished contributors to this volume, on all sides of the oceans, for their thoughtful analyses and assessments, which, it is hoped, will stimulate further discussion of some of the old and new issues that are likely to plague the West in the months and years ahead.

Finally, a note of special thanks, for the considerable patience and help in seeing through the project to the very end, is due to the efforts of Liz Seeber, executive assistant to the editor of *The Times*, and to the members of the paper's staff, too numerous to mention here.

Joseph Godson
London, 1984

INTRODUCTION

Charles Douglas-Home
EDITOR OF *THE TIMES*

Anniversaries should not simply involve retrospection. They help to put contemporary situations in a more understandable historical setting. They also give focus to the future perspective, by endowing the dynamics of contemporary events with some sense of direction – whence and whither – so that we can all appreciate that the present is but a single moment in the great cycle of time.

Thus, in celebrating NATO's 35th anniversary we have to remember the international circumstances which led to the creation of the alliance in 1949, in order both to assess its remarkable success over the last 35 years, and to question and explore its continuing relevance to most of its members today.

It was with this purpose in mind that *The Times* commissioned a series of articles, published throughout the first half of the anniversary year. The series now appears, expanded and enlarged in book form. Our contributors range widely over the significance of the anniversary. They place emphasis on different aspects of the alliance, both in its past development and in their recommendations for its most likely or appropriate future preoccupations. However, none seeks to deny that it was the existence of a threat in 1949 which caused the formation of the alliance and that such a threat continues to exist today. Superficially the nature, intensity and direction of that threat may have changed, but its fundamental existence remains unquestioned.

What was that threat? What is it today? And how and where does its contemporary character condition different responses from different members of the alliance? There are many answers to these questions within the series.

We have to begin by recalling that in 1949 the European Recovery Programme initiated by the United States had been going for two years. European society in 1945 had been threatened with a disintegration as total as the physical destruction of war-torn Europe, but the collapse of liberal politics had not been accompanied by any collapse in the discipline and preparation of the communist parties, which were ready to take over.

The threat in 1947 was not that the Red Army would continue to march westward, but that the Soviet Union would be able, by political means, to achieve the same strategic objective – the Sovietisation of war-torn Europe. However, the very success of the European Recovery Programme seemed to lead to communist coups in Eastern Europe, and to a natural fear in the West that the Soviets, having been thwarted in their attempts to subvert Western Europe from within, might choose to intimidate its further political recovery by the proximity of enormous military force which had been maintained from the war while the Western allies had already substantially demobilized.

The treaty thus helped to bind the United States to Europe, both to deter Soviet leaders from thinking that they could use the Red Army to expand their zone of control, and to reassure Western European members of NATO that, in the development of an active political culture, they would not be intimidated by the proximity of the Red Army in the same way as Finland has been intimidated on many occasions since its uncomfortable treaty with the Soviet Union in 1948.

It is worth recalling this aspect of the treaty because with the passage of time it tends to be forgotten in favour of too strict an analytical approach to the threat of formal invasion from the East. If 'the threat', which resulted in the creation of NATO, had been confined to an expectation of formal full-scale invasion then, understandably, confidence in the need for a fully manned defensive alliance, let alone a perception of its relevance to the future, would be easy to undermine as time and peace contributed to the apparent remoteness of such a threat.

A subtler strategic perception is required. That is why it is sensible to recall that the circumstances of 1949 are not so different fundamentally from the circumstances of 1984 in at least one respect: that the Soviet Union still seeks to intimidate and manipulate the course of events wherever it can by use of military power, military proxies or just the threat of their use. Though the actual perception of the likelihood of Warsaw Pact forces carrying out a direct attack on West Germany might vary enormously within the alliance, the common view, which one can sense in this series of essays, is that Soviet power and Soviet strategy is inherently malign and will exploit weakness wherever it can find it.

Now, because the alliance has been so successful for three and a half decades, the Soviet Union has been forced to react to the fact of European strength without letting up on its search for weaknesses. There are two consequences from this reaction. The first, within the alliance, is that the very success of deterrence and alliance cohesion over 35 years has inevitably led to some lowering of our guard. It has led to more disagreements about the nature and direction of the threat, and even in the wings, to some element of public opinion questioning the need for an alliance at all.

Secondly, in Soviet strategy, the success of NATO maintaining formal defences has led to two natural tactical reponses. One has been to attempt to weaken alliance resolve from within, by fomenting political unrest wherever possible and encouraging all kinds of doubts about the United States, whose membership of the alliance and continuing commitment to it is an absolute *sine qua non* of its past and future. The other response has been to try to weaken the strategic position of the West by threatening its line of naval communications – hence the growth in Soviet maritime power – its access to raw materials in the Middle East, southern Africa and south-east Asia, and the freest possible movement of people and trade in the Third World as a whole.

In both cases the response within the alliance has been varied, as our essays show. There is bound to be some political complacency in Europe after the successful regeneration of the European economies in the absence of war. Moreover, there are few votes to be had in pessimism. But differences in the attitudes on each side of the Atlantic go deeper than that.

On the European side can be seen the view that the deterrence of war and instability in Europe is NATO's primary purpose, in which the focus inevitably centres on the frontier between East and West – from Norway to Turkey. The Atlantic view, on the other hand, springs from a wider strategic perception of the struggle between East and West. In that the security of the front line is only one part of the whole. Hence we see attempts to develop a much greater readiness in NATO to construct an out-of-area role and, on the part of the United States, a desire to remind Europeans that the struggle with Moscow is a world wide one, in which the successful containment of the military threat in Europe could too easily be undermined by an unwillingness to see the whole picture. In that picture the economic and social struggle with Marxism in the long-term is probably even more important than the military one; but they all go together.

35 YEARS OF NATO

A message from
Lord Carrington

Institutions are rather fond of anniversaries. The thing can be over-done, and 35 is not traditionally one of the great milestones on the road to distinction. But 35 years of peace with freedom in the difficult political circumstances of post war Europe is no mean achievement; and NATO can be justly proud of its contribution. Besides, the celebrations provide a fitting occasion for the alliance to pay well-deserved tribute to Joseph Luns; and I enjoyed by way of bonus an unprecedented flow of good advice across the breakfast table as *The Times'* special series of articles unfolded.

As Secretary General designate, I see myself as a reader rather than a contributor. My message will therefore be short.

The parties to the North Atlantic Treaty expressed in its preamble their determination to safeguard the freedom, common heritage and civilisation of their peoples, founded on the principles of democracy, individual liberty and the rule of the law. Their success is a matter of record. We owe it to a partnership between North America and Western Europe which will be just as important in the years to come.

The alliance is by no means the only manifestation of this partnership, but it is fundamental. NATO will have to face new challenges and adapt to new circumstances, as it has in the past. But its two main functions will remain as they were described in the Harmel Report at the end of 1967: first, to maintain adequate military strength and political solidarity to deter aggression and other forms of pressure, and to defend the territory of member states if aggression should occur; second, to pursue the search for progress towards a more stable relationship in which the underlying political issues can be solved.

These functions are not alternatives. If we neglect the first, we shall not succeed in the second; while to succeed in the first alone would be to fall short of the quality of peace we would like our children to enjoy. Meanwhile, the allies have made it clear at the highest level that none of our weapons will ever be used except in response to attack; we do not seek to deny to others the security we want for ourselves; the door to dialogue and negotiation is open and will remain so.

The strength of the alliance will continue to depend on the shared commitment of its member states to these general principles and objectives. My own view is that this shared commitment is still very much there – which is not to say that it will always translate easily into agreed solutions to problems such as those which have been discussed in these articles. But we have good reason to face the future with confidence.

London
May 29, 1984

PART ONE

A global approach to Western security

THE WEST AND ITS VITAL INTERESTS

Lord Home of the Hirsel
FORMER BRITISH PRIME MINISTER

On the evidence of the 20th century, foresight is not a gift with which man is well endowed.

Early in the 1960s the British government sent a military expedition to quell a revolt against the Tanzanian government of Mr. Nyerere. When the action was successfully concluded I asked Lord Mountbatten on how many such occasions since the end of the war in 1945 had we sent out armed forces abroad, and in how many cases had the situation been foreseen? His answer was 48 – and none!

In the remaining sixteen years of this century what factors of political strategy are sufficiently predictable for the Western allies to pay a military insurance premium in advance? Some general assumptions seem to be valid.

The Soviet communist doctrine that the use of force is legitimate to achieve a political aim will continue. Moscow will still pursue a global policy of supporting revolutionary movements to undermine Western influence and extend its own. Nuclear weaponry will still be part of the military structure of both the Warsaw Pact and NATO; the defensive and offensive power of conventional arms will have been developed and improved. The Western allies will have added to their armoury of such weapons, and the Russians will have done so too.

It is likely that NATO will have retrieved some of the present deficiency in that respect, but the balance of power is unlikely to have been significantly changed.

Do these general forecasts mean that the outlook is stalemate?

It is probably reasonable to expect that there will be some modification in Russia's military deployment. However, every possibility has to be qualified by a 'but'. . . .

The Marxist revolution is more than 60 years old, but the decisively military twist given to it by Stalin still has priority. Russia, in the words of Mr. Chernenko, has to be made 'invincible'. It will denounce imperialism, but will continue to keep its grip on the *cordon sanitaire* of Eastern Europe and Afghanistan. Strategic nuclear weapons are likely to be reduced, but a large overkill retained.

The economic situation inside Russia should, on any reasonable calculation, limit its scope to subsidise these countries which it uses to

2

promote revolution at second-hand (Cuba, for example, is a heavy drain on its resources), but there is a strong feeling of nationalism in Russia on which the Kremlin can call for discipline, even to the point of a tightening of belts.

On the available evidence, Russia, by the year AD 2000, although facing considerable difficulties, will remain immensely powerful militarily. NATO, therefore, will not be able to lower its guard. Too much will be at stake, for if law and order, and political stability, were to be broken in Europe and the Atlantic, there would be chaos everywhere. The defence of Europe, the Atlantic Ocean and North America must, therefore, continue to be given priority by Britain and its allies, while they pursue what is called 'détente'.

The basic difficulty of agreeing on anything in the political military field with the Russian Communists will continue to be that they deal in ideology, and that they do not speak the same language or hold the same values as do the democracies.

Mr. Brezhnev's definition of détente, to which Mr. Chernenko subscribes, is a convincing illustration. Brezhnev talked of it as a continuing aspect of the global 'struggle' and 'confrontation', and forecast that both would have to be intensified. No democratic statesman could conceivably talk of 'confrontation' and 'struggle' in the context of détente, the essence of which is not aggression, but compromise and co-existence. To add to the dilemma of the democracies, this Russian interpretation embraces the whole world, from Vietnam and Cambodia, through Ethiopia and Angola to El Salvador.

The Soviet leaders have two options between now and the next century; and both are consistent with communist doctrine. They can maintain political and military pressure upon the European and Atlantic front, or they can deliberately create a tactical lull, in which they would concentrate their propaganda on insisting that it is the West which threatens aggression, and that Russia is the aggrieved peace-maker. They are likely to seek the best of both worlds. They will aim to split the NATO alliance by trying to persuade the European members that it is no longer in their interest to tie themselves to the United States, and at the same time they will use cats' paws to keep the pot of social unrest in the world at large on the boil.

The communist threat of subversion and takeover is undoubtedly global, and the Western allies will have to decide whether NATO as such should adapt its policy to meet it by operating outside the original treaty area.

In this context, it is worth recalling that Russia has had its setbacks. Egypt escaped Soviet clutches; in Angola the tenure of Cuban troops hangs in the balance; Mozambique has gone sour and has marked its protest by co-operation with South Africa; Ethiopia is restive; and

3

generally the Soviet invasion and continued occupation of Afghanistan has shocked the Third World.

Those who are ready to organise self-defence can properly and profitably be helped. NATO could not be a universal policeman, but there are strategic interests of the West with which communist Russia cannot be allowed to interfere.

Such situations include interference with the freedom of the seas; action to disrupt the passage of oil from the Gulf, or essential minerals from southern Africa; and an attack on any country to defend the security of which NATO is pledged.

Once such Western interests are identified, the important thing is that they should be defined with precision, so that the Russian leaders understand the limits they cannot exceed without calling forth forceful retaliation. Communists will adapt their policies to conform to plain and inescapable reality. It is on the uncertainty and irresolution of their opponents that they thrive and make hay.

There remains the question of whether NATO is the right body to assume these new responsibilities, which go beyond its original obligations. To do so would certainly conform to the facts of life, as it is NATO which stands between the free world and a possible takeover by force. The only argument against the use of this particular umbrella is the survival of the myth of neo-colonialism, which might in some instances prejudice NATO's effectiveness.

The alternative is that the leading NATO countries which possess the resources should, on an ad hoc basis, combine for the defence of common interests. The pattern would be that of the American task force off the Gulf, to which a British unit is attached and adapted as required in any given situation.

If Soviet coups on the pattern of Angola and Grenada are to be anticipated and avoided, it will be necessary for countries situated in areas of strategic consequence to make contingency plans. The Caribbean archipelago is an obvious example. The volume and value of trade which passes through that area is enormous and had the Cubans, with Soviet support, been able to establish themselves across the trade routes, and in proximity to the Panama Canal, the disruption caused would have been traumatic.

All West Indian countries, as well as the United States, Canada and Britain, have an interest in the political and economic stability of that area. So too in the South Pacific. In that complex of islands, newly independent and with few defences, many are vulnerable to Soviet infiltration and takeover. Australia and New Zealand, Singapore and Malaysia should be acutely conscious of the threat that could be mounted to freedom of passage through those seas. So, too, should Japan.

NATO, or those countries of the alliance which have the means, can take on a lot of the work necessary to ensure that communist Russia does not strangle free democratic peoples. Nevertheless, none can rest in comfort until others put teeth into regional collective security.

Finally, it can be little use to plan for the periphery if the core of the alliance falters.

Whenever (as will be inevitable) there are discussions and debates on the proportions of responsibility which Europe and America should carry, it will be necessary to remember one fact. In two wars in this century against a first-class power it took the combined might of Europe and America to win. To deter Russia from aggression Europe or America will not be enough. Both will be required. That truth should be written in emphatic capital letters over the chair of the Secretary General at every NATO Council meeting and should be given equal prominence in the Foreign and Defence Ministries of each member of the alliance.

On the unity and cohesion of NATO the peace of the world depends.

THE SOVIET DIMENSION

William G. Hyland
EDITOR OF *FOREIGN AFFAIRS*

East–West relations are bad. The outlook is for a further deterioration. This state of affairs represents a continuation and deepening of the trend that began with the invasion of Afghanistan. The responsibility rests to a major degree on the aggressiveness of Soviet policy which, in turn, has reflected the Soviet view of the consequences of a favourable change in the 'correlation of forces'. But it also reflects a growing confusion and uncertainty in the West over the nature of Soviet policy and how to deal with it.

There are sound reasons for believing that the present is a transitional period in East–West relations. The détente phase of East–West relations has virtually ended for both Europe and the United States. But the character of the next period remains to be seen. It could develop into a major confrontation of global dimensions. Alternatively, it could evolve into a significant easing of tensions. Or it could remain a mixed relationship with elements of conciliation and confrontation coexisting.

Soviet factors in themselves (especially internal developments) will be of major importance, but the direction is not a choice solely for the Kremlin. In a broad sense the future direction of East–West relations will depend more on the West; on the ability of the Atlantic allies to develop an effective strategy over a protracted period. In the winter of 1983–84 there was no such strategy. This unfortunate fact happens to coincide with a gathering crisis in the Soviet empire, with potential changes in the policies of the major Asian powers – China and Japan – and the financial–economic crisis in the Third World. In short, it is a time of unusual fluidity in world affairs, but for the West it could prove to be a time of unusual opportunities.

The objectives of Soviet foreign policy do not change often. There is a staggering continuity. Moscow's attitude toward the division of Europe into two spheres, for example, has not been altered greatly since the Yalta Conference in 1943. Nor do the main elements affecting the formulation of Soviet policy change much. Military power is as important for Chernenko or Andropov as for Brezhnev and Stalin. Propaganda, agitation, threats and peace campaigns have become all too familiar. What has changed, and will continue to change, is the international environment in which Soviet policy must operate. Soviet policy yields to objective factors (including Russian geography), even as it seeks to shape these factors. Soviet policy also yields to internal factors, but the causal relationship between foreign policy and the domestic situation is far more difficult to interpret. And, finally, Russian history plays an important role (which some observers believe is decisive).

Soviet policy in Europe has been animated by two clear aims: the preservation of Soviet dominance in Eastern Europe, and the weakening of the Western coalition, especially the links between the United States and Europe. The Soviets have succeeded in retaining their dominance in the East, while failing at every major turning point to wreck the Western alliance. On the whole, however, the Soviet Union has made gains in expanding its influence over the policies of Western Europeans, mainly through the policy of détente as pursued during the 1970s. It was in this period that the Soviets believed that they secured the ratification of their concept of a divided Europe. And it was in this period that Soviet policy began to undermine the American–European connection, as the American nuclear guarantee began to lose credibility and American attempts to restore that credibility threatened the European gains of détente and strained the alliance. In addition, the Soviet leadership seemed to assume that in Europe they had a relatively free hand in the military sphere. Hence, their build-up of the force of SS-20s was not accompanied by even a minimal effort to consult or appease their détente partners.

The great irony of détente was that the temporary Soviet gains in the West came to be offset by a massive crisis in the East. There is good reason to believe that the Polish crisis was in some part the result of the relaxation of European tensions. The upheaval was not simply another periodic Polish disturbance but a far-reaching crisis of empire. The Polish communist party collapsed almost overnight and Poland came close to a genuine, anti-communist revolution. The outcome is still open. But the forced reliance on military rule, almost 40 years after the creation of the Lublin government, is a profound shock to the Soviet system. The spread of the spirit of Solidarity must be a spectre haunting the Kremlin.

The new crisis of East Europe coincided with a major defeat for Soviet policy in Western Europe, as the deployment of American missiles began and has continued. Neither blandishments nor threats proved effective in dissuading the alliance from altering the basic strategic situation in Europe for the first time since the founding of NATO and the rearmament of Germany.

In sum, in Europe the USSR confronts a double crisis which happens to occur at the very time when the Kremlin enters a leadership succession period, which in itself may be a prolonged crisis.

To be sure, the missile crisis in Europe is not over. Given the long period of scheduled deployments, the Soviet Union will have ample opportunity to affect the outcome. In particular, there is an opportunity

7

to freeze the situation after the first phase, which could produce a situation in which the Soviets retain large missile forces in Western Europe, but the West settles for tokenism.

Soviet policy will also reflect Moscow's appraisal of its possibilities in dealing with the United States. These relations have obviously deteriorated, to the point that there is little content. No serious dialogue; no economic relationship; no bilateral exchange. The relationship has been progressively reduced to little more than grain trade and the remnants of older arms control talks. And even these few remaining links are in jeopardy. The change in Soviet–American relations dates to early 1980 when the United States reacted to the invasion of Afghanistan. This marked, effectively, the end of détente. The Reagan administration in its approach has acted on this conclusion – seeking primarily to redress what it considered to be a highly unfavourable strategic military balance before trying to revive any elements of détente. This remained the thrust of American policy until the summer of 1983, when American officials began to espouse a slightly more conciliatory line, looking toward a possible Reagan–Andropov summit. In this sense, the timing of the Korean airline crisis of September 1983 was critical. (In the wake of the airline tragedy, both the United States and the Soviet Union, for obvious reasons, have tended to deny that there were any prospects for a significant improvement in the summer of 1983.) In any case, it is apparent that the Soviets have decided to freeze their relations with Washington. Even this line may depend on another factor, in the near term: the state of the succession struggle in Moscow.

It appears that Soviet policy towards China is also in a state of flux. The appearance of the Chinese foreign minister at Brezhnev's funeral gave rise to premature speculation of a major breakthrough. While tending in this direction, Andropov's initial approach was somewhat reserved. He moved slowly and cautiously into talks, but polemics did not stop. Not until late in the summer of 1983 did Andropov make a major offer to Peking for a better relationship. The Chinese reciprocated, having already softened their preconditions; but they also moved toward the United States, thus placing themselves in a position to dominate the triangular relationship.

In the Third World, the Soviets face opportunities. In the Middle East, the Lebanese debacle put the United States on the defensive. In Central America the United States faced an increasingly complicated situation. Attempts to deal with it, as in Grenada, had the effect of reviving the American–European controversy over American priorities. In Grenada the Europeans once again deserted the United States and charged that American behaviour jeopardized higher objectives in Europe. But no strategic breakthrough is likely for the USSR. Moscow remained stalemated in Afghanistan, in particular. Soviet policy thus confronts a traditional mix of opportunities and challenges. The chief new factor is that it does so with new leaders.

During the 1970s détente became the norm in Europe; a condition not subject to reversal except for the most serious of causes. In the United States, on the other hand, there was a growing revolt against détente. The differences were latent until the shock of the invasion of Afghanistan in December 1979 revealed American–European differences over East–West strategy. The United States read the invasion as a major departure in policy and an ominous harbinger of a new Soviet aggressiveness. Sanctions against the USSR were therefore a minimal reaction. Europeans saw it differently, more as an episode than a watershed.

There was perhaps some justification for differences within the alliance over a relatively remote area, but the same basic trend reappeared in late 1981, in the reaction to Poland when General Jaruzelski imposed martial law. The Europeans argued for *realpolitik*, this time even citing the Yalta agreement as the rationale for their unwillingness to respond. The Reagan administration magnified the crisis by its insistence on a policy of selective sanctions against the USSR, including terminating the Soviet gas pipeline. The Europeans saw Washington as excessively punitive, if not hypocritical, in the light of continuing American grain sales. The net effect was to leave the United States dismayed and embittered by the persistent European rationalization of Soviet advances. At issue is not simply the question of sanctions, but how to deal with the East.

The Europeans are obviously increasingly concerned by the rising tensions. Both the United States and Europe are aware that the decline in the credibility of the American strategic deterrent means that a war could conceivably be confined to Europe. Both agree on the need to redress the European balance in intermediate missiles as well as to recouple American forces to the continent; the Europeans, however, place much greater emphasis on an accommodation through arms control.

In short, Europeans viewed the primary task as managing Soviet decline; Americans saw the task as encouraging, if not accelerating it.

One effect of the European dissent has been to strengthen the views of those in America who see a dwindling area of common interests with Europe. Indeed, what began as a questioning of European policies on specific issues has spread in some cases to a questioning of the value of the entire alliance. On both the right and left, some argue that the United States' interests are no longer served by the continuation of the alliance.

As a parallel, in Europe there seems to be growing disenchantment with the United States. Some Europeans openly advocate decreasing dependence on America. Many express a renewed interest in an independent political entity, which must necessarily have an anti-

Atlanticist definition; some toy with the notion of a separate European nuclear deterrent. Europeans appear to believe that somehow they can reduce their dependence on the United States without stimulating American neo-isolationist sentiment. They argue – much too confidently – that the United States has no viable option other than the commitment to Europe. Prominent Americans counter that it is time for significant change in the alliance, before a disaster occurs.

Without a common evaluation of the East–West contest, which remains at the heart of the alliance's rationale and is the justification for its enormous and costly military effort, the trend toward separation between America and Europe is likely to continue. Each clash in the contest with Moscow risks accelerating the Atlantic separation.

It is easy to argue that the West should quickly compose its differences. It is another matter to describe a common basis that would satisfy both sides of the Atlantic. There is no 'European' opinion as such. Nor is there a single, dominant view in the United States. Nevertheless, it should still be possible to set forth a basic strategy, without necessarily agreeing on all of the tactics.

The immediate tactical choices must be left to the officials involved. Outside observers can offer only limited advice. Similarly, in prescribing for the long term, official agencies are as capable as academic institutions. It is for the medium-term, that outside advice may be of some value.

In examining the medium-term, two general assumptions should be made: firstly, that the relationship with the USSR will remain basically adversarial and competitive; in other words, no significant transformation of the contest is likely; secondly, that the basic western policy will be one of resistance to the expansion of Soviet power and influence.

In sum, the basic decisions for the medium-term are whether NATO should concentrate on establishing a new relationship with the East, or concentrate more on tending to its own problems, waiting for a more favourable moment to activate East–West relations. The answer depends on how the Western governments view the future: the changes in the military and political balance, western internal evolution (including domestic political trends), and, finally, an appreciation of the trends in Soviet politics and policy. On balance, the period of transition in the Soviet Union would seem an ideal moment for taking any soundings of the Kremlin.

BASIC STEPS TO STRENGTHEN THE ALLIANCE

Henry A. Kissinger
FORMER US SECRETARY OF STATE

There are two conventional ways of speaking about NATO. The first is to praise its achievements: the peace that has been maintained for 35 years; the co-operation between sixteen sovereign nations that has been sustained for longer than any modern alliance; the crises that have been overcome; and most recently the decision that was upheld to redress the nuclear balance in Europe.

Alternatively, it is also possible to deplore the unresolved issues: the gap between the announced military strategy and what is being implemented; the imbalance between détente and defence; the pace and direction of arms control; and the growing mistrust – nurtured by the Soviets – between a generation of Americans and Europeans who have lived their entire lives sheltered by the alliance they assault.

In the public debate within the alliance it has become nearly axiomatic that East–West relations have never been worse. Many Europeans profess to be convinced that American unpredictability and changeability have combined with confrontational and bellicose rhetoric to drive the Soviets into resentful hostility. Many Americans are of the opinion that European irresolution and domestic weakness encourage the Soviet assault on the post-war political balance in Europe.

As in all family quarrels there has been an element of truth on both sides. Since the collapse of the post-war consensus during the Vietnam War, American policy has been extraordinarily changeable. The détente of the early 1970s was assaulted by an odd and unprecedented coalition of liberals and conservatives who could never have been united but for the collapse of executive authority caused by Watergate. The liberals attacked détente for being too concerned with the balance of power while conservatives damned it for being insufficiently ideological or 'moral'. That coalition succeeded on the one hand in destroying both the incentives and the penalties on which détente was based; on the other hand, still in the thrall of the Vietnam trauma, it was not prepared to face the consequences of renewed Soviet intransigence.

The critics of détente had a point when they argued that the American public was unused to power politics; that there is no tradition in America for conducting relationships simultaneously co-operative and adversary. But that is precisely the challenge before our leaders. Any other course loses public and allied support and enables the Soviets to capture the global yearning for peace – as the Reagan administration has painfully learned.

The Carter administration announced a 'new approach' which criticised the Nixon and Ford administrations for their alleged preoccupation with resisting communism. After at first rejecting the structure of SALT II inherited from the Ford administration, the Carter team embraced it; but delayed so long that the invasion of Afghanistan defeated all prospects of ratification. The current administration arrived in office rejecting the position of all its predecessors. It derided détente, refused to ratify SALT II even while observing its provisions, only to turn in the past year towards an obvious desire to improve East–West relations, even a summit.

The issue here is not what incarnation of American policy was right. Each was professed by reasonable people pursuing reasonable arguments. The trouble has been that each new administration has felt no responsibility to the legacy of its predecessor; indeed has prided itself on starting all over. Each reassessment of American policy left victims among European leaders who – trusting American representations and briefings – had committed themselves to the previous dispensation. Each reassessment shook confidence and encouraged European neutralism to become less dependent on our restless quest for novelty.

Nor has the United States been alone in changing its view. Our allies have changed with us though in a contrapuntal manner. When President Nixon came into office he had a reputation as a hard-liner. This triggered a succession of eminent European visitors to urge him into a rapid dialogue with Moscow – even though the invasion of Czechoslovakia was not yet a year old. A few years later some of the same Europeans warned against 'excessive' détente. During the Carter administration it was European leaders who first called attention to the need to counterbalance the Soviet build-up of SS-20s. And the Reagan administration has become almost legendary if one reads the allegations of bellicosity, insensitivity and major responsibility for the current East–West impasse.

And yet amazingly while it is easy to compile a record of ill-considered remarks of the Reagan administration it is difficult to point to much in the way of rash actions. Beyond muscular rhetoric the Reagan administration has actually behaved with considerable restraint. What has it actually *done* to earn such opprobrium among our European critics? Why should intelligent leaders feel impelled to base internal politics on their ability to domesticate, as it were, the Reagan administration? Why has the recent change of tone of the Reagan administration – sometimes verging on the repentant – been largely ignored by critics and most allied leaders? Is it because the critics seek an excuse for a barely disguised neutralism and the leaders require – or believe they require – at least the pretence of 'moderating' American obtuseness and intransigence as a unifying element in their domestic politics?

European critics should remember that the wider the gulf between Europe and the United States, the more difficult an East–West dialogue becomes. And the East–West dialogue urgently needs a fresh impetus. In a world of thousands of nuclear weapons the two sides cannot risk staring each other down or seeking to drown each other's proposals in invective or propaganda. The minimum requirement is that both sides understand each other's thought processes so that crises do not escalate by inadvertence.

For crises are almost inherent in the current structure of international politics. Both superpowers are associated with countries more concerned with their local rivalries than with the global equilibrium, much less with global peace. Our period should not be compared with the period preceding World War II when an aggressor launched himself into a quest for world domination – nuclear weapons are likely to inspire great hesitation, even among the reckless. Rather the appropriate model is the period prior to World War I when client states pursuing regional rivalries drew their protectors into a holocaust by gradual increments, the full significance of which was not understood until it was too late. Which of the statesmen who entered the war in 1914 thinking that the issue would be settled quickly would not have recoiled in horror had he had an inkling of the shape of the world in 1917?

Theoretically, there are as well what the Soviets would call 'objective reasons' for a constructive dialogue. The Soviet system is in trouble. It must deal with a leadership in transition, a decrepit economy and restive allies. By any rational calculation the Soviet Union should seek a respite. It should know that a continuation of its present course runs a large risk of confrontation. Its leaders cannot be so encapsuled in their prejudices as to believe that they can defeat America without our noticing it sooner or later. The longer the process lasts, the more 'successful' current Soviet strategy, the greater is the risk of some escalation.

A number of principles ought to govern Western approaches:

1. Democracies have no reason to fear negotiations with a stagnant and brittle dictatorship. But neither should talk become an end in itself. The importance of a dialogue should therefore not be the subject of debate either within the countries of the alliance or between them. The debate should concern the subjects appropriate to an East–West dialogue, not the fact of it.

2. There is a need for calm in the domestic discourse of the various allies. There is a tendency to adjust the assessment of Soviet strength to preconceived notions of the Soviet Union rather than the other way around. The Soviets are neither as powerful or cunning as the opponents

13

of détente claim; nor are they as close to disintegration as some self-proclaimed apostles of peace allege. History will not do our work for us; but neither will liturgical rhetoric.

3. If we want to avoid that the East–West dialogue divides the alliance or becomes an end in itself, the United States and its allies must agree on a long-term East–West strategy. This will have to include the whole gamut of East–West relations including East–West trade in its opportunities as well as its perils.

4. Arms control cannot possibly carry the entire or even the principal burden of the East–West dialogue. If too much weight is put on arms control, it is more likely – in Lord Carrington's words – to expose the raw nuclear nerve of the alliance than to resolve it. Were Moscow to make a *political* decision to settle for the presence of *some* American nuclear intermediate range weapons in Western Europe, the INF issue could be settled rapidly. As for START, it is my conviction that we have not thought the problem through adequately – but at least we have tried to think while the Soviets have engaged in sterile repetitions of shopworn slogans. Still, even if attitudes should change, it will lead to a prolonged technical haggle; the subject is simply too difficult to permit a rapid resolution. And the best foreseeable outcome would be primarily symbolic. Some twenty thousand strategic warheads are in the arsenals of both sides. Even were the Soviets to accept our proposal to cut this total in half, the remaining warheads would be more than sufficient for catastrophe.

In short, arms control separated from a political dialogue cannot end the current tensions or even significantly ease them. Indeed if the quest for arms control becomes too frantic it will turn into a weapon of Soviet political warfare. Or else it will become a safety valve which the Soviets turn off to increase Western nervousness and on to reduce the impact of a new act of aggression.

5. The urgent need is for a serious *political* dialogue at the highest levels. The so-called confidence-building measures so beloved by professional diplomats cannot advance us very far. The opening of consulates or cultural exchange programmes – even the prenotification of manoeuvres – have at best a peripheral significance. In my experience every real breakthrough occurred by principals or their key aides who then gave marching orders to subordinates.

The problem is how to define the highest level. A premature summit meeting would involve exorbitant risks. Heads of state cannot talk freely at the summit; their constituencies are always with them mentally; sometimes they are even in the room. Summit meetings, moreover, leave little time for real discussion. There is an inevitable time limit imposed by the schedules of the principals; there is an unavoidable protocol; there is the time wasted on translation. The possibilities of a breakthrough are usually outweighed by the penalties of failure. When heads of state disagree, there is no appeal to a higher authority; they would hardly have reached their eminence without a strong ego; abandoning a firmly held position would run counter to psychological as well as political imperatives. Summits can put the finishing touches on agreements reached previously; they are not well suited to break the ice.

One way to avoid this dilemma would be for each side to designate a special representative enjoying the full confidence of his head of government and foreign minister. He should be authorised to conduct private, exploratory conversations on their behalf, preferably without publicity. Each of these special representatives should have access to the head of state of the other side. Both parties would commit themselves to a global review of their entire relationship. As soon as the conversation between the special representatives demonstrates hope for progress, preparations would begin for a summit meeting which would then approve a full-scale work programme for coexistence. But the method is less important – there are several approaches possible – than to decide on the direction.

6. So far, attempts to discuss political problems systematically have been dismissed as 'linkage', and linkage is supposed to be bad because it is alleged to be an obstacle to arms control. By now we should have learned that the opposite is true. Arms control separated from any political context is likely to run into a dead-end. The danger of war after all, resides less in the existence of the weapons of mass destruction than in the minds of the men who are in a position to order their use. And such men will be driven by political conflicts, not systems analyses.

A serious dialogue must come to grips with how coexistence is to be defined. Abstract though this may sound, it is at the heart of the problem. No détente can be sustained if all it does is to give rise to a political offensive designed to unhinge the global balance of power. One can cite several Western failures of omission and commission. But no spurious objectivity, no effort to find both sides equally guilty can overlook the provocations that accelerated the hardening of American attitudes. The dispatch of proxy troops to Angola and Ethiopia; the revolutions in Aden and Afghanistan followed by the occupation of Afghanistan; the Vietnamese invasion of Cambodia; the encouragement of terrorist groups; the massive delivery of arms to Cuba and thence to Central America mark a foreign policy that at least since 1976 has missed no opportunity to undermine Western positions.

I say this not to sabotage hopes for a dialogue but to define its essence. The Soviet Union must decide whether it is a country or a cause. It must be willing to define security in terms other than the impotence of potential adversaries. Some ground rules for coexistence are essential. Once that bridge is crossed, opportunities for increased co-operation in trade and culture would be high on the agenda. And out of such an exchange, progress on arms control would flow naturally, almost inevitably.

7. Such a process requires the restoration of bipartisanship in the United States and an end to the constant 'reassessments' that disquiet our friends and confuse, when they do not embolden, our adversaries. The national interest does not change every four or eight years; at some point it must be fixed in the public mind if we are not to become an element of instability through our endless quest for ever new dispensations. And it is time for our European allies to abandon the charade that their principal foreign policy goal is to moderate an intransigent America – a role more appropriate for neutrals than allies. Those committed to the proposition that the precondition for peace is to insist on the moral equivalence of the two superpowers are, in fact, tempting a continuation of tensions by abdicating their judgment. The same will be true of the impact of those who confuse foreign policy with the liturgical condemnation of our adversary. The Soviets are realists. Sentimentality on the left tempts them into aggression; sentimentality on the right tempts them to exploit domestic and allied divisions.

8. Finally, we in the West must be prepared to face the fact that even with our best efforts a thaw in East–West relations may simply not be on the cards. It is possible that the Soviet leadership is too preoccupied with succession issues to change their intransigent course. Perhaps the emergence of the secret police in leadership positions means that the Soviets are applying intelligence methods to the conduct of foreign policy. They may have come to the conclusion that a relentless political and psychological offensive will wear down the democracies and they may be far from discouraged when they study some Western pronouncements. Or perhaps the whole Soviet system is frozen in inertia.

If any of these hypotheses turns out to be accurate we have no choice except to stand on our best proposals, thoughtfully devised. The West need not panic at a period of deadlock. Its economy for all its shortcomings is more vital; its governmental structure stabler and its overall power greater. The alliance can thus face a period of holding firm with confidence – provided it preserves its unity.

It has become ritualistic to speak of the need for allied unity. It is indeed periodically reaffirmed. But it exhausts itself in tactical agreement. Too rarely – if ever – is there a real attempt to project a strategy for the rest of this century.

And yet that is the single most important problem before the alliance. I do not believe the present structure of NATO lends itself easily to such an effort. And I do not have much confidence in 'wise men' exercises. Still a way must be found to deal with the unsolved issues before us. Nothing is possible without re-examining strategic doctrine without blinking. An approach to arms control must logically parallel this effort. It will be time also to look at the question of whether every NATO deployment decided a generation ago must be sacrosanct for all eternity. East–West relations in all their manifold aspects need a sense of direction. The Reagan administration has in practice abandoned its confrontational style. Our allies need now to avoid using the past as an alibi to avoid difficult choices.

The process is overdue and since it depends on the members of a democratic alliance it provides no excuse for failure. The greatest encouragement to Soviet foreign policy in the West is the lack of clarity of the alliance about its purposes. But that problem being self-made can be undone by our own efforts. Since the democracies have this possibility, it is also their duty.

WESTERN ECONOMIC AND MILITARY COHESION

Alexander M. Haig, Jr.
FORMER US SECRETARY OF STATE

Summarizing the lessons of two world wars for the West, Winston Churchill concluded that only the swift gathering of forces to confront military and moral aggression could preserve the peace. For 35 years, the North Atlantic Treaty Organization has preserved the peace precisely because it represents such a swift gathering of forces. As a direct consequence, two generations have not known war, in dramatic contrast to their parents and grandparents. The members of NATO have been free to prosper in security.

Historic perspective, however, yields the most insights when it looks forward, as well as backward. Clearly, NATO's past is a chronicle of great challenges overcome by ardent effort and ingenious diplomacy. Yet the success of the past need not necessarily be the prelude to an equally successful future. Nations are never immune to the forces of change; they are often susceptible to the tug of conflicting interests. We face today a three-fold challenge: first, the continuous problem of upgrading NATO capabilities in the face of an unrelenting Soviet military build-up; second, an equally difficult problem of harmonizing political perspectives on East–West policy; third, persistent economic problems which, while not inscribed on the alliance agenda, none the less affect NATO's cohesion.

These challenges, of course, are not entirely new. Some are legacies from the 1970s. But they are all affecting – one is tempted to say aggravating – each other. As a consequence, NATO's future success depends upon the adoption of a global approach, one that recognizes both the interdependence of these problems and the need to act in concert even when the formal alliance structure does not entirely cover the issue.

The first challenge is to our deterrence. NATO begins with an understanding of Soviet ambitions and capabilities: the only thing Moscow fears more than democracy is war, especially nuclear war. Alliance policy has therefore always been based on an assessment that a peaceful posture on the Kremlin's part required a balance of power – the power to deter. Ever since the dawn of the nuclear era, that deterrence has meant on the military side a combination of nuclear and conventional forces. On the political side, it meant a linking of the European and American contributions so that the allies shared the 'burden' – not only

18

the expense but also the risk. Together, NATO's capabilities and unity provide the best platform for the diplomacy of reducing tensions with the East.

Over the past decade, NATO's deterrence has been undermined by the well-documented expansion of Soviet military power. NATO has reacted to this challenge only slowly and in stages. We have indulged ourselves in extensive debates over whether the strategy of flexible response was workable instead of supplying the resources – nuclear and conventional – to make it work. Thanks to our recent success in the deployment of theatre-range nuclear missiles we have taken a vital step to improve NATO's credibility. Moscow's attempt to split the United States from Europe through its build-up, combined with a diplomatic crusade intended to exploit public uneasiness over nuclear weapons, has failed. NATO's two-track decision of 1979 – to modernize and to negotiate – has succeeded.

The successful strengthening of this aspect of deterrence, however, should not stand alone. Critics of the alliance have pointed out the short-falls in the conventional force area. There too, as in the nuclear debate, we have indulged ourselves in self-defeating public controversies over burden-sharing, replete with threats to do less unless others do more. Instead, we should be using the existing alliance structure to improve our conventional forces.

Progress in overcoming the challenge to deterrence should also be accompanied by progress in harmonizing differing approaches to East–West relations. Over the past ten years, every member of NATO has come to realize that some of the brighter promises of the détente era have proved to be false, perhaps because the changing military balance has encouraged Soviet ambitions, perhaps because there was less chance for an evolution in Soviet policies than some may have believed. Still, there can be no doubt that one legacy of the détente period was to sharpen a natural, underlying difference of political perspective between the United States and its allies. To put it simply: the political and economic benefits of détente in Europe are clear to most Europeans; the political and military dangers of Soviet adventurism elsewhere in the world are clear to most Americans. The problem is how to preserve the benefits while dealing with the dangers, especially when the dangers are present in areas beyond the geopolitical boundaries of NATO.

Our approach to this problem should recognize that these different perspectives will persist and that any attempt to 'extend' NATO's jurisdiction will dilute the alliance's cohesion long before it adds any strength to the West's position elsewhere in the world. At the same time, NATO's members should realize that certain countries are better able to handle the dangers of Soviet expansionism in Asia, the Middle East and the western hemisphere than others. I am not calling here for automatic endorsement of the United States' or any other country's policies in dealing with crises, such as the Falklands, El Salvador or the Middle East. I am calling for an understanding that Western interests are ultimately at stake, for patient diplomacy to reconcile differences of approach and the consistent leadership that does not leave us wondering about each other's next surprise. The benefit of the doubt should be given to the exponents of freedom not to their detractors.

Our challenge, then, is not to work at cross-purposes based on different perspectives. As always, that remains the easiest course of action. Instead, our obligation is to work together, to try to reconcile these perspectives with the vision of a common interest.

Finally, the security and political challenges facing NATO in the 1980s occur in the context of severe economic difficulties. The industrial democracies of NATO, with their extensive social programmes, have been confronted simultaneously with a Soviet military build-up and persistent economic distress. The perennial choice between guns and butter has become the staple of domestic debate, often threatening to tear apart a hard-won and carefully constructed domestic consensus in more than one country. But this is a false choice. We must be able to defend ourselves and deal with our social problems together, or we shall be able to do neither.

The real issue is to restart the engines of economic growth before everyone succumbs to a disastrous cycle of protectionism. As we have begun again to work together successfully on the challenge to NATO's deterrence, as we strive to harmonize differing perspectives on Soviet challenges in the Third World, so we must also seize the opportunities to resolve our economic difficulties.

In 1984, the agenda has become clear with sudden force: for the United States, to control a deficit that could threaten the economic recovery and to lower interest rates in the process; for Europe, to renew both the promise of the European Community and its industrial growth; for all of us, with Japan, to resist protectionism, non-tariff barriers and other temporary restrictions which could cause permanent damage.

NATO at 35 comprises a group of nations whose underlying vitality is astonishing by any historical standard. As an American, I believe that we and our allies, working together, can surpass an already extraordinary record of achievement. To do so, however, we cannot begin with the negative proclamation that we are in disarray.

NATO may appear to some to be lame because it leads with only one foot at a time. The challenges of improving deterrence in Europe, of countering Soviet adventurism in the Third World and of reviving economic growth can be overcome if we move forward with both feet, if we adopt policies with a global approach that recognize the interrelationship of these challenges.

The stake is the same as when NATO was founded: our freedom. The opportunities are still there: to do great things together in the interests of democracy and peace. Surely we can find the vision and courage to seize them.

THE EURO-ATLANTIC LINK

Emilio Colombo

FORMER ITALIAN PRIME MINISTER AND
MINISTER OF FOREIGN AFFAIRS

The 35th anniversary of the Atlantic alliance finds a consensus of opinion in Italy that virtually encompasses the country's entire political spectrum. Reservations such as the important one concerning the Intermediate-Range Nuclear Forces (INF) are still voiced by the communists. It would be a mistake to disregard these reservations, though it is a fact that no one dares deny the usefulness of the alliance, as it would not be understood by public opinion today. This has not always been so, and grateful acknowledgements go to those men who at the end of the 1940s worked to make this evolution possible.

In recalling the lively debate which at the time attracted the interest of the country's politicians alongside the man in the street on a choice made complex by the difficulties of post-war Italy, positions such as the one taken by Alcide de Gasperi, a staunch supporter of the Atlantic option, today appear particularly far-sighted. The Christian Democratic party, still at the centre of the country's political spectrum, and the other parties, which, following our proportional system, formed coalitions solidly anchored to the Western concept of democracy, were aware that the validity of the choice would be confirmed, and would enable the settlement of disputes which accompanied its conception.

The lively debate between the two sides of the Atlantic, which has characterized in more than one instance the history of the alliance, cannot *per se* be regarded as the motive of the crisis, provided that a frank debate be established. In fact, it is only through a frank debate that moments of apparent tension can be overcome, safeguarding the individuality and the sensibility of each participant and avoiding dangerous diversities.

Two different instances come to mind. The first one is the difficulties which arose among the allies during 1982, after the dramatic events in Warsaw. I believe these were due to the fact that the political objective to be pursued – on which we were all in agreement and which was a serious and unanimous warning to the Soviet Union – had not been clearly defined. We also had to take into consideration the legitimate interests of each country as far as East–West economic relations were concerned. But this we did with some delay and not without difficulty.

The second instance which comes to mind is the fruitful dialogue which immediately ensued between Europeans and Americans on the very delicate question of INF. In my opinion, the West owes its united front to this intensive and open dialogue in which European countries gave many valuable suggestions. I personally recall on this particular instance my meeting with President Reagan in March 1983 at the White House on the so-called 'intermediate option'. The extraordinary frankness of that conversation greatly contributed to further defining the Western position on the matter.

The alliance was therefore able to respond to the psychological offensive launched by the Soviet Union as a cover for her massive programme of rearmament in the Old Continent by strengthening its solidarity and through closer forms and methods of agreement. The INF did not cause that schism which Moscow had sought in Europe, nor did they widen the gap between the two shores of the Atlantic. Europe gave its firm response to the threat of the SS-20. Of course, there still is keen concern also for the future of peace, as peaceful rallies all over Europe demonstrate, quite apart from distorted interpretations. However, I am reassured by the prevailing awareness that this present phase of peace and security requires above all a common effort on the part of each and every one of us.

On the other hand, we are concerned by the fact that political forces, such as the British Labour party and the German Social Democratic party (SPD), which have managed to firmly govern their respective countries even in difficult times, have – and I trust only temporarily – changed positions. This weakening of the attitude could prove very costly for Europe's stability.

The question of the INF has therefore once again confirmed that Europe's security is indivisible from that of the United States and it has further proved, if there were any need, the importance, I would say almost structural, of the Euro-Atlantic link for each of our countries. The search for always more efficient ways of ensuring security for all in the future can only spring from a reaffirmation of our interdependence.

Some months ago in Bonn, in the course of a meeting on European questions, I remarked that if Europe wants to play a full role, if she wants to make her voice of moderation and wisdom heard with greater authority within the Western context and the world, it must for her part take on wider and more direct responsibilities.

Politics is the art of the possible and shuns rigid contrasts. It is a fact, however, that as Europeans it will be somewhat difficult for us to make our needs and priorities better heard if we are not prepared to do more, and above all to do it together.

I am only too well aware of the effort made on the national scale by countries of great traditions, such as Great Britain and France. I also know full well that this is a very delicate question and I can understand the legitimate sensibility of London and Paris on this point. With due respect for the position of each country, the day will come when these questions will have to be addressed, that is if we have been successful in building a European framework.

While recognizing the importance of a military commitment, European countries have for many years deleted from their common political dictionary terms such as 'defence' or 'security', either out of fear or hypocrisy. Today, we talk a lot about European security.

However, what needs to be done first of all is to clear the ground of certain prejudicial obstacles. The first and most dangerous one is the idea that wider agreement among European countries for a more firmly concerted common defence necessarily presupposes third-force options, and is a prelude to a split between Europe and the United States, or even to a precipitous return of the latter to an isolationist position.

This is a concept which though well rooted in many circles on either side of the Atlantic nevertheless is based on a twofold misunderstanding. On the one hand, Europe cannot be defended without the United States: an undeniable fact recognised by all, including the French. The debate on the potential decoupling impact of the decision on INF stands to prove this point. On the other hand, the United States could survive without Europe, but the reduction and fragmentation of the free world could herald an era of growing uncertainty.

Having accepted the principle, which works both ways, that the Europeans cannot defend themselves without the United States, it remains to be seen what the Europeans should do among themselves. Unilateralism and the temptation of a restricted forum are both to be dispelled, since they have no right of existence in Europe's security.

What should be done first of all should be to try to co-ordinate our weapons industries and our procurement programmes. European industry has suffered considerable losses in the past through duplicating efforts; for some it has been possible to reach relevant market positions on a purely national basis, but this will become always more difficult with the next generation of 'intelligent weapons', on which NATO has based its conventional modernization programme. We will have to work pragmatically, bearing in mind past experiences and looking for industrial and economic compatibilities. The French idea, based on relaunching the Western European Union (WEU) to co-ordinate and rationalize European procurement, is a step in the right direction.

The key issue is of course Europe's political will to move forward, and to do so together. The timid reference to political and economic aspects of security in Stuttgart's Solemn Declaration, which was all Herr Genscher, the West German Foreign Minister, and myself were able to obtain at the end of a long negotiation, stands rather as a testimony of present difficulties than as a sign of progress. Yet, there is no doubt that progress in the field of security is essential in order to lend substance to those policies which we all are advocating as a way out of the quagmire of the lakes of milk, butter and wine in which we are now trapped. At Stuttgart we expressed a political will which did not however bear its fruits in Athens, but which cannot be ignored for too long and which will soon need to be tested.

If Europe will show her ability to face up to the technological and economic challenge of the coming years, and at the same time provide a greater contribution to common defence in the interest of the Atlantic alliance, it will have acquired a new and greater international dimension. It will be a slow and difficult process whose obstacles can only too easily be visualised, but it is something that has to be done in order to move forward. If we are able to undertake this process with clear determination we will give greater strength to the idea of a European union aimed at reinforcing closer ties among its members and at co-operating to promote a common vision of peace and interdependence with the United States.

NATO'S CHALLENGE

Henri Simonet
FORMER BELGIAN FOREIGN MINISTER

For some time now any description of the state of the Atlantic alliance and any attempt to predict its future has had to confront one simple common assumption, namely that the alliance is passing through a serious and lasting crisis.

However, despite these now ritual assumptions, it is still rare to find many people making the deduction that the alliance is becoming useless or that one can allow it to disappear without too much anxiety.

This refusal to draw the logical conclusion from a permanent state of crisis is easy to understand. The alliance is part of the East–West balance of forces. It is a symbol of that balance and it is a major factor in the relationship between two antagonistic systems – built around the two superpowers – that have been opposed to each other since the end of World War II. Deliberately to question the alliance's role would be equivalent to attempting to overthrow the whole structure of politico-strategic relations that has received much (perhaps undue) credit for averting a major and probably suicidal conflict within the industrialised world.

Where is the sensible man, the sincere democrat either of conservative or progressive, liberal or Christian conviction, who dares to proclaim frankly that the alliance is dead or dying and thus becoming unnecessary?

Perhaps a few do believe this, but the majority of our fellow countrymen, interested in the problems of Western security, are unwilling to go along with this. This is true even for some segments of responsible opinion that could be considered to be in favour of the dismemberment of the Atlantic alliance. Fear of the decease of the alliance has even been suggested on occasion by a prominent leader of one of the principal European communist parties. Such a fear certainly still prevails in Europe, for which any irreparable weakening of the alliance will mean a revolution concerning Europe's relations with the continental superpower. A set of sophisticated and complex balances would be put into question, beginning with the European *status quo* itself. On the other hand, even if such a possibility does not necessarily imply a total withdrawal of the United States to 'Fortress America' (one might imagine that bilateral linkages between the United States and various European countries could to an extent, whatever they may involve, compensate for the disappearance of the integrated military organisation of the alliance), it would nevertheless imply a radical strategic and geopolitical change with incalculable consequences.

It is generally accepted by experts that the public debt of a country is not paid off by the depreciation of its currency, but that its financial burden is lightened by this depreciation. One might transpose this situation to international relations. International treaties are rarely denounced. They lose their *raison d'être* under the impact of concealment, suspicion, ill-will and passivity from the countries which once subscribed to these treaties. Then the day arrives when it is realised that they no longer have any utility; one perceives only the disadvantages of the treaty.

If – God forbid – such an appraisal should ever have to be made of the state of the alliance, it will certainly provoke huge movements, if not among public opinion then surely in political circles. One can reasonably anticipate that these movements will be preceded by flying sparks, confrontations and attempts at reconciliation.

Analysis of the various ups and downs of the alliance over the last 30 years and the ways in which they were resolved to avoid irreparable breaks should restore confidence in its future. Moreover, when some of these vicissitudes occurred nobody foresaw then that, paradoxically, they could contribute to the strengthening of the alliance. Thus one cannot in retrospect consider the decision made by the French government in 1966 to sever its links with the NATO integrated military command to have weakened the alliance. However, the consequences of this decision leaves a margin of autonomy for the French – and sometimes their criticisms of the United States' initiatives in the alliance, provoke irritation in Washington. This irritation tends to dampen the enthusiastic reappraisal recently made in Washington concerning the consistent rhetoric used by the French government *vis-à-vis* the USSR and the various anxious analyses made by the French on the hegemonial tendencies and expansionism shown by the USSR. In the present neutralist and pacifist cacophony, it even appears that France may receive the label of 'best ally'. Such a certificate of good Atlanticist behaviour is now rarely awarded even to countries whose fidelity and solidarity have never been in question.

Another example lies in the fact that, while the Graeco-Turkish dispute has certainly not contributed to reinforcing the southern flank of NATO, Italy has barely wavered in doing her share to implement the two-track decision of 1979. I do not mention these two examples in order to shrug aside the real disquiet that should be inspired by the present challenges which confront NATO. However, these two examples show the ability to sort out these challenges in a rather less absolute perspective and in a more relative way than in the pessimistic descriptions found here or there when some analysts examine the question of alliance survival.

When it was established, the NATO alliance was conceived as a reaction to the threat posed by the Soviet Union to Western European countries. The fear of the Soviet Union led them to search – almost in panic – for the security and protection that only the United States could provide. Thus two components were essential from the start: the military dimension of the alliance; and the American involvement in it (it was a unilateral commitment since no one considered at that time the need for any reciprocity).

The political dimension of the alliance was asserted later because of the end of the Korean War and the first steps toward what would later become détente. These did much to make the European allies less keen to rearm. Furthermore, the reduced perception of a direct military threat made it less urgent for European governments and public opinion to implement a massive and lasting rearmament effort.

In any case, it soon became clear that rearmament of the West was feasible and tolerable only with German participation. This brought a new political problem and, moreover, the question of inserting the Federal Republic of Germany into an organisation that would definitively anchor it among the Western countries. Thus one can see that Western anxiety about the siren song from the East towards West Germany is not new!

Ever since the centre of gravity of the alliance moved towards strategic and military issues, it has come to be perceived differently than it was at its inception – by both governments and especially by the people.

The emphasis put on strategic and military matters, plus the Soviet–American controversy, in which American rhetoric and phraseology sometimes gave the USSR an easy alibi to justify its expansionism, gradually shifted Western Europe's perception of the role of the NATO alliance itself.

In contrast, American opinion tended to assume that NATO was a partnership, in which the United States carried the main part of the common burden.

In a phrase, NATO suffers today – at least amongst its Northern European members – from an identity crisis. It no longer seems to present a clear image of a partnership for countries deeply bound to peace, animated by a political vision of their future, and for whom military investment is not an end, but only a means for obtaining peace and security.

The history of the Atlantic alliance is sprinkled with crises. How could it have been otherwise if one considers its exceptional duration? The alliance has always overcome each crisis, but without finding a way to cure the fundamental causes. If it remains true that each crisis has had its particular characteristics, analysis of them could perhaps provide the basis for assertion about what kinds of similarities or differences the present crisis has in comparison with its predecessors.

The present period of difficulties among the allies is of a different nature.

Firstly, by its duration. Four years of suspicion, recrimination, misunderstandings, and quarrels broken by intermittent harmony and co-operation, is more than an ordinary crisis. An 'ordinary' crisis is a temporary state when the balance of forces and common interests are disturbed for a short period of time before moving towards a new balance and a new convergence of interests. But in the recent crisis, the opposite seems to have happened. Disturbances of the social and political equilibrium and national disagreement have become the norm. A solid consensus and the sharing of common interests appear to be of short duration and rather exceptional.

Secondly, by its multiform character. Practically no major political, economic and social interests of the various alliance countries are immune, either alternately or simultaneously from a clash of interests and differences of opinion. The disagreement on economic and monetary policy, and suspicion about strategic aims and long-term policy towards the potential menace that still holds the alliance together have all been present within NATO for a number of years.

Finally, there is a kind of fatalism which leads some analysts to see these recurrent disagreements and confrontations as inevitable until culminating in the twilight of the alliance.

The tendency amongst NATO countries periodically comes together with what I call 'a globalist temptation', which consists of seeking to subordinate the various difficulties sometimes dividing the alliance to a common Atlantic denominator.

It is the political challenge that appears to be most global and the most fundamental. All the aforementioned challenges are, in a sense, political. Moreover, if any one of them reaches a particular intensity, however confined initially to a particular field or particular aspect of the alliance relationship, it risks becoming a political struggle.

The political challenge is also the most fundamental. The alliance – because it is defensive – must be able to rely on a single strategic vision of the world. It will only be able to resist the peacetime tensions and conflicts of interest if it can rely on a political concept which is not grounded on insuperable divergences amongst the allies.

The achievement of a prevailing consensus about the many issues confronting the alliance and its members, concerning both the relationship between them and their political opinions, is the substance of the political challenge.

Then there is the demise of détente and the reactions to it on both sides of the Atlantic which underline the point that the alliance is bound to be in endemic crisis if it does not collectively define an *ostpolitik*.

In other words, NATO must establish a consensus about what the rules should be and how they should be applied in relationship with the USSR and the other Warsaw Pact countries. Particularly should the alliance define its objectives and the limits it intends to place on Soviet international activism and ascendancy over Eastern Europe.

Enduring disagreement on these subjects will undermine the alliance. In fact, during the disagreements within the alliance over economic sanctions in 1982, which centred around the gas pipeline question and the accompanying United States embargo, one finds the main characteristics of the two antagonistic theories of 'roll-back' and 'containment', which defined the options available to the United States *vis-à-vis* the Soviet Union at the start of the Cold War. One sometimes gets the feeling that some segments of the American leadership are indeed tempted to up-date some version of the 'roll-back' theory, looking towards the collapse of the Soviet empire from both economic difficulties within the USSR and centrifugal forces in the satellite countries.

Stemming from this assumption is the idea – totally unacceptable for the West Europeans – of taking a term from the Marxist lexicon, and exploiting the 'internal contradiction within the communist system'.

Considering the tendencies present in American foreign policy, the Western Europeans have reason to become worried about what they consider to be a dangerous mixture of intellectual single-mindedness and manichaeism. They will be close to thinking, as André Gide once said: 'it is with good intentions that bad literature is written'. They will add: 'and it is with noble and dignified principles that bad politics is performed'.

Many Europeans are so passionately committed to détente – perceived as a kind of life insurance premium for peace in Europe – that they are ready to avoid taking any initiatives on their own, or encouraging any changes by the people of East Europe in their submission to communist regimes and integration into the Warsaw Pact. Otherwise, how can one explain the speed with which high-level statements were issued to indicate that, since Poland was integrated into the Russian *imperium*, nothing will be done by the West to interfere in upheavals in their sphere of influence?

To summarise, it appears impossible for the alliance to overcome the political challenge that confronts it, if it is unable to define a comprehensive doctrine for its relationship with the East. To a certain extent it is essentially a question of how to extend, deepen and up-date the Harmel Report. Nevertheless, even though such an intellectual effort appears essential if difficult, it will not be enough. There is also an internal dimension to the political challenge facing NATO. Since this dimension is incomparably broader than it was ten years ago, it deserves the utmost attention. The internal political and moral debate spreading throughout the alliance spares few countries even if it is still limited to specific segments of our populations: the churches; youth (whether organised or not); political organisations of the left; some trade unions; and the ecological movement.

Without political vision the alliance will not be able to withstand the damaging effects of struggles for influence, conflicts of interests, national or continental selfishness, and Soviet policy.

The political vision should be based on the one fundamental shared interest, which is to avoid war in Europe and to guarantee mutual security with an appropriate, coherent and credible strategy relying on effective means of defence. This leads to the development of ideas about what I call the strategic challenge.

Without a strategy for deterrence and defence, the alliance no longer has a centre of gravity. For some years, alliance strategy has been reminiscent of those elegant and fragile antique chairs which one can admire from a distance but dare not sit on for fear of collapse.

In an era of strategic nuclear parity a strategy for deterrence is bound to be ambiguous. Its deterrent effect relies first on the total uncertainty remaining in any opponent's mind about the probability of answering an aggression with nuclear weapons. However, ambiguity should be confined only to that and should not relate to the physical capability to retaliate if necessary.

The present debate has had tremendous consequences for Western European public opinion since it places the strategic doctrine of the alliance under strain. Most of the countries of Europe have accepted, and even wished, that nuclear deterrence should remain in place and stable, because it seems to be the only way of preventing war.

Unfortunately, nuclear deterrence implies too that some consideration be given to the eventual implementation of nuclear strikes. Nuclear deterrence prevents war breaking out only if its credibility is assumed. And this credibility exists only if one plans for the possibility that deterrence could break down and so thinks about how to run that war. It is hard to imagine a country playing a game for its survival, when the probability is that the holocaust will render that search futile. 'Mutual Assured Destruction' can be considered, if need be, as a strategy; but this is impossible if suicide is certain.

The time has come for the alliance to integrate the following factors into a global strategic framework: the structure of the American deterrent and its connection with Europe's security, which has come under a cloud after some pronouncements in Washington that imply, for the Europeans, a fundamental shift in America's whole strategic thinking; the continuation of the strategic dialogue with the USSR, in order to set limits on the development of intercontinental weapons so that quantitative levels are reduced step-by-step. In most alliance countries, however, public support for such a dialogue would be in jeopardy if it were to amount to no more than the strategic codification of the arms race; and finally, reaffirmation and preservation of the solidarity of the strategic security of the two pillars of the alliance.

PEACE AND PACIFICISM

Franz Josef Strauss
PRIME MINISTER OF BAVARIA AND
CHAIRMAN OF THE CHRISTIAN SOCIAL UNION

Ever since the creation of the Federal Republic of Germany, the effective safeguarding of peace has been a central element of its political thinking. The first Federal Chancellor, Konrad Adenauer, recognised quite clearly that the peace and freedom of West Germany was inextricably linked to the freedom of Western Europe and to this day it has only been possible to maintain this in conjunction with the United States.

For this reason, in the 1950s Konrad Adenauer and the parties then in power in West Germany, decided to take West Germany into the European Community and the North Atlantic Treaty Organisation. In so doing they secured free democratic constitutional rule in our country and kept alive the hope of freedom for the inhabitants of East Germany and the other European countries behind the Iron Curtain.

That decision turned out to be the right one. The deterrent effect of NATO's conventional and nuclear strength has prevented all armed conflict between the Eastern and Western blocs since 1949. The existence of nuclear weapons on both sides of the demarcation line has profoundly altered the political and military dimension in Europe. The outbreak of a purely conventional war here is no longer even theoretically conceivable. Any armed conflict between NATO and the Warsaw Pact countries that might occur in Europe would inevitably have to take on a nuclear dimension. The Soviet Union is just as frightened as we are of the apocalyptic destructive nature of any such war. So long, therefore, as NATO maintains the credibility of its nuclear deterrent, peace will be preserved in Europe.

The past year has been an important one for NATO. If the West German government or the Bundestag had given in to the pressures of the peace movement, or had been swayed by the threats of the Soviet Union, and had refused to allow the deployment on German soil of the new strategic defences, NATO unity on defence policy would have been destroyed and the Soviets would have scored their greatest political and strategic victory since the end of the Second World War.

Today this NATO policy attracts less heated debate than it used to; the huge propaganda marches and actions of the so-called peace movement by and large petered out once Moscow recognised, after the NATO decision was ratified and rapidly implemented by the government of the Federal German Republic, that there remained little point in continuing to provide large-scale financial and organisational support to the anti-NATO campaigners. This was a repeat of what had happened in 1958, 1959 and 1960, when there was a similar movement in West Germany hostile to NATO. The aim of its supporters then was to prevent the armed forces of West Germany and the other NATO members stationed on German soil from being equipped with tactical nuclear weapons. Sizeable peace marches, in many cases organised by communists – often with the same slogans that we see today – fizzled out fairly quickly when, in 1960, the equipment was delivered.

The strong support of the unilateralist agitation of the so-called peace movement by so many young people today is an indication of the degree to which a section of our youth takes freedom for granted. Taking measures to defend our freedom is often seen as unnecessary and absurd, and sometimes even as dangerous warmongering. These young people should be made to understand that while material prosperity and social welfare are important political objectives, the most important of all is the safeguarding of peace and freedom.

I am firmly convinced that the existence of NATO and the effect it has had is the greatest peace movement in the history of mankind. It is more than merely an alliance for the protection of its members against external threat, more than the sum of the military strengths of its member states; it is the embodiment of our firm intention to defend inalienable human rights, fundamental political rights and basic freedoms, and the right to self-determination by free peoples, whenever these may come under threat from outside by any form of totalitarianism.

On June 17, 1984, the 31st anniversary of the popular uprising in central Germany, the inhabitants of the member countries of the European Community were called upon for the second time to take part in direct elections to the European Parliament.

The movement towards European unification is at the moment bogged down in a serious crisis. But that must not prevent us from raising the question of a common European foreign and defence policy, even if this is at present unattainable. Twenty years ago, in the context of West Germany, I outlined the basis of the Western alliance as follows: 'Friendship, trust and guarantees of security from the United States of America through a German policy favouring the development, safeguarding and strengthening of the European Community and transatlantic solidarity'.

In a speech to a conference in Rome on April 4, 1984, the Federal Chancellor, Helmut Kohl, rightly pointed out that NATO consisted of two pillars – a strong American element and an equally strong European element. European strength and military capability, however, leave much to be desired at present, and for this reason the American involvement in Europe is today more necessary than it has ever been before.

Although the numerical strength, aptitude and intelligence, technical skills and military training of the Europeans should enable Europe to achieve a deterrent strength capable of considerable independence from the United States, the fact remains that in reality the role played by Europeans is almost pathetic compared with their potential.

Europe is psychologically and geographically a well-defined continent, with 300 million inhabitants living in the European Community member states alone, and such facts are in the long run clearly inconsistent with a total dependence upon Washington for guarantees of the right of self-determination. There is also the question of the necessity for a greater say and right of participation in the decision-making process on issues concerning Europe itself. Since Europe cannot really claim at present to constitute a genuine political entity, the voice of Europe sadly counts for little in the international arena.

Europeans can only gain influence in matters of world affairs of concern to them if they join together and assume a greater political and military role than the individual European countries now have.

The transatlantic partnership clearly should not mean that the United States is solely responsible for deterrence, defence and the economic sacrifices these entail; nor should it leave Europe with the monopoly of détente functions and the short-term economic advantages that these bring with them. We must display a neighbourly attitude towards our American allies, and not haggle like street traders for immediate gain, because more is at stake here than mere trade advantages; we are talking about the very future of Europe itself.

The ten member states of the European Community, restricted by frequent conflicts of national interest, remain unable, for the foreseeable future, to take any major steps towards political integration. It is, therefore, especially important that we should join together as Europeans in more modest ways for specific purposes, such as scientific and technological projects, and co-operate in such fields as military technology and industry. One aim of such co-operation would be to close the gap that has developed between us and such countries as the United States and Japan in the fields of advanced and high technology, microelectronics, and bio-technology. It is in the mastery and industrial application of these technologies that hopes for tomorrow's full employment and prosperity lie.

The NATO alliance and the Warsaw Pact are as different from one another as fire and water. Whilst the Warsaw Pact is an alliance of subjugated peoples, NATO is a community of free nations, all enjoying equal rights. Within NATO, the United States inevitably plays a leading role by virtue of its military superiority. Despite this leading role, however, senior American politicians are obliged, when making statements and proposals on NATO's future policies, to pay due attention to the views of their NATO allies, and to take them into consideration.

Recent warnings by the then American Deputy Under-Secretary of State, Lawrence Eagleburger, issued for the benefit of European audiences, have conveyed the message that Europeans should not be too inward-looking and should resist the temptation to shy away from playing a responsible role in world affairs. These warnings should be taken seriously, as should his comments on the growing economic, political and military significance of the Pacific region to the United States, implying that in future the main thrust of American political attention might be turned from the Atlantic to the Pacific.

NATO clearly has vital security interests outside the narrow geographical boundaries of the area. This does not mean that German troops should become involved in events taking place, for instance, in the Middle East, in the eastern Mediterranean, the Indian Ocean, the Gulf region or the Horn of Africa. For such situations the use of the forces of NATO's maritime nations is more appropriate – those of Britain, France and the United States. These nations have had the benefit of long-standing – indeed often centuries-old – experience in handling responsibilities in far-flung parts of the world, and have at their disposal a network of traditional overseas connections. The German Empire never built up such connections and so West Germany today does not have any either. This does not mean, however, that West Germany can simply sit back and watch her allies fulfill these obligations, which help safeguard German national security, as well as those of her allies. Should it become necessary to defend our vital strategic economic interests, we in West Germany must be prepared to make strenuous efforts to make up any deficiencies in the NATO strength created by military commitments, however temporary, outside the NATO area.

It is due to the deterrent effect of NATO's flexible response strategy that we have peace in Europe today. This strategy binds the European and North American NATO allies into a closely united strategic whole. Recent advances in the technology of arms manufacture mean that America will have extensive protection from Soviet middle-range and intercontinental strategic missiles afforded them by the latest anti-missile systems, with either atomic or laser back-up. Such developments make European bases less important to American defence than they were in the past, and the West German Defence Minister, Manfred Wörner, has recently warned – quite rightly in my opinion – of the dangers of weakening transatlantic ties that might follow on from this. It is, therefore, becoming more important than ever to make efforts to maintain close military and political co-operation between the United States and Europe.

One question that often arises in political debate is how much longer the policy of deterrence should be pursued? Is there a political consensus in favour of the policy of deterrence, or to put it another way, the policy of preventing war? But, it is quite misleading to put the question in that way. The question should not be how long can a policy of deterrence be continued, but rather for what reasons is such a policy necessary?

As long as the Soviet Union continues to pursue expansionist policies aimed at promoting worldwide revolution, as long as the Russians interpret balance of power to mean military superiority, as long as the citizens of communist countries are denied even the bare minimum of basic freedoms, and as long as Soviet thinking lays such great store by military strength, then the West must maintain a deterrent strength sufficient to prevent the Russians from resorting to military aggression for fear of reprisals.

There exist today in both East and West nuclear arsenals with apocalyptic powers of destruction, and this fact has ruled out the possibility of war as a means to achieve political ends in Europe. Wars may occur in Africa, in the Middle East, the Far East and in Latin America, but are unlikely again in Europe. Unlike Adolf Hitler, whose criminal policies displayed a total disregard for the risks involved in their implementation, Soviet leaders conduct foreign policy with a keen awareness of the risk factor. Since the creation of NATO, the Soviet Union has refrained from major provocative actions and destabilizing military operations in Europe.

Instead, the Soviets have concentrated on attempts to export their revolutionary ideology and arms to the Third World. They have also tried to attack Western Europe indirectly – and without incurring danger to themselves – for example, by trying to gain control of the sources of energy and raw materials which are indispensable to the industrialised countries of Western Europe. NATO must obviously take steps to counter these endeavours.

Europe, however, is not a fertile breeding-ground for revolution. In Western Europe there is no cause for revolution; in the Warsaw Pact countries all past and recent attempts at revolution have only led to bloody, disastrous consequences without achieving radical political change. It is for this reason that the Roman Catholic church in Poland is unwilling to support policies which can only result in futile bloodshed.

But history does not stand still. Change will surely come about in different ways. Modern news reporting technology, with its enormous potential for the dissemination of information, makes it no longer possible for communist governments on the other side of the Iron Curtain to keep their people in total ignorance of the political and social situation in the free West. The inhabitants of Warsaw Pact countries are getting to know about the rights and freedoms of their brothers in Western Europe, about the prosperity they enjoy and their freedom to develop their abilities to the full. They are bound to ask questions, voice their dissatisfaction and make their demands heard. Above all, they will begin to yearn for freedom and the chance to live in a united Europe. We should not under-estimate the importance of the role played by today's mass media as an instrument of change in the long term in the social order of countries of the Warsaw Pact, adding new impetus to an inevitable evolutionary process.

The second means of promoting change is in the sphere of modern scientific research. The 1980s, and even more especially the 1990s, will see momentous strides forward in the scientific fields of micro-electronics, bio-technology and laser technology, and this progress will undoubtedly have considerable economic and social consequences. But successful modern research is dependent upon total freedom of debate and exchange of information. Therefore, researchers who must con-stantly bow to Marxist ideologies, and who have ideological constraints thrust upon them, cannot hope to keep pace with researchers operating in the academic freedom of the West. Marxist-communist countries will not be able to catch up with the West in scientific, technological and economic fields, and the gap between the two blocs will become ever wider. This will be the end of the road for the repressive communist social order. In the long term it is unable to survive; it is also unable to resort to armed conflict to secure its survival for as long as NATO maintains its military deterrent. Their social order cannot be changed by military means from outside, nor by bloody civil war from within.

But change will inevitably come about, in a much slower way, from within the system itself. We in the West must use all the peaceful means that are at our disposal to encourage this historical evolutionary process of change, wherever the opportunity presents itself.

Changes in the social order of the Warsaw Pact countries by such an evolutionary process will also bring about a transformation in the political map of Europe, opening up opportunities for the creation of a united free Europe, able to live in peace. And this would also bring an end to the division of Germany.

PART TWO

Defence, arms control and transatlantic order

PROBLEMS FACING THE ALLIANCE

James R. Schlesinger
FORMER US SECRETARY OF DEFENCE

A tone of sourness and doubt now characterizes transatlantic relations. Although relations at the government level apparently remain excellent, storm signals are rightly being hoisted. Are the strains in the relationship anything new? If one recalls the collapse of the European Defence Community, Dulles' 'agonizing reappraisal', Suez, the Skybolt controversy, de Gaulle's expulsion of NATO from French soil, or the Mansfield amendment, one might readily infer that transatlantic relations are normally tempestuous and complacently conclude that the current strains be disregarded.

Is there now a difference? In a word – yes! If we are wise, we shall pay attention. For this difference is qualitative: beneath the historic pattern of tempestuous irruptions, there is now a spreading and mutual disenchantment. At base, this disenchantment reflects a lessened conviction on both sides of the Atlantic that the alliance well serves – or serves as well as in the past – the interests of its major participants, European and American. This attitude is widespread in the rising generation, but it is by no means confined to youth.

How could such doubts arise? In a sense the mutual advantages provided by the alliance are no less than they ever were. The preservation of a free and independent Western Europe – the centrepiece of American foreign policy since World War II – is, if anything, more important now than it was then, in the light of the recovery and expansion of the European economies. For the Europeans, American support and protection, initially put forward as a unilateral guarantee, continues under somewhat altered circumstances as an indispensable element for preserving political independence.

In the absence of effective unification and a substantial strategic nuclear capability, the small and medium states of Western Europe would by themselves be unable to withstand the pressures from the East – without the stiffening presence of the other superpower. Europe's need for American support has not diminished – in the light of the steady expansion of Soviet military power. While the alliance, no doubt, serves America's long-term interest, it serves Europe's primary and immediate interest.

What then underlies the disenchantment, the storm signals? If this is not more of the traditional tempest, wherein lies the qualitative change?

40

At base, the change reflects a substantial alteration in the military balance of power – the slippage of America's military strength relative to that of the Soviet. In the past, America's nuclear might implied something close to absolute protection. Today, military deterrence must rest on something more subtle than clearcut nuclear superiority – but also, therefore, more ambiguous and even equivocal. That this change was inevitable, as the Soviets developed an effective strategic counter-deterrent, has not made it any less disturbing within the alliance.

In the past, if the Americans were irritating, there was ready compensation in that they also provided virtually absolute protection. American blunders, which in the past might have been dismissed as idiosyncracies of an all-powerful protector, have now understandably become a source of worry and resentment.

For the Americans, the protection of Europe implies strategic risks that now appear to be quite real, rather than hypothetical as in the past. That has led, instinctively if not logically, to the feeling that Europe was somehow obligated to provide steady support for American policies in the Third World.

Both attitudes may be understandable, but neither is useful. Yet, these changed attitudes that stem from the shift in the balance of power have been reinforced by other, almost ancillary, developments.

On the European side, the shifting power balance has been accompanied by some disconcerting discoveries about the United States: the weaknesses of the American Constitution (stemming from the separation of powers), the odd procedures by which we select our presidents, and the consequent zigs and zags of American foreign policy. The power and unpredictability of the Congress was discovered during the Ford presidency. It was followed by what were perceived to be the erratic weaknesses of the Carter presidency, and the erratic strengths of the Reagan presidency.

What Europeans desire to see in American foreign policy, above all, is steadiness and continuity. These latter-day discoveries have led to European doubts regarding the necessary wisdom in American foreign policy, in a period in which America's military strength, while still substantial, is relatively less formidable than before.

In the past quarter-century, international tensions have shifted increasingly from Europe itself (which is covered by the alliance) to the Third World (which is not covered by the alliance). For over a generation, Europe has enjoyed unmatched peace and stability, and for half a generation it has enjoyed a gradual diminution in tension between East and West. Both are in large degree a consequence of the alliance. None the less, Europeans – perhaps most notably the West Germans – who are basking in the lessening of tension, are in no mood to see the fruits of détente in Europe disturbed. They fear that tensions between the United States and the Soviet Union in the Third World will spill back into Europe to disrupt the *modus vivendi* that has been worked out. They have no desire to see this happen. They have no desire to join in American actions – or what they may consider American adventures – in the Third World.

Yet many Americans have come to expect, if not to demand, unquestioning European support in Third World controversies – South-East Asia, the Middle East, Central America, or the Caribbean. The spottiness of such support was the source of some disenchantment after Afghanistan, and even more at present in Central America. It is the source of a powerful, though not uncontrollable, impulse towards global unilateralism. It is also the source of disenchantment with Europe – and an invidious infatuation with the Pacific Basin and with our more docile allies and dependents.

These political differences have been exacerbated by differences regarding the military strategy of the alliance. Since the early 1960s the Americans have regularly pressed their European partners to develop a fully-fledged conventional deterrent. Such pressures have been regularly resisted initially on doctrinal lines, more recently on straight budgetary lines. In general, Europeans have regarded the Soviet military threat as far less menacing than have the Americans, and have consequently felt much less need to create the appropriate military counters to Soviet conventional strength. Put very briefly: the Americans have regularly insisted that a high-confidence deterrent is necessary for the security of Western Europe, whereas Europeans themselves have been satisfied with a low-confidence deterrent. No doubt this difference stems from internal political constraints as well as differences regarding the Soviet menace. None the less to Americans it has come as a source of astonishment – and of disillusionment – to discover that the United States appears to be more concerned about the security of Western Europe than are the Europeans themselves.

To these very real transatlantic differences have been added some substantively rather superficial but nevertheless irritating problems. I pass over differences about economic policy which, however important, remain peripheral to the central issue of security. On the European side, there is a good deal of unnecessary and unproductive sniping at the Americans. The latest manifestation (revealed in some surprising places) is to pretend to a Europe equidistant from the two superpowers. Europe could thus presumably in a detached way examine the defects of the two superpowers – the one that is the source of protection and the one that is the source of menace. Europe, in this view, has thus ceased to be the target of Soviet aspirations. It is perhaps unnecessary to add that a continuation of this view is likely to sap the American willingness to bear the costs and risks involved for itself in the security of Europe.

Another dangerous irrelevancy is to play the game of hypothetical conundrums: would the Americans exchange New York for Paris or Savannah for Hamburg? Given the nuclear strategy of the alliance, this is at best an over-simplification. But far more importantly, even in its simple form it overlooks the fundamental reality of nuclear deterrence. While Europeans – from General de Gaulle on down – would no doubt like to have 100 per cent confidence in the American nuclear response, even a much lower estimate of the likelihood of an American nuclear response will continue to have the appropriate deterrent effect where it is needed – in the eyes of the leaders in Moscow. No more than with needless sniping should the alliance tear itself apart with interesting but unresolvable hypothetical questions.

So much for the nature and causes of NATO's discontents. The alliance is troubled – but not incurably so. Nonetheless, unless the present fissures are carefully attended to, they could ultimately lead to disintegration or divorce. Ignoring these strains would be unwise. All too frequently old Atlantic buffs (including myself) seem to believe that simply singing the old litanies of the 1950s will somehow be sufficient to overcome present difficulties.

I myself believe not only that the goals of the alliance are as important, if not more important, than ever, but also that the psychological resources are available to ensure that the alliance continues to measure up to its challenge. Much of the remedy lies in those on both sides of the Atlantic getting a better grip on reality and giving up unrealistic expectations. Although the largest requirements for adjustment rest on the Americans, as is not surprising, Europe must also recognize some fundamental realities.

The Americans must realize that what has been true in the past continues to be true today: the preservation of a free Western Europe remains the pre-eminent United States foreign policy objective. There continues to be a risk that the Americans in a spirit of disenchantment – born of frustration with a Europe that fails to embrace our policies in areas outside the alliance – will throw the baby out with the bath water. While the proclivity for global unilateralism and for brushing off the views of wayward allies is less strong than at the outset of the Reagan administration, it is no doubt still there. Along that path lies folly. The preservation of a free Europe remains immensely important to the United States, for reasons as much political and aesthetic as those of military security. Fidelity within the alliance cannot and need not be global.

Americans will therefore have to make the following adjustments: whatever Americans may prefer, they must be prepared to accept a differential détente. Europe is in no mood to forfeit the advantages of diminished tension in Europe or to re-create what will appear like cold war tension because of troubles in the Third World. Americans would be ill-advised – to say the least – to insist that Europe impose political sanctions upon the Soviet Union, with damage to the *modus vivendi* existing in Europe, in order to discipline the Soviet Union for misbehavior elsewhere in the world. While some Americans may regard as irresolute such European unwillingness to face up to the East–West confrontation, avoiding unnecessary tension in Europe remains a political imperative.

Secondly, the Americans must also understand that the European reluctance to build a fully-fledged conventional deterrent is not due to their failure to grasp American arguments over the past 25 years. Europeans have a different assessment of the threat. They are unprepared to face the budgetary consequences of building a stalwart conventional capability equivalent to that of the Warsaw Pact. They remain satisfied with a lower confidence deterrent.

This means that the Americans should stop lecturing and hectoring the Europeans on this subject. The Americans have expended a great deal of political capital to push an objective that will not be achieved. Maintaining alliance cohesion is far more important than any specific military deployment or capability.

On the European side, requirements are perhaps less demanding, but nevertheless substantial. It is unreasonable to expect the United States to exhibit undeviating responsibility that no European state has ever attained. American politics, no less than European politics, reflect domestic considerations and pressures. Europeans have come to recognize that the Americans are less than perfect. There is a sense of shock – for historic reasons perhaps most notable in the German case – that the former idol has clay feet. What Europeans choose to regard as the imperfections of the American constitutional system, resulting in a lack of continuity in foreign policy, are unlikely to be altered soon. But the important thing to bear in mind is that in its most important aspect – support of the Atlantic connection – the Americans have demonstrated a remarkable fidelity over the course of the last 30 years. Properly sustained that fidelity will continue, and it is essential that it does.

A lessening of transatlantic sniping would also be helpful. Indeed, I believe, this is indispensable with respect to the supposed equivalence of the superpowers and to the presumed equidistance of the Europeans from both of them. Europeans must recognize the United States will continue to take actions in the Third World not necessarily approved by Europe. Nonetheless, so long as such actions do not feed back into East–West tensions in Europe, and the *modus vivendi* with the East is preserved in Europe itself, Europeans should find this acceptable.

Finally, and perhaps most important of all, Europeans must accept their own ultimate responsibility for the quality of the European deterrent. Ultimately they will have to bear the main burden for whatever improvements are achieved in NATO's conventional capability. In improving the conventional deterrent lies the only satisfactory alternative to continued high dependence on the threat of nuclear retaliation. But given the budgetary realities, the improvement in the conventional capability will no doubt fall short of what is desirable from the standpoint of deterrence. Nonetheless, if the European states are unable to provide for a substantial improvement in conventional forces, they ought to refrain from blaming the Americans for undue dependence upon the threat of nuclear response.

Just as the Americans should adjust to the fact that Europeans do not share their assessment of the Soviet threat or their insistence upon a high-confidence military deterrent for Western European security, so also the Europeans must accept the ultimate responsibility for the risks inherent in a low-confidence deterrent. Nations cannot, any more than individuals, have it both ways.

The alliance that protects the West can again flourish and the doubts now debilitating it can be dispelled, but it will require a sense of sober realism on both sides of the Atlantic to achieve that desired outcome.

THE CONVENTIONALIZATION OF NATO STRATEGY

Hans E. Apel
FORMER WEST GERMAN MINISTER OF DEFENCE

When it adopted the Harmel Report seventeen years ago, the alliance brought to an end almost a decade of discussions devoted to a review and successful adjustment of its strategy. Today, we find ourselves in a new phase of assessment and adjustment. The 'decreasing acceptance of nuclear weapons in Western societies' (German White Paper 1983, p. 111) has triggered this discussion. The peace movements have made it a focus of public interest.

The current military strategic debate is essentially concerned with removing NATO's dependence on the early use of nuclear weapons. Conventionalization, strengthening the conventional capability of the alliance, is the answer given by the experts. However, its translation into practice will be possible only provided that complex interrelated facts are taken into consideration; and the room for manoeuvre is incomparably smaller than these clear-cut answers suggest.

Conventionalization is conceivable only provided that, and to the extent that, the primary aim of our strategy of deterrence, namely the prevention of war, is not abandoned. For us Europeans, one major element of this prevention of war is that the superpowers share fully the risk of a war breaking out in Europe. An aggressor must continue to face incalculable risks as far as his own survival is concerned. Even though the nuclear threshold needs to be raised by strengthening NATO's conventional deterrent, it is impossible at present to renounce nuclear deterrence.

On the other hand, an improvement in our conventional capabilities cannot and must not make it appear possible to wage a conventional war in Europe. It must not be accompanied by a relapse into earlier times in which war was considered a continuation of politics by other means. Today, the decisive criterion of conventionalization is no longer its practical value in a war, but its value as a deterrent in peacetime.

A conventionalization of our defence concept will trigger highly dangerous debates in the Federal Republic of Germany. The alliance must, therefore, be aware of the extraordinarily limited political and psychological room for manoeuvre at its disposal, if it does not wish to jeopardize acceptance of its defence concept in the Federal Republic which de-nuclearization is intended to restore in Western societies.

The idea of not defending our territory in immediate proximity to the intra-German border has been discussed before. However, I doubt whether the people in that densely populated region will accept a defence concept which, in a first phase, abandons major portions of their territory, only in order to have the conventional battle fought out to the bitter end on German soil.

The alternative is being discussed in the United States. Instead of forward defence in the sense of defending the NATO area close to its borders, there is to be forward defence in the sense of advancing into enemy territory. By means of highly mobile units with strong fire power, NATO is to be able to advance rapidly into the depth of enemy territory and seek a decision there. This concept too is unacceptable in the Federal Republic. We would expose ourselves to Soviet charges that we wish to launch a conventional attack and involve its territory in a war. We Germans in particular would, in view of our invasion of the Soviet Union during the last war, find it difficult to withstand such a campaign, not least because of the Federal Armed Forces' particularly high contribution to NATO's conventional deterrent in Europe. Reflections of this kind also raise questions which might substantially change or strain East–West relations. We need more, not less, mutual confidence and understanding between East and West.

In addition to the fundamental discussion about the conditions of conventionalization, of which I have mentioned only a few aspects which are important for the Federal Republic, there is the question of implementation.

In the light of present demographic trends, it does not appear to be possible to strengthen further NATO's conventional combat power by 'more troops'. The Federal Armed Forces number 495,000 servicemen. To maintain this high level, the Federal Republic has – unlike the United States and Great Britain – retained universal liability to military service. From 1988 onwards, the decline in the birth rate will make its impact felt on the Federal Armed Forces; from that year onward there will be a steady decrease in the number of young men liable to military service and by the middle of the 1990s their number will have halved. Even though the mobilization strength of the Federal Armed Forces with its reserves numbering roughly 1.2 million servicemen will, for the time being, remain unaffected, this will ultimately mean a shortfall of some 100,000 conscripts annually. For political reasons it will hardly be possible to compensate for this decline by extending the period of basic military service. Given the fact, however, that these demographic trends are particularly pronounced in the Federal Republic, substantial additional efforts will be needed in order to maintain even the current conventional defence capability of the Federal Armed Forces.

Strengthening the conventional combat power is, not least, a financial issue – which applies even more if the decrease in the number of troops is to be offset by greater quantities of better equipment. We should not harbour the illusion that the necessary funds could be provided by a major expansion of Western defence budgets. Since the change of government in Bonn, the present government has made it clear that it too is in no position to comply with NATO's 1977 aim of a 3 per cent annual increase in defence expenditure in real terms – either in 1984 or in the years ahead. The rise of 4 per cent demanded by General Rogers has already proved illusory. The United States is the only country, after a phase of neglecting its defence, to have substantially increased its military expenditure, without regard to the overall budget. The negative repercussions of the American deficit for the European economy show clearly that this solution is not acceptable in the long term. In view of the international economic crisis, as well as of the challenges of environmental protection and structural change, national budgets will continue to labour under considerable strain. In the Federal Republic, a transfer of funds from social security to defence is ruled out. In our country, social security and justice form part of our security and part also of our catalogue of values which sets us apart from the East and on which our attractiveness *vis-à-vis* the East is based.

Finally, technological developments are the third component with which NATO's conventional capability can be strengthened. The progress already achieved or to be expected in the field of weapons technology can be used primarily to de-nuclearize anti-tank defence, anti-aircraft defence and extensive interdiction. This indeed affords the most promising opportunity of reducing NATO's dependence on nuclear weapons. However, we must not replace reality with science fiction in this field either. Even if we achieve decisive breakthroughs in weapons technology in the next few years, I doubt that such new technologies can reach the troops before the 1990s. In the Federal Republic of Germany at least, the pattern of expenditure on armaments is, until the end of this decade, fixed to such a large extent by major procurement projects that substantial change is possible only within narrow limits. We are, however, formulating and implementing our security policy in the 1980s.

An approximate conventional balance in Europe should be achieved above all, not by a corresponding strengthening of NATO, but by a reduction in the forces of the Warsaw Pact or the orientation of its force structure to defence. The Stockholm negotiations and the resumption of the MBFR negotiations in Vienna could provide an opportunity in this respect. It is essential that we explore the Soviet proposals thoroughly and table initiatives of our own. However, there is simply no guarantee that these negotiations will soon meet with success. As regards realizing our aim of 'de-nuclearization', we cannot therefore rely on them alone.

The sum total of resources available to strengthen the conventional capability in terms of servicemen, money and technology clearly shows that it would be illusory to regard conventionalization as a 'quick fix' for NATO. Only a persistent policy of small steps can, in the medium term, lead to the necessary raising of the nuclear threshold by strengthening NATO's conventional capability. There is no prospect of additional resources. The only realistic policy is to use the existing ones more effectively. To my mind, this approach holds out the promise of success for Europe in particular.

Concentrating, interlocking and streamlining European security policy and its defence resources would substantially strengthen the alliance's conventional capability – particularly since the two European nuclear powers, France and Great Britain, have, at least in the past, been committed to a balance between conventional and nuclear capabilities. They must be relied upon to maintain this balance in future too, despite the expansion of their nuclear potential.

Scepticism is no doubt justified. The Athens summit clearly revealed the paralysis of the European Community; it showed how very much the European idea has degenerated. Politicians aware of their responsibility cannot afford, however, to indulge in resignation and idleness. This applies particularly when it is a matter of mastering the challenge of this age: averting the danger of a nuclear war. A common European policy may provide a chance of achieving this.

The idea of more effectively combining Europe's defence resources and thus lending added weight to Europe within the alliance is not new. More than two decades ago President John F. Kennedy gave his speech in Philadelphia about the two pillars of the alliance, America being one, Europe the other. Some progress has already been achieved in this direction. Between 1969 and 1979, the European share in NATO's total expenditure rose from 21 per cent to 41 per cent. We must continue to pursue this course consistently and must acknowledge the necessity of assuming, through our own European efforts, greater responsibility for the defence of the European central front.

This would stabilize the alliance in the long term too, and would reduce the current irritations between America and its European alliance partners. As a superpower, the United States has global interests; rivalry with the Soviet Union is another determining factor. Europe has no global projections; its contribution to security in other regions of the world is mainly confined to diplomacy and development aid. As a regional alliance, NATO simply does not have the interests of the United States as a world power. This is why we reject horizontal escalation or an extension of whatever kind of NATO's military operational area.

Another chance of strengthening the conventional combat power consists in exploiting the possibilities of arms co-operation within the alliance. However, such opportunities will present themselves only if the development of new arms technologies and the production of military hardware do not benefit only the American economy. Without genuine Atlantic arms co-operation, the so-called 'two-way street', nothing can be achieved in this field. The United States must be made aware of its responsibility in this respect for the strengthening of the alliance.

Possibilities of optimizing the use of Europe's defence resources do exist. However, their realization depends on one factor: it will be necessary to overcome national parochialism and the preoccupation with national prestige. Optimizing the use of Europe's defence resources also entails a division of labour in Europe and, as regards equipment planning, will mean that not every weapon system can automatically expect to be modernized and developed further and that competition, at national level, among the services for the assignment of functions and equipment can no longer be resolved by the principle of proportional distribution practised hitherto in accordance with the motto: something for everyone.

Having been the focal point of two devastating world wars, Europe bears responsibility for peace and must actively fulfil this responsibility. By strengthening the European component of the alliance, it can contribute to developing, on a step-by-step basis, the policy of mutual deterrence into a policy of partnership for common security. Even if the superpowers' weight is immense, only in this way can Europe perceive its function, find its identity and use its strength indissolubly to involve the United States and the Soviet Union in the process of gradually developing a European peace order.

RETHINKING CONTINENTAL DEFENCE

Franz-Joseph Schulze
FORMER GENERAL COMMANDER IN CHIEF,
ALLIED FORCES CENTRAL EUROPE

Rethinking our defence is a continuous task and nobody will pretend that the leaders of our alliance or our national governments have neglected this obligation in the past. Why is it, then, that the problems of our security, of a credible strategy of deterrence and defence, are the subject of an ever broader public debate that is characterized by a vigorousness we have seldom experienced before?

The Atlantic alliance has accepted for a long time – indeed, for too long a time – gaps and deficiencies in its own military potential and found relief in the thought that the superiority in other areas would offset these weaknesses; in the final analysis, it has relied on the deterrent effect of the United States' superior strategic nuclear arsenal. But the times of American strategic superiority have gone, and the imbalances below the strategic nuclear level (for example, the long-standing and ever-increasing conventional superiority of the Warsaw Pact) and Soviet predominance, acquired in recent years in the field of long-range theatre nuclear weapons, have gained a different weight, rather suddenly and quite obviously.

In a condition of nuclear parity the credibility of our deterrence calls for sufficient counterweights to balance the whole spectrum of an aggressor's offensive capabilities. The defender must have the means to counter an attack in any given phase of the conflict in such a way that the aggressor realises that the initiation or continuation of the conflict will confront him with incalculable and, thus, unacceptable risks. To achieve this objective, improvements in the nuclear posture, as well as – and even more particularly – in our conventional capabilities, are indispensable.

Redressing the correlation of forces to secure a viable deterrent posture is only part of the problem facing NATO, however. The relentless growth of Soviet military power has led to an erosion of our nations' and peoples' confidence in our ability to defend them. The perception that NATO might be forced to take recourse to nuclear weapons at an early stage of conflict, has caused widespread questioning of the validity and credibility of our deterrence and threatens to undermine the political self-confidence of our countries. Thus, deterrence and reassurance must be pursued together. A determined effort must be made to reduce our present dependence on a possible early use of

51

nuclear weapons by substantially improving the conventional component of our deterrence and defence posture. Improved conventional capabilities can foster a better balance between the basic objectives of the alliance: deterrence and reassurance.

It is the aim of the North Atlantic alliance to make it evident to the Soviet Union, by a demonstrated and assured defence capability, that the use of military force, either for threatening or for attacking the West, will not offer any prospects of success.

The Federal Republic of Germany, standing on its own, would never be able to face a challenge by the Soviet Union or the Warsaw Pact forces. The same applies to all our European neighbours. Confronted by a nuclear world power like the Soviet Union, the capabilities of the European states are insufficient as an effective deterrent against the threat or use of force, and not even the capabilities of a united Europe would suffice.

It would be a tragic misconception to assume that Europe could do without United States protection, or that it could – if it were only united – defend itself alone and play an independent role in world politics. Whatever can be read into East–West comparisons of population figures, economic capabilities, or military postures, a brief look at any map and at the geostrategic pattern of Europe should be sufficient to demonstrate that the security of Western Europe can only be safeguarded by a close alliance with the United States of America.

Maintaining the full spectrum of effective deterrence and defence is beyond the political, economic and military capabilities of even the combined resources of Western Europe. Close and indivisible ties between Western Europe and the United States are the only means to ensure a balance of forces adequate to cause the potential aggressor to adopt a course of rationality in its political conduct.

The command and force structure in Allied Command Europe reflects the principle of collective defence. This is particularly obvious in the Central Region where land and air forces of six – and, if the French decide to participate in the common defence, seven – nations have to fight side by side. The deployment of our land forces ensures that each army corps has formations of a different nation as its neighbours. Behind this 'layer cake' of army formations, air defence units of different nations are deployed in two air defence belts.

Nowhere else is the principle of collective defence as apparent as here, a principle that is fundamental to NATO's deterrence. The deployment pattern of NATO forces eliminates the possibility of the aggressor directing his attack in such a way that only the forces of selected nations would be affected. This command and force structure has to be maintained, therefore, even if other solutions might seem to be more attractive from a purely defence orientated position.

Forward defence is a corollary of collective security. NATO territory must be defended as far to the East as possible. There are undeniable political and military imperatives that underlie this concept.

If NATO's strategy were to deliberately yield the territory, population, and resources of one of the member nations, how could NATO then expect that nation to stand? Forward defence, indeed, is a pre-requisite to any German contribution to the common defence. This does not apply to the Federal Republic of Germany alone, however, but equally to all Western European nations. If the Soviets take the risk of a major aggression against the heartland of Western Europe, no-one should imagine that its armies would stop at the Rhine or the German-Danish border.

Militarily, Western Europe has only very limited depth in its defence. Strategically important objectives, like the North Sea and Channel ports, are in easy reach of an aggressor. The objective, therefore, must be to stop the enemy before he reaches his stride. His mobility must be killed before his attack gains momentum.

Finally, the concept of unequivocal forward defence is in itself an essential element of deterrence. Concepts of 'trading space for time', in order to mount major counter-attacks, or 'area defence', in order to wear down the enemy armoured formations deep in our own territory, are not likely to deter a potential aggressor.

Any success in forward defence will depend on the ability to bring all available firepower and electronic warfare capability to bear. This requires a high state of readiness of our defence forces, timely measures for the preparation of their defences and the closest co-operation between land and air forces in a well-coordinated and truly combined land and air battle.

Nuclear weapons are an indispensable element of deterrence. NATO's deterrence rests on the close linkage of its conventional and theatre nuclear forces in Europe and the strategic nuclear potential of the United States. The tight and indissoluble coupling of these three elements of the NATO triad confronts the Soviet Union with the incalculable risk that any military conflict between the two alliances could escalate to an all-out nuclear war.

A renunciation of the first use of nuclear weapons by NATO would rob the present strategy of war prevention of a decisive characteristic, and the significance of Soviet conventional superiority would increase dramatically. In fact, NATO would face a fundamentally different conventional threat since the elimination of the nuclear risk would free the Warsaw Pact from the necessity of dispersing attack forces. Conventional conflicts in Europe would no longer involve any necessary risk for the territory of the Soviet Union. The USSR would be liberated from the one constraint that has kept it from using military force against

53

the European continent. With the growing risk of a conventional conflict, however, the danger of a nuclear war would also increase because, as nuclear powers are drawn into an armed conflict, the probability would grow that the conflict might degenerate into a nuclear war, in spite of such declared policies as the renunciation of the first use of nuclear weapons.

NATO countries cannot hope to escape from using nuclear weapons to deter aggression. They must make an energetic attempt, however, to reduce their present dependence on the early use of nuclear weapons as a deterrent. Efforts to improve the conventional capabilities are most urgently required and should be a task of high political priority in all NATO countries. The call for strengthening NATO's conventional capabilities has acquired a new degree of urgency and, for the first time in NATO's history, a realistic perspective. The new degree of urgency is due to the fact that the imbalances below the strategic nuclear level now have a much more serious impact, and a new, more realistic perspective appears because modern technologies can offer efficient and more cost-effective solutions. The question is not whether nuclear deterrence should be replaced by a purely conventional one. Nor is it one of achieving conventional equilibrium. A conventional capability is required that is sufficient to deny the Warsaw Pact those operational options on which rapid success and quick victory depend.

Almost all NATO nations are facing severe budget constraints. This may be a familiar challenge to defence departments, and many defence ministers have had to fight to secure an appropriate share for defence in spite of budget constraints. But for the first time, defence planners are confronted with another, more severe, constraint. The manpower resources from which NATO armed forces can recruit their soldiers, sailors, and airmen are shrinking dramatically. The result of this demographic development is one first priority: to stop speaking about needed increases in force structure. Manpower problems alone will preclude any significant force build-up throughout NATO. In exploiting modern technology we have to seek less manpower-intensive solutions.

Today NATO has a wide array of ageing aircraft, however, whose combat effectiveness is questionable, due to the lack of appropriate ammunition and the ever-increasing air defence capability of the Warsaw Pact. Their survivability and fire-power could be greatly enhanced by a stand-off dispenser system, carrying a combination of general and special purpose submunitions that would be effective against artillery concentrations, assembly areas, river crossings, choke points, and dispersal operating bases. The development of both appropriate dispenser systems and submunitions has reached an advanced stage. They could be procured in a very short time.

NATO cannot wait until more sophisticated technology becomes available, and should not block urgently needed decisions by rules and controversy between national forces and services or by focusing the discussion on the sole issue of the costs involved. Closer industrial co-operation among NATO countries, already in the development phase, could help to reduce the costs. Efforts to improve NATO's conventional capabilities should be a task of high priority in all NATO countries.

STRATEGY AND ARMS CONTROL

Johan Jørgen Holst

DIRECTOR OF THE NORWEGIAN INSTITUTE OF
INTERNATIONAL AFFAIRS

The Atlantic alliance has maintained the peace for 35 years and may be described as a major success story. It has provided military security through strength and clarity. American engagement in the security order in Europe has produced countervailing power to the military machine of modern-day Muscovy as well as reassurance to European society against the resurgence of traditional jealousies and rivalries. American protection has provided a necessary framework for West European co-operation. It has provided an external precondition for a European concentration on social reconstruction and regional reconciliation, the reconstitution of a viable civic culture in the wake of the great carnage of the Second World War. Furthermore, the alliance has provided coherence and cohesion to the security order in Europe by linking the central European region to the northern and southern flanks, areas which are flanks only in relation to the central front but which occupy central positions within other geometrical depictions of the balance of power.

For the smaller powers the Atlantic alliance has provided an arena for meaningful participation in the political process which shapes the structure of power and the conditions of diplomacy. They have obtained access and assumed roles which would otherwise have been unavailable; the alliance has become a countervailing influence to small-state propensities for messianism and escapism in international relations.

All states have a right to security and it is impossible for any state to obtain absolute security except by the total domination of other states. Hence, all must accept the fact that security is attainable only in a relative sense. This will be true as long as international society is made up of sovereign states and there is no international authority with the right and power to police international relations. States have to exercise mutual restraint in their quest for security. In the absence of such restraint they are likely to set off competitive actions which harbour the danger of exacerbating conflicts, introducing new sources of instability and resulting in ever higher levels of military forces.

In the nuclear age, states can no longer view security as a competitive goal, as a benefit to be obtained at the expense of adversaries. Security must be viewed as a shared value. The common enemy is war itself. Real security means common security. Therefore, the search for arms control and disarmament must be a pursuit of mutual gains rather than unilateral advantage.

NATO is committed to a two-pronged approach to security: the maintenance of adequate military strength to deter aggression, and a search for progress towards a more stable relationship in which the underlying political problems can be solved. Arms control and disarmament can contribute to a stabilization of East–West relations in a manner which should enhance rather than detract from military security. The two prongs are complementary in nature.

The alliance will run into internal problems whenever the dual track approach to security is obscured in practice or rhetoric. Societies will support the required military effort only when the latter is associated with an alternative vision of a more co-operative arrangement than an open-ended military competition. There must be light at the end of the tunnel for our citizens to join the journey towards real security. Arms control should be viewed as a genuine complement to military insurance, not just a sugar-coating on the bitter pills of 'military necessity'.

The Atlantic alliance has drawn the line in Europe. It provides clarity to the political lines of division buttressed by a military posture based on the concept of forward defence. Such a posture serves the purpose of containing Soviet military power. However, it cannot in a similar manner sustain a policy of political reconstruction aimed at ameliorating or overcoming the division. In a period where the Soviet Union may be viewed as a colossus on clay feet stewing in uninspiring clumsiness, a policy of containment may seem inadequate to the political aspirations of self-conscious and assertive West European societies. American 'realist' critics of the policies of détente frequently forget that the latter were policies to induce change. Furthermore, the basic instability of the Soviet imperial position in Europe flows from the barriers to social and political change, which the mechanisms of Soviet control erect in Eastern Europe. A continued military confrontation at a high level of military forces generate and perpetuate obstacles to political change, which could produce a more stable and legitimate social order in Eastern Europe.

Furthermore, to the extent that the danger of war is perceived as inhering more in the possibility of turmoil spreading from 'police actions' and insurrections in East Europe than in a deliberate Soviet western offensive, a nuclear-based forward defence posture may seem less reassuring and relevant to Western European policy makers and public alike. The classical problem of aligning political perspectives and military postures is becoming increasingly complex, as NATO faces the challenge of striking a proper balance between the need to preserve clarity and provide openings for change. Differences in European and

American outlooks may come to the fore if Americans tend to view the need to contain and tie down the Soviet Union in Europe as a means to stem Soviet global ambitions, while Europeans focus on the need to create a more open political order in Europe, wherein Soviet military power would gradually recede into the depth of mother Russia (with the option of being deployed in different directions).

The relationship between military dispositions and political development is hidden in obscurity and does not lend itself to easy demonstration. Hence, unstated assumptions, vague concepts and visionary rhetoric may come to dominate the discourse. It could manage to destroy present structures without providing viable alternatives. The danger of romantic flights could be exacerbated by a propensity to resist any change for fear of a ride on the slippery slope. The debate about NATO strategy could easily crystallize into a debate for, or against change, rather than a debate about the purpose and method of change. The alliance could lose relevance in the eyes of the 'successor generation', which does not accept responsibility for the historical roots of the post-war order in Europe, which were created by the Second World War. It could come to be viewed as part of the problem rather than the solution to the division of Europe.

NATO strategy should be assessed, then, in terms of a spectrum of potential contingencies and not be driven solely by the spectre of large-scale invasion. Moreover, attention should be paid to the potential impact of the military posture on peacetime relations and perceptions. This observation is relevant to the discussion of emerging technologies and the options they provide for large-scale deep strikes into Eastern Europe. A posture which is optimized for disrupting a large-scale Soviet offensive towards Western Europe may push Eastern Europe deeper into the Soviet military embrace. Such could be the peacetime result of a Western strategy which makes Eastern Europe into the western zone of pre-emptive military destruction.

The problems are complex as geography, and the need to fashion a credible defence against echeloned attacks from a position which lacks geographical depth, imposes a need to disrupt the enemy before his forces penetrate deeply into Western territory. However, the fixation with second and third echelon forces could cause NATO to overlook the need to cope with the first echelon forces of the first wave of an attack. A propensity to look for identifiable technological fixes to complex operational problems further accentuates the difficulty of finding prudent and effective solutions. Complex solutions inevitably become vulnerable to malfunctions or breakdowns in individual elements of the system. The problem of target acquisition is likely to prove more difficult in the fog of actual war than on the testing range. This is not to argue that modern technology should be eschewed, the point is rather to choose solutions with prudence and pay attention to ramifications beyond the rather simple calculus of battle management.

Modern warfare has developed a velocity and intensity of destruction which defies deliberate and measured control by political authorities. It conveys the danger of the military machine driving political institutions across the threshold of no return. Nuclear weapons, in particular, have compounded the problem of maintaining political control. Unreality abounds in the discussion of alternatives. A frightening example is the notion that the Pershing-II is much more threatening to the Soviet Union than the Minuteman-III because it would involve some 6–10 minutes warning, rather than 30 minutes, thus depriving the Politburo of the time to contemplate the decision to retaliate. But where do we find the political body which can be convened and which is capable of considering the ins and outs of the most momentous decision in history in the course of 30 minutes? Surely the task must rather be to make the time for decision about retaliation independent of the flight time of the attacking missiles by designing deployment options and procedures for command, control and communication so as to permit the political authorities to deliberate and not commit the future of their country and others to automated, pre-programmed responses. There is a dilemma here as deterrence might be considered stronger the more certain a massive response may appear to the would-be aggressor. However, pushing deterrence of the potential enemy to the limit may also produce immobility for fear of being manoeuvred into a position of having to respond.

In the search for viable conventional options NATO should be looking for responses which slow down and space out military operations rather than putting a premium on rapid and massive counter-strikes which threaten to consume options for restraint and early termination of the war.

NATO's reliance on large-scale and early use of battlefield nuclear weapons epitomizes the danger of losing control and of self-imposed immobility at the point of crisis. Conditions have changed since the strategy of flexible response was first conceived in the early sixties and later promulgated in 1967. Strategic parity, Soviet preponderance in intermediate-range nuclear forces and the nearing parity in battlefield nuclear forces between East and West, no longer make it a rational solution for NATO to rely on the use of theatre nuclear forces to compensate for inferiority in conventional forces. If the purpose of using battlefield nuclear weapons is not to turn conventional defeat into nuclear victory, but rather to increase the danger of escalation to the level of strategic nuclear forces in order to induce the adversary to stop the war, it is hard to see why NATO needs the thousands of nuclear warheads which will remain in Europe, even after the Montebello decision to

59

reduce NATO's inventory in Europe with 1400 nuclear warheads has been implemented. It seems to suggest rather an option of prolonged nuclear war on the battlefield in Europe, an option which seems particularly unattractive in view of Soviet nuclear capabilities and the density of population and industry in Central Europe. The spectre of being enveloped by the dilemma of using or losing the nuclear weapons, which are kept in munition sites in forward areas and intended for use by delivery systems with short-range and firing from forward positions, is one which seems bound to attract increasing concern and opposition.

NATO will be compelled to move in the direction of abrogating reliance on the option of first use of nuclear weapons. This is not a matter primarily of declaratory commitments, but rather of re-fashioning the structure of nuclear deployments so as to prevent the latter from driving decisions about the deployment of nuclear weapons. Furthermore, it seems doubtful if NATO should conclude an agreement with the Warsaw Pact countries to renounce the option of first use of nuclear weapons, as such agreements tend to breed inflated views of their importance and, perhaps more importantly, they could be exploited for purposes of claiming a *droit de regard* regarding the general defence policy of the other contracting party. Defence policy should not be made hostage to the consent of the adversary. However, it should be fashioned also in cognizance of his perspectives, expectations and concerns.

Other modes of regulation may require formal agreements concerning build-down, disengagement and thinning-out of nuclear (and conventional) weapons. It is necessary for NATO to adopt a comprehensive approach so as not to create an artificial separation between the definition of solutions in the fields of military planning and arms control negotiations. Military planning is based on a combined arms approach to force structure and war plans while arms control negotiations are frequently based on a clear separation of the nuclear from the conventional force components. Is it possible to stabilize forward defence through restructuring arms control arrangements, leading to the withdrawal of battlefield nuclear weapons and a thinning-out of armoured forces, bridge-crossing equipment and self-propelled artillery from forward areas? Is it possible to fashion a defence posture for NATO with a marked conventional and defensive accent (always recognizing that there can never be an absolute separation between offensive and defensive postures, let alone military systems)? More boldly, perhaps, it may be asked whether the American commitment to the defence of Europe could be maintained by a different posture than the present one, even taking into account the geographical asymmetries of a distant 'island power', like the United States, and a continental 'heartland power', like the Soviet Union, in relation to the central front in Europe. A combination of pre-positioned equipment, regular exercises and host-nation support agreements could possibly provide a basis for a substantial build-down of the American permanent military presence in Western Europe, provided the Soviet Union could be persuaded to build-down its permanent military presence in Eastern Europe correspondingly. There is a strong political case for maintaining the priority of Soviet and American troop reductions in the Vienna negotiations about mutual and balanced force reductions in Europe.

NATO's strategy must cover the entire alliance area, not just the central front. While the general principles upon which it rests should be valid throughout the area covered by the alliance, they should surely be tailored to the specific circumstances. In northern Norway, for example, NATO can better afford to trade space for time than in Central Europe. The principle of forward defence can be applied differently. Similarly, nuclear weapons do not have to be deployed alliance-wide, in order to extend protection to the whole alliance. Sub-regional nuclear weapon-free zones need not contradict overall NATO strategy if properly fashioned, particularly if NATO were to move in the direction of a *de facto* no-first-use posture. It is indeed possible to argue that in certain areas the need to prevent inadvertent escalation makes it more important as a confidence-building measure to clarify the salient distinction between the possible use of nuclear weapons and conventional weapons than to keep the adversary guessing about the nature of the response in order to increase deterrence. In future, NATO will need to be able to contribute to the weaving of a more complex texture of defence arrangements, which are capable of reassuring the societies of the member states, of providing credible deterrence *vis-à-vis* the Soviet Union (while at the same time conveying incentives to show restraint), and of contributing towards the construction of a more co-operative political order with an interlocking set of arms control arrangements.

During the INF negotiations, NATO developed a novel and highly effective system of consultations concerning the conduct of the negotiations, although the limits of such consultations were demonstrated when the United States took a position on the 'walk-in-the-woods' and 'walk-in-the-park' formulae for possible compromises without prior consultation with the NATO allies. Logically and politically the negotiations about intermediate range and strategic nuclear forces should be merged, in order to enable Moscow and Washington to create their own mix of forces within agreed parameters and while observing equal ceilings. However, such a merger would imply a European demand and expectation to be consulted in the broadened negotiation (at least to the same degree as about INF in the past), thereby obtaining a say in the structuring of American strategic forces. The resistance in Washington to the proposed merger is hardly unrelated to the unwillingness in many quarters to allow a greater European voice in the overall decisions about the nuclear weapons of the United States. However, if the alliance is to remain a viable and relevant institution in the future, Washington has to concede a European right to consultation and co-determination about the military posture which is designed to protect the alliance. In the absence of such a concession the alliance is likely to experience future replays of the double concerns about American decoupling from Europe and Soviet hegemonic aspirations therein, which both shaped the original 'dual-track' decision in 1979 and caused the fall-out between large segments of the public and their governments in the alliance over its implementation.

PEACE: THE VITAL FACTORS

Michael Howard
REGIUS PROFESSOR OF MODERN HISTORY,
OXFORD UNIVERSITY

Lord Ismay, NATO's first secretary general, once described the object of the alliance as being to keep the Americans in, the Soviets out, and the Germans down. For a third of a century it has been successful in these objectives except, fortunately, the third. The Germans have not been kept down but raised up; raised up, indeed, so successfully that today the younger generation finds it hard to understand that there was ever a German problem at all. The Soviets have certainly been kept out: by military deterrence, without doubt, but even more by the development of societies so successful, both politically and economically, that the same younger generation, even those of the extreme left, find it even harder to understand why anyone in the West ever regarded the Soviet system as in any sense a competitor with their own. So far from extending its rule westward over Europe, the Soviets are finding it harder than ever to maintain their hold over the territories they overran in 1945.

Still, 35 years is a long time. The settlements after the Napoleonic wars and the German wars of unification lasted only 40-odd years, while the deeply flawed Versailles system collapsed after twenty. All eventually ceased to reflect political realities or to contain irresistible new ambitions. When the existing order is no longer seen to express the real relationship of social and political forces, the chances are that someone will challenge or test its stability by the use of force. That is one way wars begin. Have we reached such a position in Europe today?

Certainly much has changed since the alliance was established in 1949. In the first place there has grown up in Western Europe a generation for whom the deeds of both Hitler and Stalin seem as remote as those of Napoleon or Alexander the Great. They take for granted the security provided by the alliance, see little point in adding to the military scaffolding so as to preserve the stability of the edifice, and in some cases would like to have the whole expensive and unsightly apparatus pulled down.

But it is not only this generation which believes that, now that the original purpose of the alliance has been achieved, we should be pressing on with the further objective, of normalising relations with our neighbours to the East; the Soviet Union so far as possible, Eastern Europe, and particularly Eastern Germany, as a matter of urgency. The states of Western Europe, and the Federal Republic of Germany in particular, are not content to remain indefinitely as the border provinces of an American-centred empire. The restoration of historic, cultural and not least commercial links with their neighbours has always enjoyed a high priority in their policies. Defence has always been seen, in wide circles in Western Europe, as a preliminary to détente.

This attitude is less widely shared in the United States. From Washington, especially President Reagan's Washington, the Soviet Union is not seen primarily as a regional danger in Europe, but as a global adversary, threatening the *status quo* all over the world. Other regions – the Middle East, South-West Asia, and increasingly Central America – appear as further fronts where the enemy is probing for soft spots in the defences of 'the Free World' in its quest for global domination. To the Reagan administration, and many other Americans as well, the European desire to normalise relations with their neighbours looks like softness, self-delusion and susceptibility to nuclear blackmail. They demand instead that the Europeans should not only undertake yet greater efforts for their own defence, but contribute to the burden of global defence in other regions of the world.

Some European governments share this global perspective, but by no means all. There is, on the contrary, a widespread feeling that the American interpretation is based on a fundamental misunderstanding, both of the nature of Third World problems, and of Soviet capacity to exploit them. There is a fear that these problems will only be made worse by the methods, both political and military, of the Reagan administration, and that American policy, so far from holding Soviet expansion in check, is in fact providing new opportunities for it. The question that worries many European observers is not whether or not American policy in the Third World is 'moral'. It is whether it is not dangerously counter-productive. And there is a yet more widespread fear that these policies, unilaterally pursued, might involve Europe in a conflict over 'out of area' issues on which Western opinion was deeply divided, and in which Europe itself might be destroyed.

These divergences in perspective exacerbate a problem which was in any case likely to develop once Western European political stability and economic prosperity had been restored; that of burden-sharing within the alliance. The failure of Western Europe to make the kind of progress towards political unity that had been hoped when the alliance was established, remains the fundamental obstacle to the creation of the kind of European 'defence entity' that would alone enable us to play the role in our own defence which our wealth and population should make possible. This is the more serious since the economic and political problems of the Soviet empire have not prevented it from achieving and maintaining a position of military parity with the United States; a position which gives it greater confidence in its operations on the world scene, and might make all prospects of a purely conventional defence of Western Europe appear hopeless but for the continuing deterrent of the possibility of general nuclear war.

Does any of this amount to the kind of seismic shift in social and political forces which destroys the underlying stability of the international order and places it at the mercy of crises and accidents? Have we moved, as is sometimes suggested, from a post-war into a pre-war era such as that of 1908–1914 or 1933–1939?

Certainly the world outside Europe is profoundly unstable. No new order has yet developed to replace that imposed by the old European empires. But the conflicts outside Europe are unlikely to result in Armageddon unless both superpowers involve themselves, explicitly and simultaneously; and this will happen only if they are prepared to accept the appalling risks of nuclear confrontation. Whatever alarming quotations may be dug out of the strategic literature on both sides, there is no indication that either the American or the Soviet leadership is prepared for anything of the kind.

As for Europe, in assessing the prospects for stability, we should look neither at the military balance nor at the nature of the weapons themselves. This has been the fundamental error of the past decade; one shared equally by the Committee on the Present Danger in the United States and the *doppelgänger* it has conjured up on this side of the Atlantic, the European peace movement. We must look deeper for the things that really matter.

Can the Soviet Union continue to control its East European empire? The tension between the Soviet determination to maintain political and military control over an area they deem vital to their security, and the desire of the peoples of Eastern Europe to share in the material, if not the political blessings of the West, will continue to require the most delicate management. If that management were to fail, and Eastern Europe were to enter into a prolonged period of turbulence, what would this mean for the stability of East–West relations? Could Western governments resist the temptation to involve themselves in these upheavals – and would the Soviet Union believe it even if they did not? And whether or not such turbulence spread to East Germany, can the Germans, East and West, incrementally develop a relationship which will not call in question the whole post-war settlement of the continent?

There is however a third and equally disturbing problem. The two decades of economic boom which brought Western Europe to such heights of prosperity now lie in the past. Western European societies are having to adjust themselves to a lower degree of expectation. At the same time technological change is speeding the decline of older industries without creating comparable opportunities in new ones. If the government of West Germany is increasingly beset by the social and ideological difficulties created by generational change, those of France and Britain

65

have to grapple primarily with the political and economic problems arising from massive industrial dislocation. These developments fuel a political radicalism which, without necessarily advocating Soviet-style solutions or being sympathetic to Soviet policies, is fundamentally anti-military and anti-American in its orientation, and provides much of the political muscle for the peace movements. For these groups, opposition to the alliance and to the American connection is part of an overall package of opposition to governmental policies in general. It has been strong enough to destroy the consensus over defence that existed between the major political parties in Britain and West Germany for 35 years, and it would be optimistic to assume that it will not cause a great deal more trouble yet. This radicalism is unlikely to gain political dominance in Western Europe; but it could do much to make the region, quite literally, indefensible.

Finally, the question arises as to whether a United States whose centre of gravity has been steadily moving away from the Eastern seaboard, and whose sentimental links with Western Europe have been gradually eroding, will continue to regard the region as so vital to its own security that it will persist, in spite of all the frustrations and humiliations involved, in maintaining so complex an alliance.

Factors such as these will determine whether the balance is stable or not: not SS-20s, Pershing-IIs or numbers of Soviet tanks. If the underlying political structure remains stable it will not be disturbed by weapons imbalances, or be at the mercy of crises, accidents and misperceptions. If it is not, then peace cannot be preserved either by anxiously matching weapon for weapon or by dramatic gestures of one-sided disarmament.

Peace in Europe is thus only likely to be threatened by a combination of the three circumstances outlined above. First, growing instability in Eastern Europe might drive a desperate Soviet Union to take the gamble of a *fuite en avant*: much as the bleak prospects in the Balkans led the Central Powers in 1914 into the actions which precipitated the First World War. Second, growing instability and political divisions in Western Europe might make the Soviets believe they would run a negligible risk in taking the offensive. And finally, American impatience and disgust with their European allies might make the Soviets misread the signals, as they did so fatally at the time of Korea, and assume that the United States now regarded Western Europe as expendable.

The first of these developments lies beyond our control, and we would be ill-advised to think otherwise. But it was to guard against the second and the third that NATO came into being, and for which it still exists. No doubt one day the inevitable process of social and political change will make it impossible any longer to preserve the alliance, or better still, may make it unnecessary. But meanwhile, anyone seriously

66

concerned with the preservation of peace should devote their best efforts to keeping the framework which has for so long made that peace possible in the best feasible state of repair. It is no less true today than it has been in the past; if we do not hang together, we shall assuredly hang separately.

FROM CONFRONTATION
TO CO-OPERATION

Bülent Ecevit
FORMER TURKISH PRIME MINISTER

After World War II, several East European countries had to pay a very heavy price for the Soviet Union's contribution to their 'liberation'. Stalin's commitments at Yalta to allow free elections and to respect governments representing the popular will of those countries soon proved to be shallow words to gain time for consolidating the Soviet Union's hold over a large part of Europe, either through military pressure or through blatant interference in the internal affairs of the 'liberated' countries.

Western Europe and the United States rightly regarded such actions as a serious threat, not only to their security, but also to their democratic heritage. NATO was born out of the legitimate concern over the Soviet ambitions and policies of those years. The Warsaw Pact, on the other hand, was established six years later, as a counterweight, to ensure the continuation of Soviet hegemony over most of Eastern Europe.

A significant difference between the two alliances is that, while nations have joined NATO voluntarily or, in some cases, have even declined from participating in its military structure, membership in the Warsaw Pact has been imposed on its partners, and the rules and conditions of membership have remained rather rigid.

Another difference, testifying to the greater freedom and independence enjoyed by individual countries within NATO, is that, while it is very difficult and risky for Warsaw Pact countries to deviate from Moscow's orthodox guidelines, NATO countries are free to follow different paths, within a democratic process, as indicated by the presence of democratic socialist or social democratic governments as well as conservative and capitalist ones in the alliance, (although the tolerance enjoyed by some individual member countries that, now and then, deviate from democratic principles are not always consistent with those principles).

Although local wars have been going on around the world during the four decades since the Second World War, there has not been a single military conflict between the East and the West. The opposing North Atlantic and Warsaw Treaty alliances have been instrumental in containing the differences, disputes and rivalries between the two sides within peaceful bounds. Both alliances, therefore, have come to be accepted as the indispensable components of a balance on which the hopes of preventing a Third World War and nuclear annihilation largely rest.

Relations between the superpowers that lead the two alliances have become markedly strained in recent years; and, in those parts of the world which are not covered by the North Atlantic and Warsaw treaties, they keep confronting each other in conflicts by proxy. Such confrontations, in turn, adversely affect relations between the East and West as a whole. The peace and security maintained by the two alliances are valid only regionally and rest on a stalemate of deterrence rather than on rapprochement and mutual confidence. In the meantime nuclear arsenals have grown excessively, posing a serious threat to mankind.

As détente deteriorates, and as the reciprocal deployment of tactical nuclear weapons escalates, the members of both alliances situated in the sensitive areas of Europe tend to become increasingly scared of being fatally engulfed in nuclear warfare at the initial stage of an East–West conflict that may be triggered on or near their own soils by either of the two superpowers.

After what the Europeans lived through in two world wars, their dread of being the first victims of a nuclear conflict, and the reaction of certain sections of the public in Europe to the deployment of new nuclear weapons, should not be regarded as signs of irrational pacifism, nor as the outcome of the Soviet 'peace propaganda'. If sufficient freedoms of expression and association existed in the Warsaw Pact countries, such reactions would no doubt be expressed there also, as strongly at least as in some of their Western counterparts. Indeed, reactions are becoming increasingly vocal in East Germany in spite of its repressive regime.

The smaller members of both Alliances are obviously disturbed by the feeling that they are not sufficiently in control of their own security and future any more, having relinquished their fate largely to their respective 'big brothers'. Such concerns or misgivings on the part of smaller allies and the recent deterioration in East–West relations should not be construed to indicate, however, that the two alliances have outlived their usefulness. The world is not yet ready to do without them.

What is needed is some basic rethinking, on both sides, with regard to the two alliances. A lot has changed since the Second World War to warrant a fundamentally new approach to collective security. This rethinking should be based on a non-prejudiced assessment of tendencies and intentions in both the East and the West.

It should be clear to any objective observer that people on either side, with the possible exception of some non-consequential fringe groups, do not want war; on the contrary, they dread the prospect of war and they have no irredentist ambitions. Governments on both sides also share this. Although the rhetoric of some governments occasionally, and the rhetoric of the two superpowers more frequently, may give a contrasting impression, they all take care to stop short of building up tension to an irreversible point. It is paradoxical and irrational that such a pervasive mood of peacefulness, such aversion to war, should be so contrastingly accompanied by an unparalleled and deadly armament race, between the East and the West, nurtured on mutual suspicion.

The open societies of the West ought to be able to muster enough self-confidence and courage to take the initiative in coming forth with proposals to demolish these suspicions reciprocally. One such proposal may be the establishment of a permanent and institutionalized dialogue, with periodic meetings between the two alliances. The suspicions, grievances and expectations of all the parties should be aired; and problems, concerning not only areas covered by the two alliances, but also those pertaining to universal peace and security, should be collectively discussed, and possibilities of increased co-operation should be explored, in the course of this dialogue. Although the Conference on Security and Co-operation in Europe (CSCE) seems to be deadlocked for the time being, after the promising start in Helsinki, this initiative has illustrated that the two superpowers and the European countries, both in the East and the West, are not averse to the idea of dialogue – that they are aware of its necessity.

In launching an institutionalized dialogue of their own, the alliances should refrain from acting as if they were attempting to sidestep or demote or duplicate the CSCE. On the contrary, they should see to it that the dialogue between the two alliances prepares their members to participate more productively and constructively in the CSCE talks and help unfreeze those talks. After all, it is largely due to the disaccord and mistrust between the two alliances that the CSCE talks have become deadlocked. Therefore, a fruitful form of communication between the two alliances may substantially ease the way for the CSCE, giving the non-aligned and neutral countries of Europe greater opportunity, in turn, to prod the two alliances to make better progress towards rapprochement and a more assuring peace.

Apart from the CSCE, non-governmental, as well as governmental meetings or dialogues of different groups and nature also take place between the East and the West, some of which are attended by a number of neutral countries as well. So the two sides already have an accumulation of experience in this regard. But these remain disconnected ventures that leave certain areas uncovered. It would be worthwhile and timely to build on such experience a systematic and comprehensive dialogue within the framework of the North Atlantic and Warsaw Treaty alliances, in a way that may change their relationship into something more constructive and positive.

It is very important that, from the outset, various social and political groups, apart from governments and the military, actively take part in this dialogue, through separate but converging platforms. This is necessary to prevent the dialogue from being clogged, either by the intransigence of certain governments, or as a result of the inherent inertia and instinctive diffidence of civilian and military bureaucrats who are rather insensitive to public opinion and are even inclined to regard it as a cumbersome and uninformed intrusion into affairs of state.

Yet public opinion has become an important factor, not only in internal matters, but also in international affairs and, at the present stage at least, it has also become a force that can enhance peace. It should, therefore, be ensured that public opinion be effectively reflected in this process of dialogue. In contrast to Western representation, the presence of true and free representatives of public opinion in the non-governmental groups from the East may, of course, be only exceptional or accidental. But this would be a moral advantage for the West rather than for the East; and this moral advantage may eventually stir a tendency for soul-searching and for increased outspokenness and self-assertiveness among the members of non-governmental groups from the East, particularly among those in the smaller countries. They would at least have a chance to be exposed to the atmosphere of freedom that characterizes the democratic countries of the West, and this might in time have a positive impact. Besides, even the governments of the Warsaw Pact countries do not see eye-to-eye on every issue; and the participation, if possible, of non-governmental representatives in the dialogue – although they may be, in effect, chosen by their governments – may provide the smaller nations of that alliance with outlets to air some of their differences in a less restrained way. It should be ensured that the dialogue is not dominated by the leading powers; for the minor partners of both alliances have reasons to be apprehensive of certain traits and styles in the ways the two leading powers handle international affairs and security matters. Such a process may not yield substantial results initially but, even by starting it, new positive forces and trends would be set in motion.

In an age when the danger of annihilation for all mankind has become so tangible, dialogue on vital matters between the East and the West cannot remain tied to summit talks held at intervals of years or decades, pending a particular presidential election in the United States to coincide with a particularly opportune succession of septuagenarial leadership in the Soviet Union.

Piecemeal bilateral contacts between individual countries of the East and the West are also not sufficient. They may yield conflicting or, at best, limited and disconnected results. The time has come for a more comprehensive and sustained participatory dialogue. The establishment of such an institutionalized dialogue would help regenerate and update the North Atlantic and Warsaw Treaty alliances in ways that may enable them to better adapt to changing conditions and to the peaceful mood of their member countries. It could, one hopes, start a process whereby the two alliances may eventually converge into a bridge of co-operation, rather than remain as opposing bastions of confrontation. It would give the smaller members of both alliances a chance to moderate between the two leading powers, not only within the context of East–West relations, but also globally, thus contributing to a general relaxation of atmosphere in the world. It could, in the meantime, help relax the political atmosphere within the Warsaw Pact community of nations, providing them with opportunities of gradual liberalization without causing excessive apprehension in the Soviet Union. And it would provide Europe, as a whole, with a chance to restore its considerably reduced influence in world affairs and over the course of civilization.

Most West European countries have become increasingly sensitive to democratic values and human rights in the recent decades. But, because of their restricted weight in the alliance, this sensitivity has not been sufficiently or credibly reflected in NATO policies and attitudes. The North Atlantic alliance is not supposed to be a partnership for collective defence alone. The text of the Treaty demands that the member countries pledge themselves to safeguarding 'freedom' and 'the principles of democracy, individual liberty and the rule of law'; and that they contribute to 'peaceful and friendly international relations' not only through military measures, but also by 'strengthening their free institutions', by 'bringing about a better understanding of the principles upon which these institutions are founded', and by caring for the 'well-being' of the people.

But these aspects of the alliance have been overshadowed by the priority given to considerations of security in the military sense, largely because of the dominant role that the United States plays in NATO. For, despite the American nation's unquestionable dedication to freedom and democracy, most United States' administrations seem to think that a superpower with global interests and responsibilities cannot afford to be very particular about democratic values and institutions in international relations.

This approach has resulted in tolerating occasional deviations from democracy and human rights in one or other of the NATO countries. It has also led to the identification, not only of the United States, but to some degree of the West as a whole, with some of the most absolutist or anachronistic regimes in certain parts of the world.

Yet such digressions from basic principles and objectives damage the consistency and sap the moral strength of the alliance. As a result, and with the added negative impact on the Third World of the international economic policies of most of the industrial nations of the West, the democratic countries are increasingly outnumbered and isolated, and they fail to influence the direction in which the political systems of many newly emancipating nations evolve. This, in turn, weakens the effectiveness of the Western security system in international politics.

President Ronald Reagan has rightly said, in his address to the British Parliament on June 8, 1982, that 'the ultimate determinant in the struggle that is now going on in the world will not be bombs and rockets, but a test of wills and ideas' and the West's 'spiritual resolve' to uphold the democratic 'values', 'beliefs' and 'ideals' that it cherishes. It is high time that a NATO strategy reflecting this 'spiritual resolve' gains ascendancy over strategies stressing 'bombs and rockets'.

Even if mankind may not yet be mature enough to ensure its survival without maintaining a nuclear balance, such balance could be de-escalated to much lower levels, without risking security and peace, if the East and the West would jointly exert at least as much effort to build up mutual confidence as the efforts they have reciprocally exerted, for four decades, to build up piles and piles of armaments and nuclear deterrence. They could try this by engaging in an institutionalized pluralistic and participatory dialogue between their alliances, aiming at eventual transition from confrontation to co-operation.

WHEN DIVERSITY MUST PREVAIL

Thierry de Montbrial
DIRECTOR OF THE FRENCH INSTITUTE FOR
INTERNATIONAL RELATIONS

Alliances are mortal. Their birth and death depend fundamentally on the nature of the international system. Whether the Atlantic alliance will survive for the next twenty years depends primarily on whether the international system itself will maintain its basic structure. I would like to argue that such would be the case, although with a number of qualifications. Fundamentally, I believe that our fate is in our hands.

The world of 1949 could be described as 'bipolar'. After World War II, the international system became progressively structured around two dominant poles, a sea power – the United States – and a continental power – the Soviet Union. Certainly, a number of changes have taken place. The internal balance of the Western sub-system has changed greatly. While American GNP, in the aftermath of World War II, was roughly twice as large as that of Europe, they are nowadays of the same order of magnitude. Also, the decolonization process has gradually taken place and came to an end during the seventies. On the Eastern side, the USSR has been able to establish its grip on its Western flank, and to change the regional balance of power to its advantage along its southern border after the Iranian revolution. But the Soviet Union has been weakened toward the East since the Sino–Soviet split. While the East–West military correlation of forces was characterized until the seventies by a 'balance of imbalances', that is, an American nuclear superiority which was supposed to offset the Soviet conventional superiority, the situation is now somewhat more complex: there is an approximate nuclear parity, while the Soviet conventional superiority still prevails. On the other hand, the completion of decolonization has created a void that makes unavoidable – whether we like it or not – East–West competition in the Third World. In some cases, such as the Near East and the Gulf, the stakes are so high for both sides that the possibility of a major East–West showdown in a Third World area spilling over into the central theatre has become, at least, thinkable.

Concurrently, the détente phase left a probably irreversible impact in Europe. Although the reunification of Germany is excluded in the foreseeable future, the question of the normalization of inter-German relations is now at the forefront of West German foreign policy and there will be no return to the *status quo ante* in this area. Another new dominant

74

feature of Western foreign policy is their willingness to play a major role in *Mittel Europa* affairs. On the other hand, the new strategic balance between the two superpowers, together with the technological evolution of nuclear weapons (accuracy, yield, penetration, etc.) has led many, in particular in the United States and in NATO circles, to have doubts about the adequacy of NATO strategy.

The transatlantic partnership is now more troubled than ever before. The Americans too often look down on the Europeans as freeriders trying to shift the defence burden on the United States, while continuing to flirt with the Soviet empire; and many Europeans see the Reagan administration as a highly dangerous group of people, capable of putting the world on the verge of a major catastrophe.

Will, however, the whole international system break down? In theory, this could happen under three basic circumstances. First, a large-scale war. I believe that this is very unlikely. No Western country would obviously take the risk, and Moscow probably knows that it might be the surest way of bringing the great communist adventure to an end. However, an accident cannot be totally ruled out, for example, if at some point the Soviets yielded to an old temptation – to intervene in Iran.

The second circumstance would be the internal collapse of one of the two major alliances. There is considerable speculation about the future of the Soviet Union itself. The internal difficulties of the country – economic and demographic problems, the question of nationalities – should be neither over-estimated nor under-estimated. Some very painful adjustments have to take place inside the USSR; although I believe that a real collapse is excluded within the next twenty years, more and more constraints are likely to limit its ability to practise a too ambitious foreign policy beyond its immediate borders. As for Eastern Europe, the Soviet leaders have learnt to manage the situation to their advantage, and I consider an explosion there, even in Poland, to be unlikely. Overall, the weakness of the Soviet empire will develop, but not to the point of provoking an implosion.

As for the Western alliance, the situation is, of course, totally different; nobody would even consider the possibility of an American internal collapse. But, should the Atlantic alliance fall apart, it would indeed change the international system overall. The probability of a limited war in Europe would increase sharply; the 'Finlandization' of Germany, if not of Western Europe as a whole, would also surely be achieved in one or two decades.

In the long run, the blow to the United States could be mortal. The internal collapse of the Atlantic alliance could be the end point of a political process, but it could also follow from a degradation of the international economic system, especially if protectionism were to prevail. In such an event, the Mutual Security Treaty between Japan and the United States might not survive either. Japan could be tempted to shape a new model of its sphere of co-prosperity in the Pacific. Ultimately, the blow to the United States might even be more severe.

There is a third possibility for a major change of the international system – the irruption of one or more new poles. One can think *a priori* of three candidates, namely the three big Asiatic powers: China, India and Japan. The first two have two of the major attributes of formidable superpowers: space and population. However, they are struggling with underdevelopment and internal political problems, and it is hard to imagine that they could, in the next twenty years, overcome them to the point that they could challenge more than marginally the United States and the Soviet Union. As for Japan, it obviously suffers from its territorial exiguity. But, more fundamentally, I do not think that Japan is ready to change its priorities unless it were forced to do so, because of a major change in the international economic system.

This brief analysis leads, it seems to me, to a clear conclusion. Although the international system has experienced very dramatic changes in the last 35 years, its fundamental underlying bipolar structure has been preserved and is likely to survive for quite a while as long as the Western allies do not make too many mistakes in the political, strategic and economic fields.

To survive well, all the members of the alliance must remember that the subjects of the international system are the nation-states, which recognize no superior authority to decide on important matters, such as peace and war. In concrete terms, this implies that the members of the Atlantic alliance must respect and understand each other. In other words, they must respect the national interests of one another. For instance, the French must accept the West German concern to improve relations between the two German states and its interests in Central Europe, and the Americans must also accept that their current approach to the Soviet Union is not agreeable to the Europeans.

The Europeans, for their part, must make greater efforts to strengthen their own security. For sure, some of the American criticisms are unjustified. Thus, the European share in total NATO expenditure has risen from 22.7 per cent in 1969 to 41.6 per cent in 1979. However, there is little doubt that in order to maintain Atlantic cohesion, the Europeans must do more. Indeed, the primary reliance of Western Europe's defence on American nuclear weapons will become increasingly difficult to maintain.

It would be foolish to go as far as foregoing deterrence, but it seems no longer possible that nuclear weapons can carry the entire burden. Although the French and the British deterrents are significant contributions to the alliance, as it has been recognized since the Ottawa Declaration of 1974, it is not reasonable to assume that they could play a central role in strengthening the defence of Northern Europe in the foreseeable future. The French, and probably the British, have a vested national interest in modernizing their nuclear systems, and this happens to be positive for the alliance as well. But this is not enough, and Western Europeans seem obliged to think more and more in terms of classical defence.

This has four very practical consequences. First, each European country must contribute more to the conventional defence of its own territory. Secondly, the national initiatives have to be coordinated within NATO. Thirdly, significant actions must be taken to promote European armament industries. Fourthly, the European countries, individually and collectively, must increase progressively the percentage of their GNP allocated to defence. The four points constitute a whole. There is no way to lower the nuclear threshold for free. Being above all a national matter, the survival of the group is based on the individual efforts of each of its members, and on the coherence of these efforts. Also, it is unlikely that the Europeans would accept to do more for their defence while buying only American weapons.

To the Europeans, the philosophy of the Harmel Report of 1967 is still valid. Defence and détente are complementary policies, not substitutes. Détente is not dead. Arms control negotiations must resume between the two superpowers. The French, for their part, do not exclude the possibility of entering a five-power negotiation (with the United States, the Soviet Union, Great Britain and China) if and when the two superpowers have made significant cuts in their arsenals. East–West trade must continue on a basis of mutual advantage and subject to COCOM rules. However, deals, such as gas, should be coordinated among the Europeans before they go to Moscow.

One of the big international issues in the past ten years has been the question of 'divisibility of détente'. Since the end of decolonization, there is no *status quo* in the Third World to refer to. It is wrong to want to establish a link between arms control issues and East–West competition in the Third World. It is also wrong to expect that the Western allies could agree on the nature of, and the way to deal with, every regional conflict.

The Atlantic alliance is a defensive alliance aiming at protecting its members against a direct attack. Of course, everything is related to everything else, and as we have seen, a full-scale conflict could result from the degeneration of a regional crisis. Nevertheless, the surest way to ruin the cohesion of the NATO partners would be to demand too much unity. The other side of the same coin is that the Atlantic partners should try – even more than they did in the recent past – not to hinder those who are involved in a local crisis, if their national interest is at stake (as in the Falklands issue or, to some extent, Grenada) or if they are resisting indirect Soviet pressures (Chad), or even more generally if they are wishing to stabilize a situation whose degradation could be detrimental to the Western allies at large (Lebanon, the Gulf). In some circumstances, however (Central America), Western disagreement cannot be totally papered over. In those instances, it is essential that the diverging views be expressed in such a way as not to undermine the cohesive forces within the alliance.

In the economic sphere, I have pointed out that the preservation of an open trade system is vital. Although it is quite remarkable that the GATT system has lasted rather well, this cannot be taken for granted in the next decade or two. I also claim that it is vital to save the European Community. If a global agreement cannot be found soon, we could very well see the beginning of a dismantling process, which would, over the years, destroy the very fabric of the Western alliance itself. The survival of that alliance and that of the European Community are closely associated.

There is a bright future for the Atlantic alliance if the members are willing and able to pay the political and economic costs of adjustment to the continuing evolution of the international system. The Atlantic partners should be self-confident; they should be convinced of the superiority of their economic and social structures, and trust that in the long run, the Soviet empire cannot win against them. They should, however, remain continuously on their guard against making the kind of political mistakes that, if too frequent, would amount to committing suicide.

PART THREE

Economic challenges and responses in the 1980s

THE GLOBAL ECONOMY AND SECURITY

Bunroku Yoshino
PRESIDENT OF THE JAPANESE INSTITUTE FOR
INTERNATIONAL ECONOMIC STUDIES

How do global economic policies help or hinder Western security, and what should be done about it? As we gradually emerge from the longest and deepest recession since World War II, we discern many uncertainties that are threatening international economic security and hindering a steady recovery of the world economy. The present recovery has been triggered mainly by the long-awaited upsurge of the United States' economy, and the countries that are not greatly dependent on the United States' market are not so far, at least, direct beneficiaries of this recovery. The areas that are not immediately affected by the rising demands of United States' imports will eventually come to enjoy the spill-overs of the immediately affected countries, but this is totally dependent on how robust and long-lasting the United States' economic recovery will prove to be.

Another element of uncertainty is high and almost unchanged levels of unemployment prevailing in most of the Western countries. The causes of this high rate of unemployment are not solely attributable to the low state of business activities. High labour costs based on high social charges prevalent in advanced Western countries make it more difficult for individual businesses to retain personnel over and above their minimum requirements. Increasing numbers of women workers entering labour markets to be liberated from household drudgery or to earn more money to meet rising costs of living may be another cause of the over-supply of job seekers. Technological advances, enabling more efficient production or management of work with less human labour, undoubtedly aggravate the situation.

On the other hand, this unabated high level of unemployment has become a serious social and moral problem for modern society. Not only does it consume a disproportionately large share of government expenditure, but the long-term social costs to be borne by coming generations may be incalculable. Indeed, the present-day economy of the Western world needs an urgent restructuring, in order to cope with this situation.

Another feature sharpened by this high state of unemployment is increasing protectionism. Protectionist trends and movements are always present in modern society as conservative human nature joins forces with vested interests. But when unemployment rises steeply and economic and social adjustments are not able to keep pace with this situation, industry and labour, and even government, take to protectionism.

Although inflation seems to be under control in most of the Western countries at the moment, it is potentially a no less dangerous threat to our society. The history of the recent inflation is well known. It began during the Vietnam War, the United States' dollar was then detached from the gold standard, and the major currencies of the world floated in the beginning of the 1970s. The following successive sharp rises in oil prices accelerated inflation further. The recycling of oil money, to alleviate the plight of those afflicted, further contributed to this situation. This business of recycling also called forth the unmanageable problem of the high debts of many developing countries, which are now threatening the global financial system.

In this connection, we must also view with great alarm the prospect for United States' federal budgets that continue to show a yearly deficit of an inordinately increasing magnitude. Because the United States is endowed with an enormous potential in natural resources and an unparalleled capacity for agricultural production, American budget deficits amounting to 5 or 6 per cent of GNP through a few more years may not be alarming if all other parts of the industrialised world are able to activate their potential economic power simultaneously. With the current low state of the global and national economies, harassed by unemployment and lurking inflationary trends, a concerted upswing of national economies cannot be expected or even hoped for, however, even disregarding the prevalent belief that we are at the bottom of a long-term cyclical trough. On the other hand, if the United States fails to 'grow itself out' of deficits, the American monetary and financial system may suffer a temporary collapse, bringing about a worldwide financial crisis. I am not a Cassandra, crying for this to happen. On the contrary, I believe in the American political system and hope that it will prevent such a disaster from taking place. Meanwhile, however, the American public should know that the whole world has been watching most anxiously to see how the United States' fiscal deficits will be halted or reduced.

The extraordinarily high level of interest rates prevailing in the United States is another source of concern. Not only has the United States' dollar's position as the major world currency been strengthened since the oil crisis, in spite of the weakening in the latter part of the 1970s, but the United States is now regarded as a safe haven of the first order in this turbulent world. It is only natural under these circumstances that large amounts of savings from all over the world should flow into the United States and the prevailing high plateau of interest rates strongly reinforces this.

Also, there are the heavy debts of most of the developing countries,

81

perhaps the most serious element of instability in the present-day world economy. That half of the total external debts owed by these countries are directly from private financial institutions hangs over the head of our capitalist society like Damocles' sword. Moreover, groundswells for recovery and development of the world economy are most likely to arise from those countries that have insatiable demands and abundant potentialities for growth – if these are released under appropriate strategies. Indeed, a failure to recover these past debts might be dwarfed by the enormous loss that the whole of humanity might suffer should this great reservoir of human energy and other resources be left untapped, prevented by debt burdens.

But to find a solution or remedy to each of these uncertainties is a truly daunting task. There may not be any appropriate treatment to be found immediately. These uncertainties must be removed gradually and step-by-step, in the course of world economic recovery, in a long process of policy mixes and their cautious application. But the world economic recovery hinges on how successfully we are able to solve these problems.

We are fortunate that the United States' economy has finally made a breakthrough in this world stagnation, and it is even pulling some of us in its trail. We should not sit back and leave the whole effort of leading the way to the Americans. We need the concerted efforts of every country in the world. What little any country can contribute should be reinforced by the co-operation of others. The sum total of all these endeavours will become a massive force that will utlimately pull us all out of the current doldrums.

In order to start such concerted efforts on a worldwide scale, my proposal is for the major trading nations to call for a new round of General Agreement on Tariffs and Trade (GATT) negotiations. The necessity for concerted efforts for world economic recovery has been well recognized by most of the world leaders for some time and has been repeatedly reconfirmed in past summit meetings. But up to now, most Western countries have been absorbed in their own domestic affairs and, being depressed by their own poor economic performances, have not been in a position to take the initiative in this matter. A new GATT round will provide a good start for such concerted efforts on an international scale.

This new GATT round should have a quite different character from that of the three major rounds in the past decades. It should represent the beginning of a concerted effort to find a key to the solution of the main uncertainties causing the present economic woes. What would be the main items of the agenda of this new round?

To come to grips with the complexities and magnitude of the problems involved, the agenda for the round must be most extensive and comprehensive. This might alarm some countries, especially those of the developing world. To enlist the full participation of the less developed countries (LDCs), access for the Third World's products to the Western markets must be a first priority on the agenda.

In the increasingly integrating international economy, the importance of the linkage of trade and finance and other issues must be recognized. This has been reaffirmed by the recent meeting of trade and finance ministers. A new GATT negotiation on trade issues would attain no great results without the participation of finance ministers of both developing and developed countries. Honest and serious efforts must be made to ease the real access of the LDC products to our internal markets.

But this would pose to the Western world a most discomforting task. The inroads of cheap-labour manufacturers already present a great menace to the existing industries of Europe and the United States. Should the Western world reject or limit the entrance of these products into their markets, however, not only would our developing assistance made over the past decades be lost, but the overall recovery of the global economy would be retarded. A groundswell of economic recovery, which we have been expecting to arise from these developing countries, may be stifled. The prospect of debt repayments would become still darker.

Protectionism, however, is spreading not only against the manufactures of developing countries, but also against the products of industrialised countries. The long, drawn-out stagnation and unabated high unemployment encourages this trend. Industries and even governments lend their hand to this situation. But we know that under the free enterprise system, especially after the world economy has become integrated, protectionism does not provide any answer for a stagnant economy. What then are the real measures to be taken by us all to ward off protectionism?

To start with, I believe we should recognise that the world economic structure has been undergoing great change. We have seen how the Bretton Woods system of fixed rate currencies crumbled through inflation and high energy prices. Through the success of our development efforts and investment policies, many developing countries have meanwhile become industrialised, and their products are now competing with ours most successfully all over the world. With the advent and transfer of high technologies some of these countries are quickly modernizing their industries to increase their competitiveness.

To meet this great challenge, it is urgent for Western countries to recognise the necessity of adjusting and restructuring their own industries in response to this changing world. Indeed, restructuring and modernizing our industries and economic system, not only to meet competition from the newly industrialised countries, but also to cope with changes arising from our own social advancement, has been long overdue.

In this connection, some concern has been expressed by certain quarters in the United States that the American supremacy in high technology fields seems to be challenged by other Western countries and that the United States' government and industry should make additional efforts to rally to such competitions. They propose to subsidize the relevant high technology industries to make them more competitive. Although we like to see the United States remain strong, both militarily and economically as the number one country in the free world, it does not follow from this that American industries individually should always be almighty in every field. In some sectors of a certain industry, the United States might lose its supreme position without yielding the political and military leadership of the free world. After all, through the rapidly advancing trends of economic integration, the Western world is quickly becoming one world. Industries and enterprises operating in this world are contributing to the strengthening of the whole world. Indeed, competition among enterprises in the world is an essential factor in a free economy and open world trading system. It is important that in the field of defence industries and connected technological applications, we should be ahead of the Soviet Union, and in this respect American supremacy should not be lost.

To be noted also is that with the proliferation of protectionist measures, the so-called grey zone in world trade has been expanding. GATT Article 19 provides that if any product is being imported into the territory of a contracting country in such increased quantities and under such conditions as to cause or threaten serious injury to domestic producers in that territory of like or directly competitive products, the contracting party shall be free to take an emergency action to prevent or remedy such injury. But this action has rarely been taken by GATT participants. Instead, they have mostly taken recourse to bilateral or unilateral actions, aiming at restricting such imports, which are out of the context of GATT Article 19.

To place on the agenda one of the most controversial items, 'services', seems to be a key to the success of this new round. The service sector of the national economy has been growing very rapidly in past decades in the Western world; it now occupies more than 70 per cent of gainfully engaged people in the United States and more than 60 per cent in Japan. This trend will be accelerated with the advent of computers and robotics and with the upsurge of information industries.

GATT members have also been struggling to find a consensus on how to tackle agriculture, an important but up to now rather neglected subject. In this rapidly integrated world economy there is no reason to keep this area of production out of the GATT regulations. Great controversies may, however, ensue if we are too hasty in handling this taboo subject. Patience and quiet persuasion may be necessary.

There is, of course, the rather tricky problem of which international organisation is the most suitable forum for the negotiations I have proposed. The Organisation for Economic Co-operation and Development (OECD), or the Group of 10 to 20, or even the UN may vie for legitimacy as a forum for some of these issues. But we should not be involved in a trivial squabble of international bureaucrats; we should be more concerned with who could provide more expertise on these subjects.

We may perhaps be on the threshold of another industrial and technological revolution. Two hundred years ago, when the steam engine and locomotive were invented, a new industrial age dawned, with high hopes and expectations. With the coming of computers, microchips, bio-technologies, and space shuttles, we may now be entering another era of technological and industrial revolution. Whether it will bring us a brighter and better future is still unknown. At the moment, however, the world economy and international security seem to be more readily affected by political and military affairs than by changes occurring in the course of global economic evolution.

BRING BACK THE SPIRIT OF '49

Roy Jenkins
FORMER PRESIDENT OF THE EEC COMMISSION

The North Atlantic Treaty was signed by the twelve founder members in Washington on April 4th, 1949. Only seven of them had been involved in the detailed negotiations. It had all been put together in a period of just over a year. It would have been a most formidable feat of political engineering in any event. As the period was bisected by a most keenly fought presidential election, which the incumbent was expected to lose, in the country which had to make overwhelmingly the greatest contribution in terms both of resources and of sacrifice of tradition, it becomes simply prodigious.

It makes the present habit of the ten members governments of the European Community, of grinding through Council after Council, turning them each into an accountants' wrangle, but reaching no solution even to the accountancy problem, let alone embracing wider issues, seem not merely puny but a disgraceful abdication of leadership. Sir Geoffrey Howe, *pace* Mrs Thatcher, may be a 'brilliant negotiator' in this forum but it is an impasse and not a constructive solution which is too often the outcome of his, her, and everyone else's current negotiations. If the present leaders of the Community, and not their wider-perspectived forebears, had been in charge of North Atlantic affairs 35 years ago, I doubt if the United States would have been committed, Berlin saved, the Marshall Plan implemented, European recovery got underway or European security underpinned.

In view of the two preceding paragraphs it may seem that the overwhelming share of the credit for what happened in 1947–49 must be due to the United States. It is certainly true that the Western world owes an enormous debt to Truman and to two of his Secretaries of State, Marshall and Acheson, to a few exceptional State Department officials, and to some Senators, most notably Arthur Vanderberg, for he was a Republican who refused to play politics. They all had the rare combination of a prescience which enabled them to see that the long-term self-interest of their country required commitment and generosity, and of a courage which enabled them to stand against those of shorter sight and more superficial patriotism.

Yet when Sir Nicholas Henderson, with the benefit of all his accumulated experience, wrote a 1982 preface to the account of the birth of NATO, which he had recorded in 1949 as a young participant in the negotiations, he stated that if one figure bore the central responsibility for the act of creation, it was the British Foreign Secretary, Ernest Bevin. I agree with him. Just as after Marshall's Harvard speech, Bevin's quick and confident reaction made a historical turning-point out of what might otherwise have been merely a tentative exploration of an issue, so his re-bound from the break-down of the London Council of Foreign Ministers in December, 1947, when he completely took the initiative with Marshall, Bidault (the French Foreign Minister) and the Canadians, was the first decisive step on the road to NATO. Bevin's stubby fingers had a capacity for constructive creation which seems to have escaped any subsequent Foreign Secretary.

Contrary to the 'revisionist' view that the Americans encouraged the Cold War in order to enable them to create NATO and thereby dominate Western Europe, they were distinctly hesitant in the early stages. Nor did the French help much. They were in favour – Gaullist detachment came later – but thought principally in terms of the maximum immediate shipment of American military supplies to France rather than in wider or longer terms. The Federal Republic did not exist, so there could be no question of West Germany being admitted at that stage. Even the admission of Italy was a matter of considerable controversy until towards the end, but more on the grounds of her geographical position than because of her ex-enemy status. Norway, Denmark, Iceland and Portugal (in ascending order of exclusion) played little or no part in the negotiations. Those who were crucial to pushing the United States forward were Britain, Canada and the Benelux countries. The Canadians were much to the fore. It was not merely the preponderance of United States power which made it a *North Atlantic* Treaty. This British and Canadian role may have helped to fuel Bevin's deeply mistaken later suspicions of the purely European Coal and Steel Community.

The still more crucial attribute of the new organisation was however the preponderance within it of American power. In the late 1940s it was overwhelming: militarily, politically, economically, monetarily. The mainland of Western Europe had a great history, and maybe a future, but in the then present it was only just beginning to crawl up from a pit of poverty and near despair, and escape too from being a strategic vacuum. Britain was different. We were the simulacrum of a great power, one of the victorious Big Three. But our resources were grossly over-stretched, and in reality our economy was almost as weak as that of France or Germany or Italy, without having the advantage of being so stripped down as almost having to start again.

What was the history of the alliance over its first decades? First, it contained the Soviet thrust to Western Europe. The position never again looked as menacing as it had done in 1947–48, with the communist parties in France and Italy almost poised for a takeover and Berlin beleaguered. Second, it maintained the peace on the central front where the armies and influence of the superpowers were in immediate juxtaposition. Third, American leadership maintained the broad loyalty of the other members, in spite of the strains of Suez and of Dulles's brinkmanship in the fifties, the United States' disaster in Vietnam in the late 1960s and early 1970s, and then, partly as a consequence, the collapse of the dollar-centred Bretton Woods monetary system and the partial collapse of the dollar itself.

Fourth, and fairly steadily, there also proceeded an eastwards shift in the balance of power within the alliance. In every sphere, except that of nuclear strike-power, which itself became less important (but not less dangerous) as the Soviet Union moved towards a position of equality, Europe became both relatively and absolutely stronger, and the United States relatively weaker. The emergence of the Federal Republic as an economic wonder and a major conventional military power too, the unprecedented general European surge to prosperity associated with the first fifteen years of the EEC, the weak dollar and somewhat apologetic tone (although often far from foolish actions) of the Carter presidency all contributed to this process. It was fortified by the growth of political co-operation in Europe and by the Schmidt/Giscard leadership (not always good but at least discernible) of the Community. It was epitomized by Herr Schmidt lecturing the President, more in sorrow than in anger, but in a way that it would have been impossible to imagine Adenauer doing with Eisenhower. It was statistically supported by the Community overtaking the United States in total income.

That phase now looks to be over. Already, to take the last point first, the combined national income of the Community countries has fallen back to 93 per cent of that of the United States. In the short-term the gap is widening daily, but the longer term prospect is much more serious, with Europe falling behind in the technology of the new industrial revolution to such an extent as to take it out of the league of America and Japan. At the same time the political cohesion of the Community is being increasingly lost as the budgetary rows endlessly dominate the available time in the meetings of heads of government and foreign ministers. The much talked of strengthening of the European pillar of the alliance is not merely not happening; such strength as the pillar had already achieved is being eroded.

Atlanticists who were cool on Europe might argue that this did not matter if it coincided with a prospect of Washington resuming its old effortless captaincy and this being again freely accepted throughout the West. This is almost the reverse of the truth. 'Effortless' in some senses the leadership of the White House may currently be, but it certainly creates more conflict and suspicion in most of the other fifteen members of NATO than at almost any other time in the past 35 years.

This contains great dangers. For the foreseeable future the Atlantic alliance remains as necessary as when it was created. The greatest threats to the peace and indeed the survival of the world are in some ways a paradox. On the one hand there is the menace of an unimaginative belief that all that is necessary is to learn the lessons of the 1930s – rearm, don't appease, try to out-missile the enemy – and the world will be safe. But on the other hand there is a great need for a steadiness of hand. An inconsistency of purpose could be fatal. The delicacy of the nuclear balance requires predictability on both sides. The worse dangers could arise from a disintegration of NATO, which might well encourage Russian foolishness, or from a sudden break-up of the East European empire which, particularly if it coincided with a dispute between the military and the party in Moscow, could turn the Soviet Union into a lurching giant.

The latter we can do little about, except to encourage Russian confidence rather than to believe that abusive 'megaphone diplomacy' helps. The former is something to which this country, with West Germany, is pivotal. American actions, and still more, American talk, sometimes rightly assumes distrust and disapproval. But the continuing need for the alliance transcends our view of a particular President – or for that matter a particular Prime Minister.

Nor should we ignore the fact that the European allies are not now in very high standing in Washington. We are seen as disorganised and vacillating. President Carter's administration was criticised from this side of the Atlantic for one set of faults. President Reagan is criticised for the reverse. This springs from a dangerous dichotomy in a lot of European feeling about America. We are torn between a fear that she will desert us, and an apprehension that she wants to use us as, for her, a relatively safe nuclear battleground. That is totally unrealistic because there can be no such thing. But we should have the imagination to see how aggravatingly contradictory this can look from the other side of the ocean.

If we are to avoid an unnecessary and damaging de-stabilization of the world, a little more of the spirit of 1949 is necessary across the Atlantic as well as in Europe.

THE MANAGEMENT OF ECONOMIC ISSUES

Robert S. Strauss
FORMER SPECIAL US REPRESENTATIVE
FOR TRADE NEGOTIATIONS

The latest round of quarrels among the NATO allies illustrates how time has changed the nature of the alliance itself but not its institutions. Born at the close of World War II, the alliance was founded on the premise that Western security could be largely based on military might. Today, however, NATO has become the centrepiece and principal symbol of a complex web of transatlantic ties of which a military alliance is only one aspect. The threat to peace posed by increasing Soviet military strength is intensified by growing differences on economic issues among the NATO allies.

The global recession has taken its toll among the partners of the alliance and created new tensions. The common goals and unity of purpose which sustained NATO in the beginning have not translated into co-operation on economic issues. In the long run, the alliance will be able to maintain its military strength and counter the Soviet challenge only if its members can renew their economic vitality and not permit economic conflict to undermine political relationships. This requires, among other things, the creation of new mechanisms for dialogue and co-operation between the United States and Europe. Through these mechanisms we will be able to foster a new consensus on the future of the international economic system and the management of international trade disputes.

The past decade has been marked by the rise of the economic component in NATO relationships. As the volume of trade has grown among the allies, the opportunities for disagreement have increased. The United States–European confrontation over the Siberian pipeline marked a new low in NATO economic relationships.

The dilemma now facing the allies is how to manage the economic change inherent in free market economies without further upsetting ally relations and jeopardizing the efficient operation of NATO. Part of the problem lies in the structure of the alliance itself. The 1949 treaty is a concise, mutual defence pact, with a single sentence in Article 2 pledging the signators to seek to eliminate conflicts in their international economic policies.

The changing nature of the relationship today presents a montage of issues which require careful management by all members of the alliance. Only through consensus-building and leadership on the part of the

United States can such a broad spectrum of issues be managed. The day is past when the United States can dictate policy or economically intimidate its allies as was attempted in the case of the Siberian pipeline.

A major source of contention in the alliance today is that, although there has been a steady evolution in the relative strengths of its member countries, the institutions of our alliance have remained unchanged since 1949, when American military and economic superiority were over-whelming and unquestioned. Systemic responsibilities have remained much the same and NATO is still an alliance substantially managed directly and indirectly by the United States. American postwar policies, which promoted the economic rejuvenation of Europe and Japan, have had the logical consequence of a relative decline in American power. The United States no longer has the capacity to play the role of world manager – a role which requires the ability to both police the system and contain financial and trading crises. Accordingly, the allies must become more effective at managing vexing economic issues or the trend to division will accelerate.

Slumping demand in the industrialized countries, coupled with increasing competition from developing countries has demonstrated to the allies the vulnerability of their economies to changing global market conditions. Even if the current recovery spreads, the scars of the recession will not heal soon. Unemployment is likely to remain high throughout the rest of the decade and will be a steady source of protectionist sentiment. We must seek to avoid a repetition of the 1930s, when retaliatory policies followed close on the heels of financial disorder and dragged the world economy into a long downward spiral.

The liberal international economic order formulated during the 1940s, and originated in the United States, was premised on the theory of free trade. There were many reasons for the American insistence on an economically open world system, but the simple truth is that it served the American national interest. It should not be forgotten, as many often do, that American policy was widely supported in Europe. Indeed, the post-war economic system, created by the United States, proved extremely beneficial to Europe.

In his 1983 State of the Union Address, President Reagan reminded Congress of America's traditional policy and position: 'As the leader of the West and as a country that has become great and rich because of economic freedom, America must be an unrelenting advocate of free trade'. Nevertheless, the Reagan administration has implemented protectionist measures in various sectors including steel, textiles and automobiles. While politically understandable, the rhetoric goes one way – its actions frequently the other. Many Americans now feel that the fundamental premises of liberal trade policy are no longer valid. The prevailing attitude in Washington, as well as in Detroit and Pittsburgh, seems to be that if no one else is going to play by the rules then why should we? This is a difficult argument for politicians to counter, and if economic pressures continue to mount we may see a further erosion of a liberal trade policy.

The first part of the 1980s has seen the allies increasingly ignoring the basic premises of the General Agreement on Tariffs and Trade (GATT). The political imperative of preserving jobs has led directly to protectionism. In short, governments are having a difficult time dealing with the fundamental result of the post-war expansion in trade: greater interdependence.

During earlier, more prosperous years, the close correlation between growth in trade and an expansion in economic welfare was happily acknowledged. The experience of the Common Market provided a clear demonstration of the benefits to be derived from the removal of barriers. Interdependence was seen as a goal, not, as it is today, as an unfortunate consequence. The socialist experiment in France during 1981–82 demonstrated this interdependence, showing that no nation can afford to pursue an independent policy out of step with the world economy.

The NATO allies now face the difficult task of resisting pressures and avoiding a further worsening of transatlantic relations. Every state has many powerful economic interest groups and deteriorating economic conditions intensify their vigour and competitiveness. However, current disagreements should not make us forget that Europe and the United States have similar economic structures and face similar problems. One of the most pressing is structural adjustment and the dilemma of ageing industries that will never again operate at full capability. Crisis management, which usually means protectionism, is a poor substitute for long-term economic policy. We need to coordinate an overall positive strategy.

First of all, the West should develop a greater consensus on the future for the world economy. Simple calls for free trade are not the answer. However, we must continue to pursue efforts for trade liberalization. In the absence of movement toward a more liberal trading system, protectionism will gain momentum.

The rules of the game of international trade are slowly being changed. Tariffs and quotas are being replaced as policy tools by 'hidden' barriers such as trade-related investment requirements, tax credits, loans, and government capital infusions. Governments must work to coordinate and control these new barriers or risk falling into a zero-sum system of competitive subsidization.

Such coordination will require new and more comprehensive trade regulating organizations than those currently in force. A major problem with the existing system of rules and institutions is that they are designed to avoid unavoidable conflicts rather than provide for their resolution.

Trade disputes are to the interdependent world economy what political disputes are to democracy: necessary and, if properly structured, healthy.

Transatlantic trade is worth more than $90 billion annually. Yet the mechanisms for ensuring the smooth flow of this vitally important trade are notoriously deficient. Regular liaison between economic policy makers is now inadequate. The dialogue between career officials of our governments should be improved in order to create a greater understanding of policy problems, and to develop shared ideas about the future of the international economic system. Toward this end, the NATO governments should explore setting up regular working groups composed of under-secretaries, section chiefs, and other specialists. These groups would ensure a greater continuity of discussion and greater understanding of each side's positions and policies.

NATO can only maintain its strength by maintaining its economic vitality, by intelligent management of trade disputes and by developing a shared vision of our economic system. The alliance will not be able to meet its responsibilities to preserve our security if acrimony over trade issues sours political relations, and if economic stagnation persists it will take too heavy a fall. Ignoring the problem is a luxury the West cannot afford.

TOWARDS A REVITALIZED ATLANTIC PARTNERSHIP

Robert D. Hormats
FORMER US ASSISTANT SECRETARY OF STATE
FOR ECONOMIC AND BUSINESS AFFAIRS

The recent debate over missile deployment in Europe may have temporarily diverted the attention of governments away from underlying economic and social pressures on NATO, but the public reaction to it brought them into sharper form. As large numbers of our citizens insist that NATO relies less on a nuclear strategy, our governments depend increasingly on it. And economic problems within and among our countries undermine confidence that Atlantic economic co-operation is beneficial to the average American or European, and reduce the will and the resources needed to improve conventional forces and thus to decrease the probability of the use of nuclear arms. Unless leaders on both sides of the Atlantic act promptly to allay deep nuclear and economic concerns, and thus strengthen NATO's neglected human and moral foundations, a deterioration in Western defence and economic relations is inevitable.

NATO, at its heart, is an alliance among democratic peoples. Its strength and credibility, which are prerequisites for Western security, depend on broad popular support. Until recently, the benefits of the alliance, and of close United States–European economic ties, have been apparent to large majorities on both continents. Today, many have doubts.

In recent months, much emphasis has been placed on the issue of missile deployment. But too little attention has been devoted to what, according to a recent Atlantic Institute poll, most troubles Americans and Europeans – unemployment, nuclear weapons and fear of war. Trade disputes, high United States' budget deficits and interest rates, and economic stagnation in Europe affect industrial and agricultural jobs on both continents. Profound concerns are raised – notably, and effectively, by women, young people, and religious groups – about the threat of nuclear war. Among young people, apprehensions about the future are particularly acute, as large numbers see the possibility of nuclear war cutting their lives short, and despair of being able to find fulfilling jobs, or any jobs at all. Economic and security issues are closely related. Transatlantic trade and monetary disputes, and Europe's internal problems, undermine possibilities for improving conventional deterrents – a major step toward reducing the number, and risk of use of, nuclear weapons.

The West needs a strategy that addresses these problems and their interrelationships. Specifically, it must meet: the needs of the United States and Europe for maintaining a high level of security with minimum reliance on nuclear weapons; American desires for Europe to assume a greater share of the conventional burden; Europe's desire for both a greater portion of NATO conventional production and an improved American dialogue with the Soviets; and the need for each side to be more responsive to the impact of its trade and financial/monetary policies on jobs and economic growth in the other.

Fears are voiced in the United States that it could become involved in a nuclear war to defend Europe. It is also argued that Europe is not devoting sufficient resources to its own defence – making the need for the American nuclear shield all the greater but, in the eyes of some, less merited.

Europe, for its part, has wanted in recent years to 'lock in' the American nuclear deterrent – which is why it originally asked for deployment of Pershing and cruise missiles in response to Soviet deployment of SS-20s. But many Europeans have become apprehensive lest Washington's contentious attitude towards the Soviets leads to increased East–West tensions. The administration's approach has softened recently; but, as the former French Foreign Minister, François-Poncet, has pointed out, past statements harm the credibility of current policies.

Europeans who doubt the credibility of the American nuclear deterrent, and those afraid that United States–Soviet frictions heighten the nuclear risk, are increasingly negative about NATO and supportive of neutrality. For Europeans, genuine security depends both on military strength and progress in reducing the tensions with the East. Inadequate attention to the latter erodes support for the former.

The weakness of European economies makes the nuclear problem all the more difficult to resolve. The need for nuclear weapons in Europe can be reduced by improvement of conventional ones. But this is expensive. The relatively low cost of nuclear deterrents is an important reason for the current heavy reliance on them. Facing increases in unemployment (from 15 million in Western Europe in 1982 to 20 million today; over 25 per cent of which is for over 12 months, as opposed to 7 per cent in the United States), high government budget deficits, and large social needs, European leaders are reluctant to undertake the increases in conventional military expenditures required to cut back significantly on nuclear weapons. They are also unwilling to diminish support for their national defence industries – that have created an inefficient proliferation of weapons systems, while most leaders recognize that significant intra-European specialization would reduce costs, they fear that it would reduce domestic jobs as well.

95

Unemployment and deep divisions within the European Community over agricultural subsidies, budgetary burdens, and cutbacks in steel overcapacity compound the problem of security co-operation. Originally intended to heal old animosities and give Germans an economic stake in co-operation with their neighbours, the Community is vital to Western economic cohesion and security. Its current weakness – and growing German alienation from it, particularly among unemployed youth (which have more than tripled in number in four years) – could jeopardize its future, as well as that of NATO, by reducing constraints on economic, and ultimately political, nationalism in all European countries.

United States–Community economic differences further weaken Western ties. High United States' interest rates draw capital from, and hold up interest rates in, Europe – slowing growth and investment, and thus limiting resources available for social programmes and conventional defence. American farmers feel deprived of their just share of foreign markets by European subsidies, and fear additional impediments. Steel producers in the United States complain about the impact of European practices on the American market. Europeans, on the other hand, argue that they do not disrupt American agricultural exports, and fear that their steel industry will be hurt by new American restrictions. Defence sales in NATO run 7–1 in favour of the United States, causing Europeans to complain about absence of a 'two-way street'. And, threatened by growing ties between American and Japanese firms, they are concerned – as former Chancellor Schmidt has noted – about being left behind on new technologies.

Because security and economic problems feed on one another, the Atlantic nations need a strategy to address both. It should aim at making Atlantic economic relationships more supportive of sustained growth and a reduction in monetary and trade frictions, which in turn would improve prospects for improving conventional deterrents. And it should aim at making Western deterrence less reliant on nuclear, and more on conventional, weapons – with a better sharing of costs and benefits.

No country is in a mood to make economic concessions simply to improve 'co-operation'. But each can take measures, in its own eocnomic interests, that would also improve collective prosperity. Reduction of the United States' budget deficit, which would reduce American interest rates and enable some European governments to do likewise, would strengthen prospects for a sustained recovery here and in Europe. Some European countries, for example Germany and the United Kingdom, could relax fiscal policy. The European Community, as a whole, could benefit by lowering subsidies and internal barriers to technology trade. The United States and Europe also need to develop a more activist approach to reducing structural unemployment – both among young people who will become increasingly alienated if they cannot find entry level jobs and fall further and further behind, and among older workers displaced by technological change or layoffs from industries cutting back on capacity.

United States–European trade disputes could be ameliorated by working toward a new, and more promising, type of multilateral trade negotiation. A major new round of negotiations, like the Kennedy or Tokyo Rounds, would involve unwieldy numbers of participants and much preparation. A permanent and less legalistic negotiating process – involving the United States, the European Community, Japan and other major industrialized and developing trading nations – should be established in, or alongside of, the GATT to reduce trade barriers, resolve trade disputes, and establish procedures to ensure that government intervention (subsidies, import barriers, and 'industrial policies') is monitored internationally, is phased down and out as promptly as possible, does not shift burdens to other countries, and lastly encourages, rather than retards, domestic adjustment. This would recognize the inevitability that governments will, from time to time, intervene in economies, in order to avoid sharp drops in employment in important sectors, while limiting the duration of such intervention and its damage to other nations.

Finally, the cavalier American attitude toward exchange rate misalignments and volatility – a major irritant to American business and labour, as well as to Europeans – could be improved upon. Currency intervention is hardly a panacea; but well-timed and coordinated, and in adequate amounts, it can moderate erratic swings and demonstrate determination to reduce volatility. And, periodic meetings among trade, finance and monetary officials could identify exchange rate 'danger zones' – zones which are likely to produce trade distortions, with an adverse impact on domestic economies. They could also identify the types of fiscal/monetary policy mixes most likely to keep currencies from entering those zones. Making the avoidance of such zones an important objective of the monetary and fiscal policy of the major economies – including the United States, Japan and Western Europe – would be a major step forward.

Reduced reliance on nuclear deterrence requires an economically and politically sound programme for conventional weapons production. David Abshire, United States Ambassador to NATO, sensibly argues for a 'resources strategy', which emphasizes efficiency of production, technology sharing (including Japan), and a better balance in defence trade and expenditures. Desirably, Europe should assume a greater share of the cost of the NATO conventional defence burden (which would lighten the United States' budgetary burden), but also receive a greater share of NATO defence production (which would create European jobs)

– a genuine 'two-way street'. NATO, as a beginning, has established roughly 75 new co-operative ventures. To further this process, governments will have to emphasize strongly to their private sectors the need for transatlantic industrial and technical co-operation. And Europe needs time to harmonize, and reduce duplication of, its many separate and often inefficient procurement and production programmes.

The United States and Europe also need to address frankly, and to narrow, differences over the nature, and best ways to counter, the Soviet threat. NATO has recently embarked on such an effort – which should lead, as soon as adequate progress has been made, to a meeting of foreign ministers, in order to reach agreement at the political level. To demonstrate a commitment to reduce tension and the risk of war, and to convey firmly the need for major improvement in Soviet conduct and a reduction in SS-20s and other weapons, the United States President should suggest biannual summits with the Soviet leader. He should also elevate the head of the Arms Control and Disarmament Agency to cabinet rank. And the idea of Senators Nunn and Warner and the late Senator Jackson, to establish nuclear risk reduction centres in Washington and Moscow, should be actively pursued. Further, NATO should develop, and obtain public acceptance of, a broadly shared approach to arms control negotiations on both nuclear weapons in Europe and intercontinental weapons. A shared approach that has obtained public support will do much to enhance credibility *vis-à-vis* the Soviets and within our own societies. It would demonstrate NATO's commitment to arms control as well as, and as part of, deterrence.

Sometimes it is easier to accomplish much than to accomplish little. More progress is likely to be made by pulling these interrelated elements together in a broadly agreed Western package than by attempting to reach separate understandings – particularly because lack of progress, or misunderstandings, in one area limit progress in others. An integrated United States–European strategy to reduce the nuclear risk, improve the economic outlook, and fairly share benefits and responsibilities will considerably strengthen popular support for Western security and economic co-operation.

PART FOUR

Public opinion and NATO

SUSTAINING THE CONSENSUS

John E. Rielly
PRESIDENT OF THE CHICAGO COUNCIL ON FOREIGN RELATIONS

My objective in this paper is to examine public attitudes in the United States and Western Europe on selected issues related to NATO.

Before dealing with the specific questions related to American support for NATO and European security, one should discuss briefly the subject of overall support for United States security efforts.

In a comprehensive survey of American attitudes done by the Chicago Council on Foreign Relations we found that the American people at the end of 1982 were confident about their military defence and less concerned about an unfavourable military balance with the Soviet Union. About two-thirds of the public and four-fifths of the leaders believed the United States was either equal to, or stronger than, the Soviet Union in the military field, a substantial change from four years earlier when 56 per cent of the public and 29 per cent of the leaders felt the United States was falling behind the Soviet Union militarily. It is this changed perception of the United States–Soviet military balance, more than any other single reason, that has led to a reversal of the trend toward higher support for increased defence budgets and growing resistance to the further increases proposed by the Reagan administration. The number favouring maintaining defence spending at the current level (beginning of 1983) has remained about the same – 34 per cent at the beginning of 1979 and 36 per cent at the beginning of 1983. Later polls taken by Gallup indicate that this trend has continued through 1983.

At the same time that support for an increased defence budget has diminished, concern over the possibility of war has increased. In the Chicago Council study published in early 1979, so few respondents spontaneously mentioned war or nuclear war as foreign policy concerns that the response was not even separately reported. Four years later 10 per cent mentioned war as a major issue and the proportion of those concerned about the nuclear arms race doubled. There is evidence that this concern has continued to increase throughout 1983 and according to an Atlantic Institute study published in November, 1983, now includes 45 per cent of the American public.

At the same time the 1982 results showed strong public support for arms control measures, with three-quarters of the public favouring arms control agreements between the United States and the Soviet Union. When asked about a mutual verifiable freeze on nuclear weapons, half the public believed the United States should stop building nuclear weapons only if the Soviet Union also agreed to do so. 19 per cent of the public believed the United States 'should stop building nuclear weapons, even if the Soviet Union does not', while 26 per cent of the public agreed that 'the United States should continue to build nuclear weapons regardless of what the Soviets do'.

Simultaneously, the Council's study shows a continuing erosion of the post-World War II consensus that the national interest of the United States requires active participation by the United States in world affairs. Only a bare majority of the public now holds the view that such international activism is best for the future of this country; a third now say it would be better if the United States stayed out of world affairs.

On the specific question of support for NATO, however, the study shows that in the beginning of 1983, two-thirds of the American public (67 per cent) felt that the United States should either keep the commitment at the same level or increase it; 58 per cent favoured the same level and 9 per cent favoured increasing it. These figures are exactly the same as those at the beginning of 1979. Similarly on the question of decreasing the commitment, there was no significant change from those (13 per cent) who felt that way four years ago.

An indication of the capacity of both the American public and American leaders to discriminate between involvement in Europe and elsewhere is shown in response to the question about commitment of American troops in crisis situations. Despite diminished support for a larger defence budget, Americans in general seemed more willing to support the use of troops in crisis situations at the end of 1982, than they were at the end of 1978. What is most significant is that willingness to support the use of American troops in case of a Soviet invasion of Western Europe continues to be stronger and enjoys much broader support than is the case in any other area of the world. 65 per cent of the American public and 92 per cent of the American leaders would support the use of American troops in such a situation, representing an increase of 11 per cent on the popular side during the past four years.

Troop support for Europe contrasts sharply with Central America in the limited support for use of troops if 'leftist guerrillas were about to defeat the government of El Salvador'. Only 20 per cent of the public and 10 per cent of the leaders favoured the use of troops in the latter case. This ability to distinguish between involvement in Europe and other parts of the world is not new, but has persisted over the last decade.

Even on the pipeline issue, which led to serious friction between the United States and Europe in 1982, American opinion was surprisingly cautious in criticizing Europe. Only 27 per cent favoured putting diplomatic pressure on Europeans and a modest 15 per cent favoured economic sanctions if other methods did not work.

On the much debated issue of deployment of medium-range missiles in Europe (only asked of the leadership in our study), 67 per cent of the leaders agreed that deployment of the missiles should begin but 'stop if the Soviets agree to limit their own missiles in Europe'. Only 19 per cent picked the response 'go ahead deploying missiles in Europe', and 10 per cent selected not basing missiles there at all. More recent popular polls on the missile issue show similar results with a November 1983 Harris poll, showing 50 per cent in favour of going ahead with the deployment and 43 per cent opposed. The issue did not generate the keen popular interest that was true of Europe.

On all the above issues related to Europe, American leadership opinion tends to be more strongly pro-European and more strongly committed to honouring America's commitments in Europe than is popular opinion. In rating foreign policy goals, the goal of defending our allies' security is considered very important by 82 per cent of the leaders, and together with world-wide arms control (86 per cent) is their most popular goal. 98 per cent of American leaders think it is best that the United States continue to take an active part in world affairs; and 67 per cent of the American leaders favour eliminating tariffs and trade restrictions (compared to 22 per cent of the public), an important issue for American relations with Europe. Also 69 per cent of the American leaders oppose restricting United States–Soviet trade, 81 per cent oppose forbidding grain sales to the Soviet Union and 94 per cent favour cultural and educational exchanges with the Soviet Union. On all of these, American leadership supports, in substantially larger margins than the populace as a whole, current American commitments in Europe.

In concluding this brief analysis of American public and leadership attitudes toward Europe, one should note that attitudes toward Europe do not divide along political party lines. This contrasts with the situation in a number of European countries – especially the United Kingdom and the Federal Republic of Germany, where the division on security issues is increasingly along party levels.

Finally, I should mention that the above analysis of American opinion is confined to political and security issues. It does not cover commercial and financial issues – where there are a number of critical voices in the United States on European policies on trade and monetary questions.

The Council study published in early 1983 indicated a stability among both American popular and élite attitudes on foreign policy questions and a high degree of continuity with the recent past. A review of selected European survey research, analysis and commentary suggests that the contrary is true in Western Europe on such questions as support for the NATO alliance, attitudes toward the use of military force, nuclear weapons, neutralism and attitudes toward the United States.

102

The election results since 1981 in the four largest countries in Europe – France, Italy, Germany and Great Britain – indicate strong continuing support for political parties which favour NATO and the Atlantic alliance. Yet European analysts of varying political perspectives indicate that basic changes in ideas and political culture have occurred which have grave implications for the Atlantic alliance, including considerable movement in the direction of neutralism in a number of Western European countries. When asked whether Western Europe would be safer if it moved toward neutralism in the East–West conflict, a larger number favoured such a move than opposed it in West Germany, Great Britain and France.

Yet most Western Europeans continue to believe that NATO is essential to protect the security of their country. Between 60 and 70 per cent of the British, Germans, Dutch, Italians and Norwegians who responded to a USIA poll in March 1981, expressed support for NATO. But less than a majority were confident that NATO could prevent an attack on Western Europe. Similarly, if Europe should be attacked by the Soviet Union, either with nuclear or non-nuclear weapons, the will to resist is not overwhelmingly high. When asked whether military force should ever be used, even in response to an attack by the Soviet Union, a surprisingly high percentage (Britain 20 per cent, Germany 26 per cent, the Netherlands 28 per cent, Italy 33 per cent and France 44 per cent) said it should not be.

On the most disputed question of the year and the one which has been the focus of attention on arms control and peace in Europe, the 1979 NATO decision to deploy Pershing missiles and ground-launched cruise missiles beginning in December, 1983, it was widely reported that the majority of people in many European countries oppose the deployment.

When the missile question was linked closely to the choice of remaining in NATO or withdrawing from NATO, a more favourable response occurred for deployment.

Whereas the Chicago Council study indicated that after two years of the Reagan administration the American people felt more confident about their military security, this has not been the case in Europe. Over a third of the Europeans in seven countries list a fear of war as their top foreign policy concern; worry about an inadequate defence was last on the list, under 7 per cent in most cases. Europeans seemed far more concerned about insuring productive arms control talks than about improving defence collaboration among European countries.

There is further evidence that Europeans are shifting their priorities on security matters. The recent Atlantic Institute study indicated that 'where previously effective co-operation between Europe and the United States and a military balance with the Soviet Union were the highest priority items in many countries, now it is productive arms control talks and/or continued dialogue with the Soviet Union which dominates at least as much and usually more'.

Current opinion polls do not support the view sometimes expressed in the press that Europeans have become uniformly negative about the United States. In polls taken in 1981–82, respect for the United States outweighs by two-to-one hostile or unfavourable attitudes. Approximately 50 per cent of the people in each of the major nations of Britain, France, Italy, Germany and the Netherlands are confident that if their security were threatened by the Soviet Union, the United States would come to their defence and risk retaliation on the United States. If Europeans have increasing doubts about the leadership of the United States government, this does not necessarily mean they believe the United States is no longer committed to the defence of Europe's security. But concern about the American leadership is growing – and is reflected in diminishing confidence in the United States.

To go beyond conclusions suggested by specific survey research data, it would appear that of the last four United States administrations, only the Nixon and Ford administrations enjoyed the confidence of Europeans. A principal reason for their popularity was that they followed a European balance of power approach to international politics and supported a policy of détente with the Soviet Union.

Both presidents who followed Ford eschewed this approach to diplomacy. Europeans were appalled by the neo-Wilsonian moralism of Jimmy Carter, who condemned power politics and sought to influence internal Soviet behaviour through his human rights policy. Carter left an impression of weakness both in America and Europe. President Ronald Reagan came to power partly to restore American power in the world. But, like Carter, he also rejected balance of power diplomacy, this time in favour of a demonic world view which presupposed the Soviet Union as 'an evil empire', which is the source of all international instability. Europeans originally welcomed the reassertion of American power under Reagan. But today, although they respect American power, they fear American aggressiveness. They disagree with the Reagan administration because it rejects détente – still a policy Europeans strongly support. But more important than their disagreement with specific Reagan policies, they lack confidence in the judgement of American political and governmental leaders.

NATO AND AMERICAN PUBLIC OPINION

Norman Podhoretz
EDITOR OF *COMMENTARY*

It seems remarkable in retrospect that public opinion in the United States should for so long have been so steadfast in its support of NATO. Yet steadfast it has been, in spite of the seductive allures of the isolationist temptation, which runs much deeper in the American character than is generally understood in Europe nowadays. To be sure, once the West European economies had recovered from the wounds of World War II, proposals were made every few years or so to get American troops out of Europe. But such proposals (usually associated with the name of former Senator Mike Mansfield) always excited more alarm in Europe than support in the United States. Not only did they get nowhere within the American foreign-policy establishment; they did not even make much political headway among the mass of ordinary Americans who might have been expected to resent the huge sums of money and the dangers of war entailed by their country's commitment to the defence of conspicuously ungrateful foreigners.

All this seems all the more remarkable when it is compared with the climate of opinion surrounding NATO today. If in the past the foreign-policy establishment in the United States was unambiguously and unshakeably committed to NATO, today many leading members of that establishment, including some who were proudly present at the creation of the alliance, have turned against it. Not, of course, in so many words, and sometimes even loudly protesting their continued devotion. Yet these excessive protestations, like those of Shakespeare's lady, only betray what they are meant to conceal (in this case, possibly, as much from the protesters themselves as from others).

The most vivid example of this change is the 'no-first-use' of nuclear weapons advocated by a group of former government officials who have come to be known as the American 'gang of four': George F. Kennan (the great theoretician of the containment strategy in the Truman administration), Robert S. McNamara (Secretary of Defence in the Kennedy and Johnson administrations), McGeorge Bundy (National Security Adviser to Presidents Kennedy and Johnson), and Gerard Smith (Nixon's representative at the SALT negotiations).

It is still, I think, not fully recognised – least of all by the gang of four themselves – that a pledge of no-first-use would be tantamount to a withdrawal of the American commitment to the defence of Europe. But there is no escape from that conclusion. The threat of a nuclear response has always been, and remains, NATO's strategy for deterring the Soviet Union from exploiting its superiority in *conventional* forces to overrun Western Europe. American troops are there not to fight the invaders off but to make the nuclear threat 'credible' by serving as a 'tripwire'. Under no-first-use, American troops, no longer needed for this or any other military purpose, would be withdrawn, thereby further weakening, and perhaps altogether cutting, the lifeline tying the United States to the fate of Western Europe.

What we have here, then, is the reappearance, in a nuclear-age mutation, of the isolationist tradition. That isolationism should once again have become an influential presence in American political life is not itself surprising; on the contrary, it was to be expected and was indeed predicted as a consequence of the defeat in Vietnam. But what *is* surprising, and portentous, is that isolationism should have returned under the sponsorship of men who once stood at the very head of the Atlanticist establishment.

Perhaps because such men are still unable to face up to the fact of their apostasy, the gang of four simply refuse to admit that no-first-use for all practical purposes means a withdrawal of the American commitment to the defence of Europe and the dissolution of NATO. Within the intellectual community, however, proponents of this doctrine like Irving Kristol and the late Herman Kahn have been willing to acknowledge its implications. Yes, says Kristol, no-first-use would spell the end of NATO, but good riddance to it. The time has come for the Europeans to assume responsibility for their own defence and for the United States to go it alone. Kristol is by no means certain that the Europeans would take on this responsibility. But he is confident that a United States disentangled from NATO would play a more forceful and energetic role in countering Soviet expansionism. Since this is the last thing the gang of four would like to see the United States do, one has to distinguish between their brand of isolationism and Kristol's go-it-alone strategy. Yet these two schools of thought, so antagonistic in their objectives, are equally dangerous to the future of NATO.

Thus, for the first time in its history, NATO now confronts a loss of support and even serious opposition from influential segments both of the foreign-policy establishment and of the intellectual community. And to make matters worse, the alliance also confronts a growing degree of resentment within the populace at large. I gather that this is not yet clearly reflected in public-opinion polls, but no one sensitive to the political climate in America can doubt that the resentment is there. Night after night watching demonstrators on television vilify the United States for agreeing to deploy intermediate-range nuclear missiles in Europe, more and more Americans have begun wondering out loud why 'we should have to beg those people to let us defend them'.

This is certainly one reason the 'freeze' movement, which calls for an immediate halt ('mutual and verifiable', goes the pious and politically prudent qualifier) to the building and deployment of nuclear weapons, is so popular in the United States even among voters not normally given to dovish, let alone pacifist, sentiments. For in the present state of the military balance between the United States and the Soviet Union, a freeze would all but dissolve the American guarantee to Europe. On the one hand, it would prevent deployment of the intermediate-range missiles from going any further, thus 'decoupling' Western Europe and the United States; on the other hand, it would prevent modernisation of the American strategic force, thus forcing America into a 'minimum-deterrence' posture (which is the nuclear-age equivalent of a 'Fortress America' strategy and consistent only with an isolationist foreign policy).

On both sides of the Atlantic, in short, the effects of a freeze would add up to a withdrawal of the American commitment to the defence of Western Europe. If this is not consciously grasped, it is, I suspect, intuitively sensed; and if it is not the greatest of the freeze movement's attractions for many people who endorse the idea, it is at any rate not the least of them.

Do these changes in American public opinion mean that NATO is doomed? Not quite. If the survey data can be trusted, most Americans still regard the isolationist temptation as a delusion. Since I count myself among them, and since I think my own feelings are reasonably representative, let me speak personally here instead of trying to read the entrails of the public-opinion polls.

It is not because I am immune to the seductive power of the isolationist temptation that I resist it. I resist because I believe that an American withdrawal from the Western alliance would result not – as some of my political friends and allies predict – in an assumption by the Europeans of the responsibilities and burdens of self-defence, but rather in a collapse in the face of Soviet power. Far from envisaging a rise in the production of troops, tanks, and missiles, I foresee an increase in the number of neutralists, pacifists and appeasers, leading ultimately to the condition of political subordination to the Soviet Union which has come to be called 'Finlandization' but which I prefer to call 'Red Vichyism' – all without a shot having been fired.

This would be calamity enough, but even this would not be an end of it. For – and here too I disagree with some of my political friends and allies – I cannot see how freedom and democracy in the United States could survive their demise in Western Europe. Trotsky used to say that socialism could not exist in one country. No more can democracy. Isolated behind a wall of nuclear missiles in a world increasingly shaped

107

by the influence and the will of the Soviet Union, the United States would, in my opinion, be unable to hold on for long to its own political culture. There too the number of appeasers would rise as the power of the nation declined, with Red Vichyism coming to look like the safest of all political arrangements.

In defending NATO in these terms, which amount to saying that the United States is now bound mainly to Western Europe as a kind of hostage, I am poignantly aware of how wan, how lacking in vitality, the case has become. But what else can one do? Like millions of other Americans, I have grown more and more to resent the apparent absence in West Europe of any enthusiasm for the alliance, or any appreciation of its achievement in preserving both the peace and the freedom of the countries living behind its shield. We are repeatedly told that there is a 'silent majority' in Europe – and again, if the polls can be trusted, a very large one – that does appreciate these things. But mostly we hear from the raucous minority, and what we hear is foul and offensive: that the United States is as bad as, or worse than, the Soviet Union, and that Ronald Reagan is a greater threat to the peace of the world than was Yuri Andropov. Even when this preposterous neutralism, or the pernicious hatred of America that often goes with it, is challenged by Europeans, it is usually done in language that seems weak and defensive, for example, 'as between Moscow and Washington, on the whole, and with all due reluctance, I suppose I prefer Washington'.

This kind of thing has already begun taking the heart out of American backing for NATO. If the coalition of neutralists, pacifists, and Soviet apologists known by verbal usurpation as the 'peace' movement had succeeded in preventing deployment of the intermediate-range missiles, NATO would by now have been finished in all but name. But deploying these weapons will not by itself be enough to save the alliance. The silent majority in Europe will have to find its voice, and it will have to be a voice loud enough to cross the Atlantic and resonant enough to force its way through the resistance of the media and into the American ear.

The fact is that Americans who support NATO need the support of European supporters of NATO. We need to hear from those Europeans who know that the free world is a reality and not a counterfeit construct, to be referred to sardonically in inverted commas; that its institutions represent an immense human achievement not easily duplicated; that its survival is threatened by an imperialism fully comparable in political, moral, and military terms to Nazi Germany in the late 1930s; and that the future of liberty and democracy depends on the power and resolve of the United States, not in Europe alone but in such other vital areas as the Middle East and Central America.

These were the ideas which gave birth to NATO 35 years ago. They are as valid today as they were then, indeed, they are made even more compelling today by the tilt in the military balance away from the United States and toward the Soviet Union. Since to some degree the rise of neutralism in Europe and of its isolationist cousin in the United States is a frightened response to this development, the first order of business must be a military build-up aimed at creating a greater sense of Western security. And if, as many advocate, such a build-up should include a strengthening of the conventional forces of the West along with a modernization of its nuclear arsenal, so much the better.

But to repeat, though indispensable, military measures are not enough. They will have to be accompanied by a more positive European affirmation of solidarity with the United States in its efforts to contain Soviet expansionism and even to reduce it in areas outside the jurisdiction of NATO, especially the Middle East and Central America. Otherwise, the isolationist temptation will prove impossible to resist, even for Americans like myself. Though we believe that isolationism is not a viable policy, if the only alternative is being dragged down by our allies, even we would be forced to take our chances at trying to go it alone.

TELL AND TRUST THE PEOPLE

Lawrence Freedman
PROFESSOR OF WAR STUDIES, KING'S COLLEGE, LONDON

The available evidence, based on polling in a number of key NATO countries, suggests that NATO does not suffer from a serious problem with public opinion. As David Capitanchik and Richard C. Eichenberg, the authors of a recent survey for Chatham House conclude, 'public support for NATO remains high in all the European member states. Nor is there any sign that the legitimacy and utility of military institutions have been rejected as a matter of principle . . . Even on the issue of nuclear weapons, public opinion is not nearly as hostile as is commonly assumed'.

The degree of comfort to be derived from this widespread support is qualified by the apparent lack of enthusiasm with which it is proffered. The evidence is quite contradictory when it comes to endorsing the official position on the more controversial issues, such as cruise missiles, and far stronger feelings are exhibited by those in the anti-nuclear movement. As we confirmed by last year's CND conference, this movement is hostile to NATO and all its works, and not just the particular weapons that have inspired the latest protests.

Does this matter? The fact that the opposition does not represent a majority view and is generally out of power within NATO, with the exception of Greece, has allowed established policies to continue undisturbed. However, the influence of the anti-nuclear movement on centre-left parties in Europe (here with the dramatic exception of France) promises trouble for the future. In three or four years time, perhaps for reasons more to do with economies than defence, there could be substantial change in the policies of key member states.

So while governments might hope that with the arrival of the first cruise and Pershing missiles the immediate fuss will die down, the sort of concerns currently at the fore could return with a vengeance. This is likely to inhibit NATO decision-making for some time: proposals to 'modernize' other segments of NATO's nuclear arsenal are unlikely to be warmly embraced by weary ministers, and there will be anxious protestations of a commitment to arms control.

Not handing the protest movements any more ready-made issues may be one way for the NATO establishment to avoid future trouble, but it does nothing to recreate a positive consensus behind the alliance. Hence, the calls for an effort to educate and inform public opinion to counter what are believed to be the mischievous and erroneous impressions fostered by the enemies of the alliance in recent years.

A little more information on current policies in an area that suffers badly from official secrecy and reticence will not come amiss, but it would be illusory to believe that it can turn the tide. For a start, many in the protest movements are often remarkably well-informed and some-times better than those sent to oppose them in public debate. The suggestion that the protestors are merely dupes of Kremlin propaganda is unhelpful, inaccurate and does slight justice to the real concerns that animate the protest.

Before NATO can improve on its communication with the public, it needs to sort out exactly what is to be communicated. One source of the current difficulty is that the prevailing sense of international crisis is not solely the responsibility of the Soviet Union. It is the United States, for example, that has failed to ratify any arms control agreements for over ten years. European governments might find it easier to counter criticisms of the United States if they did not, themselves, agree with many of them.

It is this background of international crisis that has given the nuclear debate its edge. For NATO this should warn of a serious weakness in alliance strategy. If it is the case that talking loudly about nuclear weapons at times of moderate tension triggers such widespread dissi-dence, what would happen if a crisis looked like turning into a real confrontation? For it is precisely at such times that, according to current doctrine, deterrence would have to be fortified by reminding the Soviet Union of the nuclear risks it would face as a result of aggressive action. Our recent experience suggests that the public in the West would not respond calmly to dire threats being uttered on its behalf.

Thus the difficulty in communicating NATO policy may be that certain key aspects of this policy are flawed. Politicians and officials engaged in the nuclear debate tend to bemoan the 'difficulty' and 'paradoxical' nature of the whole concept of deterrence. The implication is that this fundamental idea, upon which international order is said to depend, can only be understood as a result of a prolonged intellectual effort. It is too complicated to compete with simple slogans that fit neatly on tee-shirts or banners.

This is nonsense. The concept of deterrence is perfectly simple – even intuitive – and familiar to anyone who has brought up children, worried about crime or been involved in industrial disputes. If it appears difficult or paradoxical it is because of the particular form in which it has been adopted in the West. The excessive reliance on the threat to use nuclear weapons first in a conflict forces NATO governments to pretend to be more irrational than they actually are and definitely more than they wish to appear to their public. NATO is caught between the need to warn the Soviet Union that it might escalate in a conflict, despite the suicidal

111

implications of such a move, and to reassure the public that it would not be so reckless. Faced with such a dilemma the natural inclination is to talk in vague generalities.

Because its policy is difficult to explain, the NATO establishment is happiest when it is not called upon to do any explaining. However, the recent debate should be seen as a valuable warning. Without it the alliance might not have discovered until too late just how divisive its strategy could be at precisely the time when unity is at a premium. It, therefore, has time for remedial action, to develop a new strategy less dependent on incredible nuclear threats.

Of course, no change short of disbanding NATO's total nuclear arsenal is likely to satisfy the most ardent protestor. Perfectly reasonable policies should not be dropped simply because a sizeable opposition has been drummed up by one means or another. The reason why change is necessary is that in democratic societies, security policies that excite more public disquiet than support are unlikely to be effective and will eventually reflect badly on the organisation which seeks to promote them.

A more difficult question is whether public support will be difficult to sustain for a programme of reform. There are a number of reasons why this might be so, and not just that a renewed stress on conventional forces promises to be more expensive.

The recent preoccupation with nuclear means of destruction has led to a neglect of the extent that conventional means, while not so overwhelming, are frightful enough in their own ways. Those appalled by trends in nuclear technology will find little to comfort them in trends in conventional technology. As attention switches from the nuclear to the conventional then programmes that might have passed unnoticed before will become extremely controversial. This has already begun to happen, for example with proposals for 'deep-strike' weapons. These are being criticised for their 'offensive' character, by those apparently unaware that NATO has always had a long-range air force able to operate to the rear of enemy lines.

However, the main sources of domestic objection to a greater stress on conventional forces have little to do with the weapons themselves, but their cost. Even as the Western nations move out of the recession the competition for resources will be intense. The military professionals may feel that the expenditure of the past few years has been barely sufficient to stop the gap with the Warsaw Pact widening – and the target of three per cent annual real growth in defence-spending has been honoured far more in the breach than in the observance. Nevertheless, the perception outside the military establishment is that the shift away from civilian spending has now gone far enough. There is no point in basing reforms of NATO strategy on a substantial increase in resources.

Does this rule out reform? Not necessarily once we recognise (as the

British Prime Minister has been constantly reminding us in the civilian sphere) that policy problems are not solved simply by 'throwing money at them'. The need is for a thorough examination of the strategy theories and methods behind the current expenditure. Again, we should be taking advantage of the openness of our society to have the same sort of debate about conventional strategy that we have just had on nuclear strategy.

This requirement for public support is considered by some NATO supporters to put the alliance at a severe disadvantage to the Warsaw Pact. Because the Soviet leaders are accountable only to themselves, and the satellite countries are in no position to reject the policy line handed down from Moscow, they are presumed to have a capacity for decisive and, if necessary, ruthless action. A comparable capacity is unavailable to a diverse collection of sovereign states, each with its own distinctive public opinion.

Such a view betrays a striking lack of confidence in the political philosophy which the alliance seeks to defend. Because the Kremlin's decisions are not subjected to critical attention, expensive mistakes remain uncorrected and often unacknowledged, while deeply entrenched prejudices rest unchallenged. The quality of Soviet policy suffers from the ease with which it is formulated, just as the quality of NATO's policies suffered when they were put together by an élite temporarily relieved of the requirement to explain itself.

The permanent isolation of the Soviet leaders means that they do not know whether they enjoy the trust of the people and the actual reception accorded their pronouncements. In explaining their security policies the appeal is not to reason but to heady national symbols, and in particular to the memory of the millions killed from 1941 to 1945. These were, in fact, the symbols revived in the hurriedly renamed Great Patriotic War as Stalin discovered the limits of the masses' loyalty to the Party as the Germans advanced. Similar uncertainties as to popular attitudes especially in the East European satellites, would seriously effect the Kremlin's room for manoeuvre in a major conflict.

The intensity of the recent debate in the West may seem like the other extreme. Certainly, it has encouraged a polarisation and a dogmatism that does not help the search for a consensus. But this is in part a consequence of the previous lack of serious discussion of NATO policies. The most immediate causes of the current debate have been the general sense of international tension and the prominence of a number of nuclear weapon issues. With a more relaxed political climate and no new issues then the debate may fade. But it would be a shame if the opportunity was not used to encourage a constructive scrutiny of NATO policy and implement the sort of reforms necessary to ensure that the alliance is on much firmer ground next time public attention is turned to its strategy and plans.

FRENCH SUPPORT FOR THE ALLIANCE

Michel Tatu

EDITORIAL CORRESPONDENT FOR *LE MONDE*

For some three years now, France has surprised her neighbours by being apparently immune to the 'pacifist' wave so noticeable in other West European countries, by supporting NATO's Intermediate-range Nuclear Forces (INF) decision more actively, especially with the leftist government of François Mitterrand in power, than some other members of the alliance, and in general by renewing, and in some cases reinforcing her pledge to the alliance at a time when others have equivocated and expressed doubts and negative feelings about it. What are the reasons for this remarkable development?

Certainly, this renewed support has to be qualified by a heavy caveat indeed: it is, of course, easier to approve deployment of new weapons when those are destined to other countries, not to one's own, to hail an alliance when one has distanced oneself from it and renounced any direct subordination to it. Except for a few isolated voices, France's approval of the Pershing II and cruise missile deployment has never gone as far as acceptance of any of those missiles on French territory.

As for NATO itself, the French consensus has been even more monolithic on one point: there is no question of Paris returning to its integrated military command. On the contrary, the recent evolutionary process in Western Europe has convinced the political élite as well as the average citizen in France, that President de Gaulle was right with his two basic decisions of the 1960s: the withdrawal from the NATO command structure and the creation of an independent nuclear force.

The first decision is now seen, in the light of the present malaise in the NATO structure, as more correct than it was at the time: an affirmation of French independence and a rebellion against the so-called Anglo-Saxons. If the Germans, the Dutch, and, to some degree, the British, now have second thoughts about American protection, it is, according to French thinking, because the present NATO structure, with heavy American power and strategy, has deprived them of the indispensable feeling of responsibility for their own defence. Instead of complementing the national effort, as was normally the case with alliances throughout history, NATO has seemingly superseded it. That is why, even if a growing tendency among the French establishment pushes in favour of a stronger commitment towards their European allies (the establishment of a rapid deployment force, capable of use in Germany, goes in that direction), the mood remains hostile to any NATO integration: indeed, it is NATO which has to come closer to France and not the reverse.

The second decision, namely about the French nuclear force, is more than ever an 'article of faith', as the French say. To be sure, some questions are raised about the use of that force, such as counter-city strategy or the 'massive retaliation blow', which continue to be official dogmas for the French general staff – if not necessarily for the government. But the debate remains limited on this subject, and it comes as a normal and logical consequence of the development of the French arsenal: as in other countries, the sophistication of the doctrine follows the sophistication of the hardware, not the other way around. But the acceptance of what used to be called the *force de frappe* has not been questioned since the parties of the left also accepted it in 1977: the communists, for some obscure reasons, came first, the socialists last, but since then François Mitterrand redeemed that delay by supporting the nuclear military programme with a double zeal, without even the slight hesitations about nuclear doctrine demonstrated by Giscard d'Estaing in the first years of his term.

All main political parties follow this trend. Thus, the government has given unconditional support to the deployment of Pershing-II and even the communist party, while organizing demonstrations against it, has markedly failed to press for any cuts in the present French nuclear force. Only a few radical groups have put forward such a demand – the two small groups which may be considered as the counterpart of the so-called European anti-war movement concede that such a policy is, under the present circumstances, less than realistic: the ecologists prefer to campaign against the civil nuclear defence programme and the Committee for Nuclear Disarmament in Europe (CODENE) gears its fight against the arms race of the two superpowers as a whole.

As far as public opinion is concerned, there is undoubtedly a large consensus in favour of the nuclear deterrent, based upon the premise that this force remains in French hands, and that there is not too much debate about its use.

In fact, some critics call it a new 'Maginot line' – the average citizen is satisfied with the presence of this ultimate and national guarantee to French security, but prefers to think that it will never be used, and that it is, in fact, a 'non-war' weapon. Indeed, opinion polls indicate that in case of attempted Soviet aggression many, if not a majority of Frenchmen, still prefer negotiations to a nuclear war.

However, the fact remains that the possession of nuclear weapons by France and, more than that, the considerable development of a French nuclear arsenal in the years to come does not encounter any significant opposition. Unilateral disarmament, as in Britain, and the strong emphasis put in West Germany or in the Scandinavian countries on arms control negotiations with the Soviet Union, have no deep roots in France.

Perhaps the Roman Catholic cultural background, more precisely the tradition of a strong hierarchical church closely connected with the State and its defence imperatives, gives part of the explanation for the absence of an anti-nuclear movement in France. French bishops have adopted a nuclear deterrence stance much more favourable to this idea than any of the churches elsewhere.

Interestingly, countries with similar Catholic traditions, like Italy and Spain, have been more immune to pacifism than their heavily Lutheran or Evangelical friends in the north. But there is more to it than that.

France has often been the odd man out in Europe as far as the evolution of public opinion is concerned. This has been the case with the ideas generated by the French revolution at the beginning of the 19th century, with the ideas of 'social Catholicism' at the beginning of this one, and with the perception of socialism and the Soviet Union during the early years of the Atlantic alliance.

At a time when Stalin's totalitarianism was anathema to most people, including the intellectuals in Western Europe, the French intelligentsia, heavily influenced (if not intellectually terrorized) by a strong communist party, leant overwhelmingly to the left, a left for which there was no salvation outside the communist and so-called progressive camp. Anathema was not Stalin, but American imperialism. Anti-communism and anti-sovietism were synonymous with fascism and Nazism; the most reasonable option for some moderate intellectuals was a kind of neutralism between East and West. A pro-NATO stance was not fashionable, to say the least.

Now all this has changed, again not in tune with the evolution of the mood in neighbouring Western countries. At a time when the previously anti-communist intellectuals of Germany or the Netherlands question the legitimacy of the Atlantic alliance and look with a much greater indulgence on the Soviet Union and her positions in Europe, the French left intelligentsia has broken its sentimental ties with so-called Soviet socialism, which to them has become the main enemy instead of the model.

This startling change began with the Soviet invasion of Czechoslovakia in 1968, and was consolidated with the very strong impact of Alexander Solzhenitzyn's *The Gulag Archipelago* some years later. Last, but not least, some criticism of the Soviet Union by the leadership of the French communist party between 1975 and 1977 lifted (even if those strictures were cancelled later) the taboo which communist ideological influence had imposed upon the intelligentsia: from that time on, one could express anti-Soviet views without being labelled a fascist. This in turn helped many young 1968 radicals – who had already been converted to an anti-Soviet position by their Maoist leanings – to develop the so-called new left ideology, away from any existing socialist model, and, progressively, away from social-democratic and welfare state traditions as well.

The culmination of this evolution came in the very last period, which saw André Glucksman, a previous Maoist radical, become the apostle of the 'defence spirit' against the European peace movement, and Yves Montand, the famous singer and actor and a well-known fellow-traveller of the fifties, advocate some kind of Reaganism and Thatcherism in the economic field.

Curiously enough, the victory of the left and of François Mitterrand in 1981 did not reverse this trend; it only accentuated it. While, in domestic policy, the present *politique de rigueur* is a late adaptation to this mood as well as to the economic realities, in foreign affairs and as far as East–West relations are concerned in particular, the adaptation has been a reality from the very beginning, due in no small measure to the personal convictions of the President. Nobody has been more aware than he very early on of the SS-20 threat, and the need to re-establish a balance of forces in Europe which he considered dangerously destabilized by the Soviet build-up. Except for the communists, whose opposition had to be subdued anyway, this line has been supported by all French parties in Parliament.

This is not to say that there is no real or potential problem. First, French immunity to the pacifist mood has been due mainly to the strong personal commitment of François Mitterrand, as President, to a strong defence and to a tough line towards the Soviet Union. Without him, or simply with a return of the socialists into opposition, the way will be opened to a more pacifist trend through the combined action of three currents of opinion: the pro-Soviet communist line, the anti-military mood of the remnants of the radical left and the traditional leanings of old-time socialists towards disarmament talks and collective security.

Secondly, some dogmas of the original French doctrines, such as deterrence 'of the weak to the strong', 'massive use' and 'counter-city option' are likely to be eroded by the influence of new technologies and debates about their credibility.

Thirdly, the problem of European defence, more precisely the implementation of the concept of 'extended deterrence' to German territory, has yet to find a satisfactory answer.

Precisely because of some of the dogmas mentioned above, any idea about a division over the nuclear decision (particularly on French tactical nuclear weapons, such as the Pluton or the future Hades), is considered a taboo, and the much publicised strategic consultations between Paris and Bonn do not seem to go very far.

But, most of these questions remain a matter for specialists; French public opinion at large is not really concerned. Indeed, this will continue to be the case, as President de Gaulle wished it, at least as long as French nationalism remains broadly satisfied.

PUBLIC SUPPORT FOR NATO – A GERMAN VIEW

Karl Kaiser

DIRECTOR OF THE RESEARCH INSTITUTE OF THE
GERMAN SOCIETY FOR FOREIGN AFFAIRS

Treaties, General de Gaulle once remarked, eventually wither like roses and young girls. Can this be said of the treaty which established NATO 35 years ago? Interestingly, no substantial force on either side of the Atlantic, except for the (old) red, the (new) green and very rare neo-conservative forces on the margin, would argue that way. When it comes to popular and élite support for NATO, all available survey data show a remarkable continuity of adherence even 35 years after the creation of the alliance.

Somewhat spectacular proposals for United States withdrawal from NATO, advanced by conservatives like Irving Kristol, and equally spectacular but somewhat misinterpreted opinions by Henry Kissinger, will always make the headlines, while distracting attention from the basic fact (which may appear dull to journalists always on the search for the unusual), that American élite and mass opinion remains remarkably steady with regard to its commitment to Western Europe and its internationalism. Even when one turns to the Federal Republic of Germany, where concerned and at times agitated observers commenting on the Greens and nuclear protests speculated much about the country's future support of NATO, there is no sign of a significant change in recent years and the national consensus continues to attract some 75 to 80 per cent of those polled.

Mass support is not NATO's problem, but conflict and divergence at the level of élites. Those who view the future of NATO pessimistically usually argue that sooner or later the conflicts and disagreements among administrative and political élites are likely to affect public opinion and erode support for NATO. While strong common interests in the field of defence against a common adversary still exist, the divisive impact of intra-alliance debates on East–West relations, conflicts in the Third World or nuclear deterrence, according to this school of thinking, assume an ever-increasing importance. The strong malaise concerning nuclear weapons among the Western public, they argue, reveals a disaffection that may well go to the roots of support for NATO.

Such a line of reasoning may at first sight appear convincing. But a closer look at the history and present structure of the organisation reveals that NATO has always lived with internal disagreement and nevertheless

119

evolved in spite of everything. It was a 'troubled' alliance from the very beginning.

However, the subject areas that are regarded as relevant to the alliance and which form the object of intra-alliance communication have strikingly expanded from the more narrowly East–West oriented issues of the early years associated with such matters as the distribution of costs for troop-stationing to an extraordinary array of global subjects, such as the Near East, Central America, Third World crises, North–South problems, the management of the world economy, etc. Needless to say, as the topics of alliance dialogue increase, the potential for disagreement inevitably grows as well. These disagreements attract all the attention in the media but the common interests and areas of co-operation almost none. The assessment of NATO's capacity for handling internal divergences consequently takes on a pessimistic twist. If there is a lesson to be drawn from NATO's 35 years of managing – and often only muddling through – internal conflicts and disagreements it is one of more than ordinary resilience in dealing with divergences, than is generally assumed. Even if one were to believe that NATO's present and future problems are likely to be more severe than those of the past, one should at least be cautious in assessing their impact.

Among the problems that have a potential of undermining support for NATO in Western societies public doubts and protest about nuclear weapons and nuclear deterrence are usually cited first. Although the debate on these issues is led and conducted by élite minorities on both sides of the Atlantic, they receive undue attention in the media and have, indeed, spread to large segments of public opinion in the form of a vague, but nevertheless significant concern about the necessity and potential consequences of nuclear deterrence. None of these issues are really new; what is new is the unprecedented public scope of the debate on nuclear weapons. The issue is relatively quite simple. Deterrence threatens the destruction of what it aims to protect: human life. The principle is old of course and has always posed very serious ethical problems. Nuclear deterrence aggravates these problems in unprecedented ways. It aims at preventing war by threatening to impose unacceptably high damage in case of aggression.

This formula, which was contested only by small minorities in the post-war period, is now increasingly questioned by wider circles, because the public view on the relationship between the threatened damage and the aim of war prevention has shifted. Large numbers of people have come to believe that war can be prevented while at the same time lowering, if not preventing, the potential damage of nuclear weapons. Here lies the crux of the present public debate in NATO. Many people no longer accept that the East–West relationship, and notably Europe, has remained an island of peace in a world of numerous and bloody wars with millions of victims, because the potential risk of nuclear war decisively contributed to preventing the outbreak of military conflict.

Many opinions critical of deterrence, including voices from the churches, acknowledge the stabilizing role of nuclear deterrence, but at the same time call for a replacement of the deterrence system by other ways of maintaining peace.

Two problems arise in connection with such a demand. First, nuclear deterrence cannot be eliminated *within* a system of deterrence since the threatened damage remains the prerequisite of its effectiveness. There are possibilities of stabilizing deterrence and of lowering its real and potential cost. However, a replacement of the principle, to prevent damage by threatening damage in order to prevent war, can only be attempted *outside* the deterrence system by changing political conditions, through interdependencies, co-operation and the gradual elimination of the roots of conflict. Needless to say, that is a task for generations. Second, change in the deterrence system is only possible if all parties in a conflict agree to participate. Even the most radical policy alterations in Western societies will not change the deterrence system, unless the Soviet Union decides to reciprocate; if that is not the case the likelihood of war might, in fact, increase.

The potential for political change, which simultaneously tries to preserve stability, therefore, lies in two areas: the improvement rather than the replacement of nuclear deterrence, as well as a general détente policy which aims at improving the political relationship between East and West.

It now appears that the public debate in NATO countries is returning to a more sober assessment of the possibilities of change with regard to nuclear deterrence. The calmer mood in the debate and the protest movement that occurred in 1984 is due to several reasons. First, the decision of majorities to deploy missiles in answer to the lack of progress of the INF negotiations. That decision, notably the vote of the West German parliament, had a clarifying effect as parliamentary decisions by majorities always do. Second, the peace and protest movement of 1984 no longer corresponds to the movement of the beginning of the 1980s. The Soviet Union gravely misjudged the impact of its own nuclear behaviour on the peace movement. The Soviets remained totally unperturbed by the anxieties and aspirations of the movement through-out the protest years and relentlessly built up their own nuclear arsenal week after week, even adding totally new systems aimed at Western Europe, in the mistaken belief that this would either remain unnoticed or, for some reason, be acceptable to those who fought the deployment of Western weapons. The effect of Soviet arms build-up, on the contrary, has been to reduce the number of those in the peace movement who advocated a departure of the Federal Republic of Germany from NATO.

Third, the nuclear debate has calmed down as a result of the learning effect which any debate is likely to have. The situation in the Federal Republic of Germany may be indicative of the general situation in NATO. After the outburst of energy that resulted in protest and discussion since 1981, a certain constellation has emerged. First, the group that opposed nuclear deterrence in principle. It looks for genuine alternatives, and it will remain an institutionalized minority constantly challenging the majority view on security policy. In Germany the Greens form the core of this group.

There are, second, the strategy reformers, comprising the overwhelming majority of those Social Democrats who went into opposition to the NATO double-track decision. They are now engaged in a process of looking for improvements in NATO strategy, although that search takes place under the heading of 'alternative strategies'. Having rediscovered that genuine alternatives to nuclear deterrence are not available, efforts of this kind look at two different avenues for the evolution of strategy: the reduction of dependence on early use of nuclear weapons in case of aggression – sometimes called raising the nuclear threshold – and the strengthening of the European components of Atlantic defence. Interestingly, neither of these subjects is confined to the opposition, but is also the subject of concern in the governmental majority as well. It would, therefore, appear that Germany, like most NATO countries, has entered a phase of consolidation of its public debate on nuclear deterrence.

When several prominent Americans, including former Secretary of Defence, Robert McNamara, launched the idea of an East–West agreement on the no-first-use of nuclear weapons, they found and reinforced a critical European mood engaged in reassessing the necessity of nuclear weapons in the defence of Europe. Thus, American concern over being implicated in a nuclear war that starts in Europe, joined forces with European concerns about becoming the battlefield between the two superpowers.

In the meantime, however, the debate has produced certain intermediate results. Although there are still proponents of a no-first-use agreement, something like a majority consensus has emerged around the notion that one should decrease dependence on early first-use by strengthening conventional defence. Since General Rogers, the Supreme Allied Commander of NATO, launched his so-called 'Rogers Plan', numerous studies have been made and countless debates have taken place in various countries on the problems associated with raising the nuclear threshold. To be sure, conventional technologies will be available in the near future that can take the place of some missions with nuclear weapons. However, the political debate on these approaches is skirting a reality which the proponents of approaches to raise the nuclear threshold have always made clear, namely that additional defence expenditure would be unavoidable. European defence budgets are far from fulfilling the target of a 3 per cent real increase once formulated by a NATO summit and are, in fact, jointly moving towards stagnation and slight real decreases. Even those politicians who favour concrete measures to decrease dependence on early use of nuclear weapons generally, see no possibility to produce the kind of increases in defence expenditures that would be necessary to significantly change the present posture of relying on nuclear weapons. The Federal Republic of Germany, the most crucial country in this connection, has a special problem: as a result of the decrease in the number of draftable men in the forthcoming years, major efforts involving additional expenses will have to be made to maintain the fighting power of the *Bundeswehr*. It is simply unrealistic to expect major additional financial commitments on top of these measures in order to finance alternative conventional technologies on a significant scale.

If there is no radical alternative to nuclear deterrence and desperately little margin of manoeuvre for gradual improvement in the direction of raising the nuclear threshold because of higher costs, what are the likely and the desirable consequences? The likely consequence appears reasonably certain: given the continued build-up of nuclear arms, in combination with the crying need for additional resources in an impoverished Third World, the gap between demands and realities will grow even greater among those who oppose nuclear deterrence and even among those who only want to improve it. The nuclear issue will remain an open wound and constantly challenge the consensus that represents the foundation for alliance policy.

For those who oppose nuclear deterrence in principle the gap between demands and possibilities remains unbridgeable for a long time to come. But the large number of those who have legitimate doubts and concerns can be influenced by policies. Approaches dealing with them are likely to strengthen legitimacy among the majority that supports NATO security policy. Such approaches must work credibly on two levels: first, the stabilization of nuclear deterrence by improving calculability, balance, and crisis management. Stability is possible at a significantly lower level of nuclear potential. Moreover, any progress in the area of stabilizing conventional arms competition and restoring the balance represents a step in the same direction since conventional conflict remains the paramount trigger of nuclear conflict.

The political framework of nuclear deterrence constitutes the equally important second level. Though resolution of the conflict that lies at the origin of nuclear deterrence will be the task of generations, a great deal can be done to affect the political conditions of the East–West relationship. A minimum set of agreed rules on global and regional behaviour, as well as co-operative links in non-military areas, in particular in the economic field, are likely to improve and stabilize the environment within which nuclear deterrence plays a continued role. Since the millennium of the non-nuclear world is not around the corner and since nuclear deterrence remains essential to prevent war, the political dimensions of stability need strengthening.

JAPAN'S ROLE AS 'A MEMBER OF THE WESTERN ALLIANCE'

Shunji Taoka

SENIOR DEFENCE CORRESPONDENT FOR *ASAHI SHIMBUN*

Since Japan's Prime Minister, Yasuhiro Nakasone, defined Japan as 'a member of the Western alliance' and expressed his desire in early 1982 to make Japan 'a huge aircraft carrier', both expectations and concerns are spreading at home and abroad that Japan is going to play a more active military role in global politics. But the real defence policy of the country will be determined more by objective circumstances such as public opinion, state of finances, the strategic environment, and relationships with foreign powers, than by the personal character or political posture of one politician. And a closer look at these factors will show that Japanese defence policy will have to maintain the same course it has followed for the past three decades, which is a gradual increase of defence capability in pursuit of the goal of strict self-defence.

The trend of growing public acceptance of the Self-Defence Forces (SDF) seems to strengthen the impression abroad that Japan is now changing its course to starboard right under the captainship of ex-Lieutenant Commander Nakasone, following in the wake of the United States, the flag ship. We have to first closely re-examine, however, whether or not Japanese public attitude toward defence matters is rapidly changing. Although it is true that in recent opinion surveys (1981), 82 per cent of Japanese were in favour of the maintenance of Self-Defence Forces, while only 3 per cent were opposed, this is not really a new phenomenon at all. Six years ago in 1978, the percentage of SDF supporters was 86 per cent, in 1975 it was 79 per cent and in 1972 it was 73 per cent. Even in 1950, only five years after World War II, which was so disastrous for Japan, an opinion survey conducted by *Asahi Shimbun* showed that 53.8 per cent of Japanese were in favour of rearmament. The increased support for the SDF, about 30 per cent in more than 30 years, can by no means be regarded as a rapid change in public attitude.

Because anti-military feeling among Japanese is mainly derived from their memories of World War II, the change in public opinion will be as slow as the fading of Japanese memories of the tragic battles, horrible devastation, and the narrow-sighted, arrogant military leaders of pre-war Japan.

125

Although the passage of time is perhaps the biggest influence on public opinion, there are also several other factors that contribute to this very slow, but steady increase in support for the SDF. These include the growth of Japan's economic power which has redeveloped the sense of national pride and demand for national prestige; the low profile of SDF personnel and their patient effort to gain public acceptance, which has contributed to their current image as decent members of society; and finally anti-Soviet feelings, arising from the Soviet occupation of the southern Kurile Islands and fishery conflicts in the Sea of Okhotsk, the detention and ill-treatment of 300,000 Japanese war prisoners in Siberian labour camps for several years after the war, the Soviet military build-up in the Far East, the invasion of Afghanistan and the shooting down of a KAL plane, and Japanese contempt for corrupt bureaucracy and inefficient economic systems.

On the other hand, there still remains a strong scepticism toward the military, and the Japanese public is reluctant to spend more money on defence. In a 1981 national opinion survey, 51 per cent were in favour of keeping the present force level, 23 per cent were for an increase, and 10 per cent for a decrease. Reflecting this unenthusiastic acceptance of the SDF, the government has kept the defence budget within a limit of 1 per cent of GNP for the past 17 years.

Judging from the past trend in public opinion, it seems that, while Japanese public support for defence will continue to rise, the transition will be a very slow process. Parallel with this, Japan's defence policy will have to move toward a gradual increase or modernization, as has been the case during the last three decades. If foreign leaders expect a dramatic change in Japan's defence policy and a bigger role for Japan in global security in support of the United States, based upon a misinterpretation of the trend of opinion polls, there will be terrible disappointment and frustration.

A more serious problem for defence planners, is the financial situation of the Japanese government, in spite of the bright outlook for the economy in general. The outstanding amount of government bonds reached the level of US $46,000 million in 1983, which is about 40 per cent of Japan's GNP or an amount about equal to Britain's GNP.

The repayment of the bonds will start from FY 1985. In that year alone, the government will have to repay US $40,000 million, which is four times the defence budget and about 30 per cent of this year's tax revenue, and it will sharply increase in the several years that follow. Because such a large amount of repayment is apparently impossible, the government will have to roll over the debt with a higher interest rate, making financial problems chronic for decades to come.

As a result of this financial situation, a general increase in government expenditure, with the exception of defence, had to be

126

reduced to a meagre 1.4 per cent in FY 1983 by freezing the salaries of government workers and cutting education and social welfare services. Due to an American request, the defence budget was increased by 6.2 per cent in FY 1983, forming a 'salient' in Japan's thrifty budgetary structure. Realistically, this exceptional increase in the defence budget was aimed at accommodating the United States, which is a big importer of Japanese goods, rather than defending Japan from any military threat from the Soviet Union. As one leading Japanese politician remarked, 'A rich merchant has to donate more for his town's festival, in order not to be regarded as stingy or blamed by the town's people'. The Japanese at present are more concerned about the criticism in the United States of Japan's so-called free-ride that might aggravate American frustration with Japan, than with the possibility of a Soviet armed attack against Japan. Incidentally, the accuracy of the assertion that Japan has a free-ride with United States military protection must seriously be questioned. Successive American commanders in Japan have testified in the United States Congress and stressed in press interviews that the image of Japan's free-ride is inaccurate. As a matter of fact, Japan is spending US $1,000 million annually on the maintenance of American military bases in Japan and the building of housing facilities, aircraft shelters, and navy reservoirs. It is also paying various kinds of allowances to 20,000 Japanese employees of the United States' forces to eliminate the salary gaps with equivalent Japanese public servants.

In contrast to this, in June, 1983, the United States concluded a new five-year base agreement with the Philippines. In this agreement, the United States agreed to pay US $900 million to the Philippines to keep its base rights at Subic Bay and the Clark Field. Instead of demanding rent, Japan is paying US $1,000 million to maintain American bases and will continue to do so, in spite of serious financial difficulties. But many uninformed Americans fail to take cognizance of this Japanese contribution and instead blame Japan for a free-ride.

Although it is true that West Germany is paying much more in order to maintain 200,000 United States Army troops and twelve fighter squadrons, let it be stressed that Japan is spending twice as much money per each serviceman to support the 51,000 American military personnel stationed in Japan.

A more important difference between Japan and West Germany is the degree of the threat of a direct invasion. West Germany is facing about 100 Warsaw Pact divisions, including 20 very well equipped Soviet divisions deployed in East Germany, which could at any moment move into the West.

But in the Far East the situation is quite different. Although the Soviets have 39 divisions (360,000 men) in two military regions in the Far East, most of them are guarding the long Chinese border. In the vicinity of Japan, there are only two Soviet skeleton divisions (the 79th and 342nd) in Sakhalin and garrison troops in the Southern Kurile Islands. There are only about 20 amphibious ships in the Soviet Pacific Fleet, which is barely adequate to transport two lightly armed naval infantry regiments of 2,300 men, each with their equipment. The only way for the Soviets to invade Japan would be to take a sea port in the northernmost part of Japan by a surprise attack of naval infantry or airborne troops, and transport the main body with its heavy equipment and supplies by civilian cargo ship that would be pressed into military service. Against this possibility, in the northernmost island, Japan deploys four fairly well-equipped and well-trained divisions out of a total of thirteen divisions (156,000 men). Even if this island could be occupied, the distance from the northern part of Japan to Tokyo is more than 1,000 kilometres, making the quick subjugation of Japan by ground troops almost unthinkable, which is in sharp contrast to the situation in Germany.

The increased ranges of the new types of Soviet tactical fighter (SU-24, MiG-23 and 27) have become a more realistic threat. Although the old MiG-21, with a very limited range, could cover only the northernmost part of Japan, the modern SU-24 (Fencer), an equivalent of the F-111, is capable of low altitude penetration throughout the Japanese archipelago. Also the supersonic TU-22M (Backfire) bombers cannot be considered an easy target for some 3,000 Japanese interceptors, as could the TU-95s (Bear). But the distance of 1,000 kilometres from the Soviet Far-East Maritime Provinces to Tokyo and other vital areas is still a great advantage in air defence, compared with Western Europe.

Japan's biggest vulnerability is in its economic structure's heavy reliance upon sea traffic. To support a population of 110 million and the second largest economy in the free world, Japan is annually importing 600 million tons of raw materials and food, equivalent to the cargo load of roughly 30,000 ships. It is estimated that even on a wartime economy, 197 million tons would be required annually to maintain the Japanese living standard at the minimum level set for social welfare recipients.

Because such a large quantity of imports cannot be protected by a convoy system, unless Japan had several hundred escorts, Japan's Maritime SDF has had to conceive two complementary strategies to defend its shipping from the Soviet submarine threat. One is to blockade the three straits between the Sea of Japan and the Pacific with mines, surface ships, submarines, and aircraft. The other is to patrol Japan's Pacific sea-lanes with ships and aircraft up to 1,000 nautical miles from the Japanese coast. But the argument persists in Japan against these strategies. If Japan blockades the three straits at the time of a United States–Soviet confrontation, the Soviet Union would inevitably invade the coastal areas facing these straits to secure the passage of their submarines, or the Soviet Union might resort to nuclear blackmail. Therefore, the Japanese government had to promise in the Diet that Japan would not execute this strategy unless Japan is actually attacked.

Against the threat of Soviet nuclear weapons, Japan has realistically no response, whether the threat is new SS-20s or old SS-4/5s and SS-11s with variable range. Even if Japan decided to accept the visits of American ships carrying nuclear-tipped Tomahawks, discarding its 'non-nuclear principles', it would not be an answer to SS-20s. In Europe Pershing-IIs and Tomahawks can reach vital areas of the Soviet Union, but in the Far East, with 2,500 kilometre range, Tomahawks can hit only shabby local towns in Siberia. Tokyo cannot be exchanged for Khabarovsk or Vladivostok.

Like the countries of Western Europe, Japan has a common interest in maintaining free institutions, unmolested sea traffic, the general *status quo* of the world and peace. The Japanese people also have a deep respect and admiration for the civilization developed in Europe, which has been the main basis of present Japanese culture for the past 130 years.

To sum up, although it is true that the political trend in Japan is toward a greater acceptance of defence forces and a recognition of a Soviet threat, it would be wrong to expect that Japan will, in the near future at least, play an active military role in global politics.

PART FIVE

Regional security problems
outside the alliance

NATO AND THE
OUT-OF-AREA CHALLENGE

Amos A. Jordan
PRESIDENT OF THE CENTER FOR STRATEGIC AND
INTERNATIONAL STUDIES, GEORGETOWN UNIVERSITY

Reconciling allied responses to threats outside the North Atlantic region with collective security within it has been a problem for NATO almost from its inception. Hardly a year has elapsed since the formation of the alliance without the engagement of one member state or another in extra-regional military action. And virtually every such case has produced some measure of discord within NATO. In a few cases – Suez in 1956, Vietnam, and the Middle East in 1973 – the level of dissension has seriously threatened to rupture alliance unity.

In a way, that is scarcely surprising. When the twelve original signatories of the North Atlantic Treaty agreed in 1949 to join in an unprecedented peacetime collective security effort, they brought with them a sense of common interest possible only for nations which had barely survived a catastrophic war, together with a common perception of threat deriving from Soviet pressure in Europe. But commonality of interests was an early casualty of increasing European economic recovery and self-confidence – in a sense, proof of NATO's success. Similarly, the common perception of threat was an inevitable victim of the passing of bipolarity and the emergence of new centres of power and instability.

Under the circumstances, what is surprising is not that out-of-area challenges have posed difficulties for NATO, but that these difficulties have been successfully surmounted for 35 years. History records scarcely another case in which sovereign nations with such widely differing foreign policy traditions and interests have so successfully insulated their association from the pressures placed upon it by their external involvements.

Even so, many on both sides of the Atlantic today worry about the durability of this success. Others worry that even if that success can be sustained, continued insulation of NATO from out-of-area challenges – and vice-versa – will make the alliance increasingly irrelevant to the course of international events. Such concerns reflect several significant changes in the security environment confronting NATO.

One such change is in the nature of the threat. While the potential danger to NATO posed by the regional power of the Warsaw Pact has not diminished in absolute terms (indeed, has if anything increased), other threats have become relatively greater. The past decade has witnessed an enormous intensification of global instability and violence, ranging all the way from terrorism and civil strife to outright conventional war. Once limited by geography and technology, such violence now readily transcends political and geographic boundaries, in the process confounding both understanding and management.

Still another change is in the relative vulnerability of Western nations. Complex, technologically fragile, and increasingly dependent on external markets and resources, developed Western economies are vulnerable to disruption in a way heretofore inconceivable except in actual major war.

The third change – and by far the most critical – is the decreased ability of American power to control global events. Although this is in part a question of United States' capabilities – the now-familiar 'strategy-force mismatch' problem – it is at least as much a matter of American will, stemming from post-Vietnam domestic disillusionment with the exercise of power and increasing reluctance to invest lives and treasure where the threat to American interests is not clear-cut and immediate. (Indeed, not the least of the ironies associated with American pressure for greater allied involvement out-of-area is that it reverses the policy position with which the United States entered NATO. It was the United States, not its European allies, which insisted that NATO limit its purview to the North Atlantic region.)

Together, these changes present the West in general – and NATO in particular – with several dilemmas. Firstly, the threats to which the nations of the alliance are increasingly vulnerable are also those least susceptible to common understanding, both as to their nature and as to the appropriate response. Secondly, Soviet achievement of global projection capabilities increases the risk that a regional conflict could escalate to a global one. A commitment of military forces by one or more NATO states out-of-area thus risks increasing the danger of Warsaw Pact – NATO conflict, even as it diminishes defence capabilities in the NATO area. And, finally, both these conditions inhibit agreement on concerted Western action at the same time that American willingness to act unilaterally on behalf of Western interests is diminishing.

Together, these dilemmas significantly increase the possibility that a future out-of-area crisis – in the Middle East, for example – could confront the alliance with a choice between fatal disaccord or paralysis.

NATO is aware of this risk. Ministerial guidance agreed by the allies in May, 1981 acknowledged the increasing vulnerability of Western interests to out-of-area situations, and called for both consultation prior to out-of-area deployment by any ally, and efforts by non-participating allies to facilitate such deployments and to compensate for any associated draw-down in NATO area capabilities.

While such formal recognition of the problem is welcome as far as it

133

goes, the 1981 agreement scarcely resolves the basic dilemmas outlined earlier. Several fundamental problems remain.

The first, and most basic, is the difficulty of reconciling allied perceptions and interests. Indeed, perhaps no aspect of the out-of-area question is more troublesome than defining what constitutes a common threat. It is possible to distinguish cases, such as a potential loss of Persian Gulf oil, which threaten the interests of all allied states, from cases such as the Argentinian invasion of the Falkland Islands, which arguably affected only one ally. But even were such a distinction analytically persuasive, it could never survive politically. In any case, the distinction breaks down in practice: whatever the intrinsic merits of a case, involvement of an ally out-of-area automatically invokes – if only indirectly – an alliance interest. (The more powerful the ally, the greater is the interest, as every American intervention from Korea onward well illustrated.)

Even were it possible to secure agreement on the nature and immediacy of a common threat, moreover, such agreement would scarcely guarantee a unified response. Differences in the domestic political structures, historical traditions, and even the constitutional limitations of NATO's members present nearly insuperable obstacles to alliance action – especially military action – outside NATO's formal treaty boundaries. And the more ambiguous the precipitating event, the greater the obstacles become. While diversity is one of the strengths of the Western alliance – indeed, in a sense its *raison d'être* – the unavoidable price of diversity is a reduction in strategic flexibility.

As a final problem, achievement of alliance unity with respect to out-of-area challenges confronts a more-or-less persistent United States–European divergence in attitudes toward East–West competition. Generally speaking, the European allies have been less willing than the United States to perceive and respond to the East in geostrategic forms, and more concerned than the United States to insulate their direct relations with the USSR and Eastern Europe from the global East–West competition. The Middle East, Afghanistan, and Central America are only the most recent examples of regional conflicts in which this perceptual divergence has inhibited the development of a unified alliance viewpoint, let alone concerted action.

Given all these problems, it is clear that any attempt formally to broaden the military purview of the alliance is foredoomed. Even NATO's current security mandate has been stressed to contain such internecine issues as the Greek–Turkish imbroglio. To suppose that NATO's commitment to collective defence could be stretched to accommodate even more divisive contingencies is simply quixotic.

On the other hand, the 'division-of-labor' alternative which the alliance is pondering at American insistence may be equally dangerous in

134

the long run. Even were the European allies prepared to compensate through regional force increases for American military commitments out-of-area (and it is not clear that they could or would), such measures hardly embody the 'shared risks and burdens' essential to continued alliance cohesion. In the end, no agreements on overflight rights, or basing, or even substitution for diverted forces, can 'compensate' for the shedding of blood. Division-of-labor might ease the United States' 'overcommitment' problem, but only at the price of intensifying American public and Congressional resentment toward unilateral American action in defence of Western interests.

The fact is, there are no simple formulas for the alliance's dealing with contingencies with which NATO was never originally intended to cope and which it is no better suited to confront today. Thus the most immediate requirement is to lower expectations – largely American expectations – which currently threaten to exacerbate alliance problems without solving global ones.

At the same time, the European allies must come to terms with the reality that collective security within the North Atlantic treaty area does not excuse ignoring insecurity outside it. The United States, too, is to a degree prisoner of its interests, historical traditions, and domestic structure. Most Americans will not support a security posture in Europe to which their own survival is hostage in the face of allied indifference to conditions outside NATO which seem to Americans both equally threatening and far more imminent.

Fortunately, a formal alliance commitment to out-of-area engagement is not required. What is required is that individual allies be willing to share the costs and risks of broader security management, and that some attempt – whether through NATO mechanisms or around them – be made to coordinate their efforts. There is some evidence that the former requirement is already beginning to be met, as the activities of Britain in the Persian Gulf, France in North Africa, and Germany in Turkey and Pakistan indicate. There is unfortunately far less evidence of a serious attempt to coordinate these efforts, and it is in this area that scope exists for early improvement. Four such improvements would go far toward meeting the out-of-area challenge.

First, all could do a far better job of pooling national intelligence. Inadequate intelligence sharing has long been a problem. There are certainly risks, particularly for the United States as the pre-eminent producer. Yet we simply must accept them. The United States and its allies cannot hope to coordinate a response to inevitably ambiguous out-of-area situations unless we begin from reasonable agreement on facts.

Second, given such improved common knowledge, we require some routine mechanism for collectively monitoring and forecasting situations which could require a coordinated multinational response. Such coordination will be difficult enough to achieve without making the task even tougher by being perpetually surprised. Not all contingencies are wholly unpredictable, and there is no reason why the allies cannot undertake limited contingency planning, and every reason why they should. A contingency monitoring mechanism in the alliance would serve as both a stimulus and an information resource for bilateral and unilateral contingency planning undertaken outside NATO channels.

The third requirement, which the first two would facilitate, is for more effective crisis consultation. While a hotline similar to the one which the United States maintains with the USSR is not needed among allies, something more is needed than the pro-forma practice of advising the others of a decision after it has already been reached. As Charles de Gaulle rightly noted during the 1962 Cuban missile crisis, this is not consultation but information.

Finally, all the Allies need to work to lower the intramural noise level. Whether over a pipeline disagreement, or the Palestinian problem, or Central America, rhetoric does at least as much damage as the dispute itself. Such self-discipline is not easy for democratic governments, and is constrained by the very public accountability we seek to preserve. But between unrestrained public argument and unacceptable censorship lies a huge middle ground.

None of these suggestions is particularly novel; even together they do not promise a 'solution' to the out-of-area problem. NATO is not a monolith, and it should not be expected to behave as one. In the end, it is not the formal alliance, but the sense of common destiny which it symbolizes, which is both our stake in the out-of-area problem, and our best hope for managing it. It is a problem which requires both patience and creativity.

NATO'S GLOBAL INTERESTS

Lane Kirkland
PRESIDENT OF THE AFL-CIO

NATO is beset by multiple crises that cannot be papered over without risking an erosion of its foundations. Soothing declarations of transatlantic solidarity may ease nerves and buy time, but the time needs to be used for a serious review of NATO's adequacy in a world that has changed radically since the days of the Marshall Plan.

The massive Soviet military build-up of the 1970s, the Arab oil embargo, and the global recession of the 1980s, have combined with injudicious rhetoric from the Reagan administration to generate fear and discord within the alliance. There is a widespread perception of wavering public support for NATO and of declining confidence in its deterrence strategy – that is, its reliance on America's nuclear umbrella. New questions are also being raised about the scope and limitations of NATO's mission. It is to this last issue that I wish to speak, the rest having already been addressed by others in this book.

But first, a preface. NATO could never have been established without the support of the trade unions of the United States and Europe, whose leaders recognized the significance of Article 2 of the North Atlantic Treaty, which pledged that: 'The Parties will contribute toward the further development of peaceful and friendly international relations by *strengthening their free institutions*, by bringing about a better under-standing of the principles upon which these institutions are founded, and by promoting conditions of stability and well-being. They will seek to eliminate *conflict in their international economic policies* and will encourage economic collaboration between any or all of them'. (Emphasis mine.) It is precisely our stake in the strengthening of free institutions – especially free unions – that explains the AFL-CIO's traditional advocacy of a strong Western defence; and it is our parallel stake in encouraging economic co-operation at the trade union level that directs our participation in the Trade Union Advisory Committee of the OECD.

Because the alliance is comprised of democracies, it must rest on the approval of electorates, not merely of governing élites. It cannot survive an American perception, accurate or not, that Europeans want American protection of European territory and of European interests in the Persian Gulf but would gladly decouple themselves from United States' interests in, say, Central America. It cannot survive a European belief that the United States is an unreliable ally that combines irresolution with reckless rhetoric. It surely cannot survive the impression on this side of the Atlantic, fostered by media exaggeration of European 'neutralism', that growing numbers of Europeans regard the superpowers as morally equidistant. The more moderate leaders of the anti-nuclear demonstrations in Europe may deny an anti-American bias, but Americans cannot ignore the fact that there were no notable demonstrations while Soviet SS-20s were being deployed.

If these concerns require a candid, in-depth re-evaluation of NATO's role, the American labour movement is not indifferent to the outcome. We have no interest in a self-destructive dialogue or in administering shock therapy to the Europeans by threatening the withdrawal of American troops. The result we seek is a renewal of public support for NATO on both sides of the Atlantic, but support based on a shared common-sense understanding of what NATO is for.

Against this background, let us turn to the Persian Gulf, upon which Europe is dependent for nearly one third of its oil and Japan for more than half. The United States depends on the Gulf for 11 per cent of its supply. Yet it is the United States that has committed itself, under the policy enunciated by President Carter, to use force to ensure the flow of oil through the Strait of Hormuz.

Americans can only wonder why, if Persian Gulf oil is vital to the European economies, its protection should not be the shared responsibility of NATO. Senator Gary Hart has raised this issue in his Presidential campaign, in a way that threatens to tap the current of isolationism that always runs under the surface of American politics and that our trade union movement has always resisted.

Foreign policy specialists may respond with arguments about the language of the North Atlantic Treaty and about the technical and political difficulties of amending it. But such arguments will not wash with the man in the street, who is not always less wise in matters of survival than the professional diplomats. There is an air of unreality about a defence arrangement that aims to prevent the devastation of European territory by war but not the economic devastation of Europe by energy strangulation.

Equally unreal, to many Americans, is what they perceive to be the negative or detached attitude of Europeans to the problems of the Caribbean, which were extensively analyzed in the report of the Kissinger commission. As the commission pointed out, growing Soviet-Cuban influence in the area does pose a security threat to the United States. The threat arises not only from the possible deployment of Soviet missiles in the region but from the hemispheric consequences of a Central American war – the massive loss of life, the destabilization of fragile democracies, and the inevitable extrusion of destitute refugees by the tens of thousands. It is naive to think that the United States, caught up in such a maelstrom close to home, would not have to divert attention from the European theatre.

The commission recognized that the problems of Central America do not begin and end with the Soviet Union. They are deeply rooted in poverty, social injustice, and the denial of fundamental human rights. The commission's proposals for addressing these ancient wrongs are sweeping and profound enough to be described as social-democratic. Certainly, in its scope and intent it bears comparison with the Marshall Plan, though on a smaller scale.

Of special interest to the labour movement is the Commission's proposal to establish a Central American Development Organization (CADO) to 'provide a continuous and coherent approach to the development of the region' in all its dimensions – 'economic prosperity, social change, political modernization and peace'. Membership would be open to the seven countries of Central America and to the United States, with each country's delegation including representatives of 'a democratic trade union movement, of business and/or the government'. Such a tripartite structure would strengthen the role of the democratic trade union movement throughout the region.

In addition, Central American participation in CADO would 'turn on acceptance of and continued progress toward the protection of personal and economic liberties, freedom of expression, respect for human rights, and an independent system of equal justice and criminal law enforcement'. This condition would apply to El Salvador and Nicaragua.

Yet the commission's emphasis on economic development and social justice has been largely ignored because the commission also insists that its proposed reforms be protected by a military shield, and in some quarters there is a knee-jerk reaction against anything 'military'. This is especially sad in view of the fact that the concept of a military shield for social reform was originated not by the Reagan administration but by the late Senator Henry M. Jackson, who believed that, if free institutions were worth building, they were worth defending.

The AFL-CIO has conditioned its support for military aid to the government of El Salvador on demonstrated progress there in the field of human rights. This reflects our conviction that there can be no purely military solution to El Salvador's travail. A government that cannot or will not protect the rights of its citizens will not have the popular base necessary to prevail against Marxist-Leninist insurgencies. A government that wins such a base is entitled to our military help.

Meanwhile, Nicaragua has amassed more men under arms than all of its neighbors combined. And while much is made – properly – of the threat this build-up poses to Nicaragua's neighbors, it has for us another dimension: it is a shield behind which trade union rights are being trampled, as workers are being forced to leave the unions of their choice and join Sandinista organizations. Yet, many of our European friends see the issue in Central America simply as one of American interventionism.

139

The Reagan administration's policies deserve criticism, but however badly it has botched things, the fundamental issue remains: what is to be the fate of the peoples of Central America? Do they have a right to free institutions or must they yield to one or the other totalitarian extreme? And should their fate concern the United States alone?

The purpose of NATO is not simply to secure real estate but to secure a political system in which people are free to create and control their own institutions. The number of countries in which such a system operates is pitifully small. This unhappy fact, in an increasingly interdependent world economy, means that every retreat from political democracy under the assault of totalitarianism, anywhere in the world, is a blow to the interests of the dozen democracies that signed the North Atlantic Treaty 35 years ago.

It would not be realistic to suggest that NATO radically restructure itself to police the world. It would be equally unrealistic to believe that NATO can meet the challenge of the remainder of this century with the structures, doctrines and mission of a generation ago and still command the public support that democracies require for their policies. Bringing NATO into a better alignment with the actual global interests of the alliance will require an extraordinary exercise of statesmanship on both sides of the Atlantic.

TOWARDS A WIDER PEACE

Bettino Craxi
ITALIAN PRIME MINISTER

If we think of the Atlantic alliance in human terms, we see a man of full awareness, with his full physical and intellectual powers. As a baby he was rather weak, and many doctors shook their heads in doubt and scepticism. But he grew from strength to strength, until every anxiety was silenced. His degree thesis, the challenge of liberty, was respected even by his declared opponents. He has developed his social relationships, widened the circle of his knowledge and, most important, has preserved the security of the Western world. Today he faces the most difficult task, the challenge of peace.

Let us leave the metaphor. The Atlantic pact is a system of alliances with no precedent in history. In this, the most ideological century in history, it guarantees the safety of all its members while allowing them to develop freely without restriction of any kind. Under its protection, the great ideological challenge between East and West has been able to develop in peaceful terms. But the political organisation of peace is a battle far from won. Peace at present is a crown of thorns – it exists but it pricks, and many are the drops of blood which fall.

In the 35 years since its inception, the protagonists and the setting – notably the boundaries of the East–West confrontation – have changed. As early as 1956, an alarm bell was rung at the outbreak of the Suez crisis, which resulted not only in a dispute between allies – the United States on one side and France and Great Britain on the other – but also an abrupt break between the West and the Arab world. The subsequent Arab–Israeli wars accentuated the awareness of the dangerous consequences which an open confrontation with the Arab world would have on the political and economic security of the West. This awareness became a dramatic realisation of impotence in the 1973 conflict. However, neither the awareness nor the realisation resulted in anything concrete. Not much good was done by the sudden, over-effusive love for the Arab world (a love which to many smelt of oil) which the major European countries began to show after 1967, forgetting their earlier attitudes in favour of Israel. An even worse result for the European countries was to alienate the sympathy of Israel, thus losing the opportunity to play a moderating part and leaving this task to the United States alone. To find a specific act or at least a show of more specific intentions by the European countries, we must go to the EEC summit of December 1973 at Copenhagen, with its declaration of readiness 'to give our own assistance in the search for peace and for guaranteeing a solution' to this conflict.

This declaration was repeated at various times, always in the same tone, by the European countries up to the Venice declaration of June 13, 1980, where the Nine went further by proclaiming their readiness 'to participate, in the context of a global settlement, in a system of specific, obligatory international guarantees, including action on the spot'.

None of these declarations stopped the course of events. Destabilisation processes continue to assail many countries in Asia and Africa, spheres of influence have continued to change and to extend, and the dividing line of the East–West confrontation remains as changing and unstable as ever.

What shall we do? Clearly we cannot give up. Equally clearly, if the whole weight of the alliance is periodically moved over these changing boundaries, the result can only be an intensification of international conflict, condemning local disputes in perpetuity. This leads us to ask: Is a global vision more useful than a regional view of individual conflicts? Does European and American policy coincide towards the individual countries of Asia and Africa? What relation is there between a stable Western policy and the instability and unpredictability of some governments of these countries?

In seeking an answer to these questions, we see an obvious need for improved East–West relations, which would greatly assist in limiting local conflicts and taking most of the danger out of them. We are living through an extremely critical stage in our relations with the Soviet bloc. Détente should not become a simple memory. Our general consideration must be kept in mind: is it possible to think that world peace can be maintained by an increasingly intense and sophisticated balance of terror? Can the world live by inventing increasingly complicated and terrible instruments of offence and by inventing equally complicated devices for defence against them? Can we continue in this way? I do not believe so. The situation today is what it is – the right to safety and the duty of defence impose choices and decisions which, on our part, we have already taken, considering them right and necessary. We are, therefore, not speaking about hypothetical questions.

I only want to assert my conviction of the need to change course, of the impossibility of continuing on our present road indefinitely. Let me make it clear that I am not thinking about a situation in which one of the two contestants will put up his hands in surrender (the solidarity shown by the West with regard to the Soviet SS-20 speaks for itself). I am thinking of an agreed, controlled change of direction; a reduction in armaments that cannot be achieved if we argue over who was initially responsible for the arms race.

Improvement in East–West relations would be an important contribution to the problem of 'external areas', such as crises and conflicts in areas outside the Atlantic defence perimeter but still affecting the problem of common safety. When *The Times* invited me to take part in the debate on the future of the Atlantic alliance, it asked me to 'think aloud, even the unimaginable'. Well, is it impossible to imagine an East–West agreement to renounce strategic and military advantages outside the area of the Atlantic or the Warsaw pacts? Is it impossible to imagine an East–West understanding on the quantity, quality and nature of aid to the developing countries of the Third World? Is it impossible to imagine consistent activity aimed at preventing a war economy taking the place of a peace economy in all these countries, or death and degradation being the price which these people must pay for their yearning to survive? Is it impossible to imagine an agreement to safeguard communications and oil routes?

But apart from general problems regarding the Atlantic alliance, there are important particular tasks facing Europe and the individual countries of Atlantic Europe. Admittedly after the Athens and Brussels summits, any talks about Europe and its tasks regarding security risks turn into a denunciation rather than a discussion. And yet discussion is necessary, in order to stress again that security is a special aspect of the European identity, the identity of this Europe whose presence as such can well be a stabilising element throughout the Mediterranean and also offer the possibility of protecting the countries in these areas from the risk of becoming vassals.

Not long ago, five European research institutes (Italian, French, German, British and Dutch) completed a joint study on the future of the European Community. Their report said: 'If Europe wishes to prevent others acting on its behalf without consultation in areas of central importance for its own safety, it must organise itself, define a policy and take specific steps to implement it'. We can stop here – everything else is implied. We know all the excuses – the complexity of the consensus which European governments must obtain in order to govern; the economic difficulties with which they are struggling, in view of the lifestyle of their populations; the lack of confidence, the criticism which is made against any proposal to act, often even when action is vital. But there is no doubt that unless Europe recovers the unity and the ideological resolve to achieve a communal policy and play an active, energetic part in world development, it will be able to do nothing except to make continual requests for information and consultation without ever having the strength to make its own decisions or to become a real factor for peace. The Atlantic pact is certainly no obstacle to European development. The very solidarity of the Atlantic alliance is a source of confidence and independence for its members.

A few words on Italy. Italy is the country most involved in the Mediterranean, the country with the best relations with all others in the same area. This is a positive development in our relationships – let us try to identify the permanent interests of the countries which face us, and try to associate these interests with our interests and our policy. We shall then succeed in stabilising and protecting them from sudden, unforeseen changes. The peace and safety of the Mediterranean are essential; we shall fight against the short-sightedness of those who want to keep us in our little shell.

We are convinced that if Italian policy is based on the aims of peace and collaboration, it will continue to play an essential part in the Mediterranean, for the benefit to all, particularly I hope to the other maritime nations. Nothing is unimportant as a contribution – no matter how small – to meeting the challenge of the end of the century – the challenge of peace.

THE WESTERN ALLIANCE: AN OUTSIDE JUDGEMENT

Abba Eban

FORMER ISRAELI MINISTER OF FOREIGN AFFAIRS

There is no effrontery in a comment on the Western alliance from someone who falls outside its registered membership. Americans and Europeans have generated a profuse literature of recrimination in which little place is given to the notion that each of them may have a case. Many years have passed since a serious statesman or scholar wrote about the alliance without an epithet of nostalgia or disappointment. The titles of the books and articles strike a sombre note: *'Troubled Partnership'*, *'The Western Misalliance'*, *'Reluctant Allies'*. A similar air of disillusion prevails in the European Community which is the central core of the alliance. Even the most loyal Europeans no longer speak of their enterprise in the old rhapsodical tones. Ministers returning from Brussels to their own capitals rarely boast of having strengthened the European idea; they usually congratulate themselves on having defended their particular national interest against the malice and guile of their 'partners'.

The disappointment would be less sharp if the expectations had not been pitched too high. The popular myth implies that in the late 1940s the United States, Canada and Western Europe entered into a relationship of great scope and intimacy from which there has been a sad decline. The truth is that nothing of the sort ever happened. The only engagement that the Western nations ever undertook toward each other is contained in the North Atlantic Treaty of April 4, 1949, which stipulates in Article 6 that 'an armed attack against one of them shall be considered an attack against all'. The commitment is austerely limited both in the territorial and the functional sense. The formulation gives an impression of reciprocity, but this was more a gesture to Europe's wounded pride than a description of reality. Europe needed America's protection against an expanding Soviet power, while America, secure in its nuclear monopoly, needed no defence from Europe. American descriptions of the NATO treaty as a 'unilateral security guarantee' were deeply hurtful to Europeans, but this does not mean that they were untrue. There were some attempts to give the treaty an ideological context by adding language about democracy and human rights, but the United States, anxious for Congressional approval, forbade any such excesses. This appeared fortunate in later years when the NATO family was joined by a Spanish dictatorship, a Greek junta, a Turkish military regime and an absolutist Portuguese government. In the meantime, democracy has scored some successes and the portrayal of the NATO countries as a democratic grouping would not be excessively pretentious. But the gap between American and European views of the world remains unbridged.

What went wrong? Many of the frustrations arise from objective circumstances. The alliance was founded in an atmosphere of exceptional deference to American leadership. The United States had contributed decisively to the defeat of tyranny, had blocked the expansion of Soviet power in Europe and the eastern Mediterranean, had created and distributed enormous surpluses of capital and productive capacity and had patiently fostered European integration and unity. If the United States did not inspire affection it certainly excited envy and emulation. This sentiment began to erode in the 1960s with Vietnam and a falling dollar. When the United States accepted Soviet nuclear parity and ascendancy in conventional arms the myth of American primacy suffered further injury. Later, Europeans winced at evidence of American hesitancies and failures – the authorization and subsequent cancellation of the B-1 bomber; the retreat from SALT II; the loud anti-Soviet rhetoric followed by a failure to restrain Soviet actions in Afghanistan and Poland; the endorsement of American wheat deals with the Soviets while punishing Europeans for co-operating with the Siberian pipeline; and, most recently, a policy in Central America which most Europeans persist in regarding as unduly nervous and obsessive. There were times when Europeans accused America of being excessively moralistic and lacking in realism. Today the tables are turned; Europe charges America with being too hard-headed and insensitive to international opinion and law. The common feature is that in European eyes America can never be right. Dissociation from the United States is the certificate of European 'independence'.

Disagreements between Europe and the United States on issues outside the NATO geographical area are not, strictly speaking, in conflict with the 1949 treaty. The European signatories never undertook to support American policies or operations in Vietnam, Cambodia, Central America, Iran or the Middle East, and the United States is under no contractual obligation to identify itself with the policies of the European powers in their former colonies or to condone their tendency to strengthen economic links with the Soviet bloc. There have been occasions, such as the 1962 Cuban missile crisis and the Falklands war when Americans and Europeans received support from each other, and there will be such occasions again. But this co-operation will have to arise from separate decisions in particular cases and not from the spontaneous solidarities of an alliance.

More serious than divergences on matters outside NATO is the

146

failure of the United States and Europe to agree on European security. This, after all, is the main theme of the alliance, and it is here that discord is most marked. It is true that America and Europe both have anxieties about the Soviet Union, but their anxieties overlap without being identical. American fear is 'only' of a nuclear attack. Europeans fear both a nuclear attack and an invasion by conventional military forces. Of these two fears, the latter, which Europeans do not share with Americans, is the least far-fetched. Soviet armies have sometimes moved into neighbouring countries while there has never been a serious prospect of a Soviet nuclear assault. In these circumstances, it is objectively understandable for Europeans to look more carefully at their relations with Moscow and to avoid abrasive rhetoric and attitudes. The more so, since Europeans are by no means certain that an American nuclear umbrella would really protect them against a Soviet conventional invasion. It must be admitted that Americans have done a great deal to nourish this scepticism. If a confirmed Atlanticist such as Henry Kissinger can tell Europeans not to rely on American nuclear protection since that 'is something that we cannot possibly mean or if we do mean we should not want to execute, because if we execute, we risk the destruction of civilization' – how can Europeans continue to dream of the United States risking suicide for their protection?

Behind this discord lie divergent perspectives about the Soviet threat. Paradoxically, Europeans who are closer to the danger are less afraid of it than are Americans who are more distant and less vulnerable. Europeans were more alarmed by a non-nuclear Soviet Union weakened by the devastation of World War II than they seem to be by the vastly more powerful Soviet Union of today. Americans talk of the USSR as of a formidably cunning and successful colossus, while Europeans see the Soviet Union as a troubled society unable to feed itself, dependent on Western technologies and tormented by its task of controlling dissident movements in Eastern Europe and managing its own invasion of Afghanistan. Europeans have de-demonized the Soviet Union while the Americans have not.

The querulous tone of European comment on the United States used to be heard with indulgence in America when the United States was confident of its hegemony and power. Today, American grievances against Europe resound not only in the traditionally isolationist Midwest, but among internationally-minded Eastern establishments as well. Americans do not understand why the European community, with a population, a steel production and a technological capacity greater than those of the Soviet Union, should not have created a conventional defence system capable of balancing Soviet power and reducing the weight of the nuclear element in Western strategy. One does not have to be an American to regard this as one of the mysteries of the post-war age.

Other American grievances come under the heading of inadequate European solidarity. Americans believe that the capacity of the United States to support European security depends on the general United States posture in the world; yet whenever America makes a show of resistance to Soviet pressure it is criticized in Europe as being excessively anti-Soviet. Europeans always understood that Britain and France could not resign themselves to a hostile power in control of the Low Countries; but Europeans seem appallingly insensitive to the concern of the United States about hostile regimes in central America. There is also a more deep-seated psychological resentment; the anti-Americanism in the discourse and rhetoric of many Europeans, especially in intellectual circles, goes beyond any reasonable limit.

If there is any value in an outside judgement I would say that the American case is stronger than that of Europe. The European complaints against America are concerned mainly with issues of tactics, timing and rhetoric as well as the notion that America is, if anything, excessively zealous in the resistance to Soviet encroachment, which is after all the central aim of the alliance. Americans discern in Europe a disquieting decline of will and purpose; there is a tormenting doubt whether Europe feels that its decisions matter, and that its basic values deserve the sacrifice necessary for their preservation.

In these conditions 'a joint Western foreign policy' is an exaggerated hope. There are no institutional provisions for such a Western 'concert' and the post-war age reveals few examples of successful multinational mediation. There are few issues in which American–European harmony extends beyond first, vague principles. The Arab–Israel conflict is a case in point. Europeans are more vulnerable to Arab oil and currency pressures than they are responsive to Israel's security. The United States is the only country in which Arab geo-political weight is counterbalanced by a strong Israeli place in domestic opinion. And only the United States can compensate Israel or an Arab state for the risks that either takes in a peace settlement; this was revealed in the negotiation of the Egyptian–Israeli peace treaty. Whenever a tension becomes dangerously close to escalation, the United States turns not to Europe, but to the Soviet Union for help in securing a cease-fire or a disengagement process. Every Arab–Israeli war between 1948 and 1973 ended with an American–Soviet consensus not on the political issues at stake but on the need for an end to hostilities.

The conclusion is that the NATO countries can help free societies outside the treaty region, not by acting upon them but by setting their own house in order. The fact that Europe has been at peace for 39 years is the alliance's transcendent achievement. But precisely because Europe is neutralized against armed violence, the aggressive elements inherent in the international system are diverted towards the Third World and peripheral areas in Asia and Africa. The alliance could help freedom by a more assertive defence of its own vision. Democracy does not have a rhapsodic sense. It lacks a proselytizing instinct. Democracy has produced more wealth and welfare than Soviet communism, but it stands before Moscow in an apologetic mood. It is not assertive enough in celebrating its own triumphs or criticising Soviet weaknesses. Moreover, there is a lack of symmetry in the decision making process. What we call the 'West' is fragmented at two levels – the level of discord between different states and the level of domestic diversity within each democratic nation. The Soviet Union, on the other hand, is a unitary source of decision.

What the alliance needs is a stronger consciousness of its own stature in history. The NATO powers, the European Community and Japan form the greatest aggregate of power and wealth in the history of mankind. Power and freedom have never come together more intimately than here. For the most part, the powerful have not been free, and the free have not been powerful. If the Western alliance were more sharply aware of its unique reconciliation of freedom with power it might escape from its frustrations into a new era of opportunity.

FOR PEACE AND STABILITY

Mario Soares
PORTUGUESE PRIME MINISTER

On NATO's 35th anniversary I wish to express some of my thoughts regarding the alliance and its future role in maintaining peace and security in Europe and to give my views concerning the problems of regional security linked with the present situation in Latin America.

The signing of the North Atlantic Treaty in 1949 gave substance not only to a defensive military alliance but also, and above all, was an expression of solidarity by the Western countries to safeguard the values of freedom and democracy that they had freely instituted.

During the 35 years of its existence the Atlantic defence system was able to preserve peace and freedom in Europe and, more important, has been an efficient deterring instrument *vis-à-vis* the overall threat from the East. NATO is a defensive alliance; none of its weapons will ever be used except in response to attack. Just recently, the NATO countries demonstrated outstanding political cohesion by commencing the deployment of Pershing-II and cruise missiles, thereby contributing to the re-establishment of the military balance in Europe. This decision has once again proved that the alliance today continues to be indispensable to European security, as was the case, at its outset, in 1949. I am convinced that the alliance will in the future continue to fulfil its collective security role against any military aggression or intimidation in the European area.

However, it must be stressed that owing to deep changes in the international community in recent years, NATO has found it necessary to reflect on and adapt itself to the evolving situation. To achieve this, it is, of course, necessary to constantly define and harmonise the international common interests of the respective member countries. The expansion of American interests to other regions of the world presupposes the creation of a new internal relationship which must involve, in my view, a certain levelling of power between Europe and America within the alliance itself. It is, therefore, essential to enhance the European presence, rethink its strategy, as well as its means and mobility.

As mentioned earlier, the geo-political and geo-strategic factors that led to the creation of the alliance have indeed profoundly altered in the course of the last few decades. Founded in response to the need to restrain Soviet expansionist military strength in the post-war period, the West also had to deal with Russian-intensified, geographically diversified, subversive ideological efforts. Simultaneously with the worsening of the international economic situation, which has generated conflict and social tension in many of the Third World countries, we are also witness to an increase in the ability of the Soviets to intervene, and de-stabilise regions outside the alliance, which are of crucial importance to the West. The various forms that this Soviet offensive has assumed depend to a large degree on diverse factors, including measures of an indirect character which frequently are difficult to analyse because of their complexities in terms of the dangers they pose to the alliance.

It should be stressed, in this connection, that the lack of foresight on the part of the developed countries has produced a system of economic relations that cannot but result in generalised dependency, making the rich countries richer and the poor progressively poorer, thereby gravely undermining a rational sharing of national resources and preventing a balanced and rapid economic development – decisive ingredients to advance and maintain international peace and security.

Consequently, the people are frequently being subjected to totalitarian ideologies and unable to defend their freedoms, aspirations and vital needs, which normally are subject to considerations of global strategy.

Latin America sets a good example of such a circumstance. It is obvious that Latin American realities cannot, under all circumstances, be placed in or reduced to the global frame of the East–West conflict. They are endowed with a character of their own, varying from region to region and from country to country, with essentially distinct and indigenous problems, as distinct in fact as their positions are in relation to the processes of democratization. But, beyond the political and institutional differences, one must not overlook the common sociological realities: economic underdevelopment, sharp social contrasts, distressing poverty and blatant deprivation of the vast majority of the population. This situation explains, to a significant degree, the political tribulations, the social contradictions and the exacerbated conflicts that have taken place during the last few decades in that part of the world.

As such, it is in a strictly regional framework that one must look for adequate solutions to solve the conflicts in a manner that would enhance the conditions to create, in the future, an area for democracy, freedom, and social justice in Latin America.

In this regard, one should mention the activities and the performance of the Contadora Group towards the development of links of co-operation and the peaceful solution of conflicts in the area.

Even when the prevailing conflicts are only local in nature, they nevertheless deserve the urgent and sympathetic attention of European countries, at least for humanitarian motives, if nothing else. An additional important factor, however, is that Europe must also concern itself with the penetration into Latin America by outside aggressive predatory forces and their policies.

The allies recognise that the security of the member countries is of a global character extending far beyond the geographical scope defined in

Article 6 of the Treaty. The political evolution of every area must be followed in such a way as to detect situations of crisis in order to analyse those that can have negative repercussions on the common interests of member nations. But decisions to support sovereign nations situated outside its frame of reference, who request assistance in countering threats to their security and independence, must always be taken by NATO member states on the basis of national decision, after due consultations, whenever they feel that their collective vital interests are at stake.

While I believe that the present situation in Latin America, especially in Central America, does not, at this time, represent an immediate threat to the vital interests of the West, it nevertheless remains within the interests of the latter to provide and extend political, economic and diplomatic support to these countries, in order to preserve and contribute to the peace, stability and well-being of the region.

Last, but not least, I must add that to pay tribute to NATO on its 35th anniversary is to place a vote of confidence in the role it has so magnificently played to maintain peace in the interest of us all.

PART SIX

Summit views on East-West and West-West relations

DETERRENCE AND DIALOGUE

Ronald Reagan
PRESIDENT OF THE UNITED STATES OF AMERICA

As the Atlantic alliance celebrates its 35th anniversary, it is particularly appropriate to re-dedicate ourselves to the great task we set for ourselves in 1949. The more closely the nations of the alliance can work together, the better we will be able to preserve peace and stability, and the better it will be for people everywhere.

The values that bind NATO together are not abstract concepts. Individual liberty, the rule of law, and respect for dignity of the individual are priceless and real. They have been handed down to us at enormous sacrifice of blood and treasure. They are the cement of the alliance and we can never take them for granted. And it is the success of democracy, not the military power of the totalitarians, that will shape the rest of this century.

The world has changed a great deal since the representatives of twelve states met in Washington, on April 4, 1949, to sign the treaty establishing the alliance. But the underlying unity and purposes of the Atlantic community have not changed. NATO remains the true and effective peace movement – and the bulwark of Western freedom.

The founding members of NATO pledged to safeguard the 'freedom, common heritage and civilization of their peoples' and to consider an armed attack against any one of them an attack against them all. Having just experienced the most devastating conflict in history, alliance leaders knew first hand the dangers of war, and the requirement for unity to deter it.

But they had more than sound historical understanding. They had remarkable foresight. The structure of Atlantic co-operation which they built has ensured the longest period of European peace, stability and progress in history, during a time when the world has undergone rapid and accelerating political, economic, social, and technological change.

The challenges which the Atlantic alliance confronts today are no less difficult than those which NATO has met successfully for the past 35 years. If we face them with the same determination, creativity, and sense of responsibility we have shown in the past, the future will be secure. If we are to achieve true peace, we must work for it.

The bedrock of our alliance is our unshakeable commitment to ensure our security through collective self-defence. There is no alternative but to maintain a credible deterrent military posture and political solidarity. The continuing growth of Soviet military power will require a sustained effort by all of us – to reduce disparities in the military balance, to broaden our co-operation, to make the necessary investments to keep the peace.

The North Atlantic Treaty is not solely a military alliance. We also seek to improve the well-being of our people. Sustained economic growth will be the key. In this regard, we need to resist protectionism while we expand our co-operation in the fields of science and technology. We, as allies have long recognized that developments beyond the treaty area are relevant to our own well-being.

Building a constructive relationship with the world beyond and the treaty area will require great energy and wisdom. We need to work together in addressing the human, social, political and economic conditions which create the instability on which radicalism and Soviet interventionism feeds. This does not mean expanding the treaty area. But it does mean working closer together in sharing the burdens and solving the problems.

Since its creation, NATO has always had to address the question of how best to deter Soviet attack. The future will be no different. And we have agreed on the outline of the answer: defence and dialogue. There is no evidence that future Soviet behaviour will be anything but a serious threat to our security and to those principles on which a humane international system must be based. The answer for the future will still be defence and dialogue, a policy of reasonable strength combined with the commitment to search for ways to reduce the risk of conflict. Our challenge is to follow a policy of realism; strong enough to protect our interests but flexible enough to spare no effort in finding a fair way to reduce the level of arms.

Sometimes, we in the free countries forget the richness of our most precious possession – freedom and human rights. People who live in tyranny, however, can see freedom much more clearly. It shines like a candle in the dark. It is our responsibility to speak out and to work hard for the dignity of mankind, to improve human rights, and to hold governments accountable for their behaviour. This challenge has no boundaries and it has no limits.

The experience of the past 35 years has prepared the nations of the Atlantic community to overcome these challenges. As long as we stand together we will remain secure. We have not learned rote formulas, to be applied to all situations whether they fit or not. What we have learned is that the alliance is truly durable. While we cannot take our partnership for granted, we can be certain that patience, co-operation, and hard work will pay off. Any undertaking will ultimately be judged by the challenges it accepts and by those it overcomes. We have accepted a worthy challenge and overcome many of them over the years. There is no reason to doubt the future.

Alliances generally do not outlive the achievement of their immediate – and usually wartime – objectives. That has not been the case with NATO.

NATO has prospered because it is adaptable. It expresses our democratic processes and reflects the very values it has for 35 years so effectively defended. The survival and vitality of the Atlantic alliance stems from one fact that overrides all others; namely, that it is based on and represents the moral and political values that Western Europe shares with North America. The alliance has evolved over time most recently through the welcome addition of Europe's newest democracy, the Kingdom of Spain.

This continuing vitality is nowhere more evident than in the deepening of alliance consultations on the question of nuclear arms control and maintenance of the alliance's nuclear deterrent. The 1979 INF decision, taken in response to the deployment of Soviet SS-20 missiles threatening Western Europe, is a shining example of the alliance's traditional approach to Western security – the dual foundation of defence and dialogue.

NATO has implemented both tracks of that decision, despite unprecedented political and military threats from the Soviet Union. NATO was responsible for the initiation of the Geneva arms control talks, which the Soviet Union at first resisted. It was through consultations within NATO that our arms control positions were developed. And, it has been the unity and determination of NATO which has made possible the actions needed to maintain our nuclear forces in Europe.

Contrary to popular assertions, the alliance is reducing rather than increasing its reliance on nuclear weapons. The alliance agreed that as INF weapons were introduced, existing weapons would be removed on a one-for-one basis. In addition, however, last autumn NATO decided to reduce the NATO nuclear stockpile by an additional 1,400 weapons. Together with the 1,000 warheads removed three years ago these unilateral reductions will bring the number of weapons withdrawn since 1979 to 2,400. The overall NATO stockpile will be reduced by one third.

The INF experience is an extremely important lesson for the future. It shows the ability of democratic governments to work together. Despite the stress, even with governmental changes in all of the countries directly involved, we will have been able to maintain a coherent policy. Contrary to the pessimism of many critics, dictatorships do not have an inherent advantage when dealing with free people. When governments remain open, people will respond in the best interests of freedom and peace.

The United States will continue to work with our allies to ensure deterrence at the lowest possible level of nuclear weapons, and to strengthen the capability of conventional forces to deter conflict and lessen the likelihood of war.

As we work to ensure a credible military posture, we are also creating the basis from which to seek more stable and productive East–West relations. On January 16, 1984, I underscored my personal commitment to building a more constructive relationship with the Soviet Union, on the basis of realism, strength, and dialogue.

The United States is prepared to pursue the dialogue with the Soviet Union in all areas of our relations, from arms control to regional issues, from human rights to bilateral concerns. While I cannot predict the intentions of the Soviet Union, I firmly believe that it is in the interest of both sides that arms control negotiations go forward in all areas which had been under discussion.

The East–West dialogue must also embrace the full range of issues contained in the Helsinki Final Act. If it does not, we cannot expect to strengthen mutual confidence and understanding. In our bilateral dealings with the Soviet Union, and in the multilateral channels of the Conference on Security and co-operation in Europe, the nations of the Atlantic community will continue to pursue improvements in the rights of the individual, in greater communication and access, and in meaningful dialogue on the whole range of issues affecting the people of the continent.

The engagement of the Western nations for peace has increased markedly in recent years, as has the difficulty of the international situation. The United States and its allies are working together, for example, in such disparate regions as southern Africa and the Middle East, in the recognition that the stability which we have enjoyed cannot endure forever if the rest of the world is embroiled in conflicts.

I am certain that the nations of the alliance will continue to live up to their responsibilities. No one should doubt the commitment of the United States to the continuing effectiveness of our coalition. The security of Europe and North America is inextricably linked, and NATO is the proven expression of that interdependence.

The United States did not come easily to the Atlantic alliance. Independence and continental isolation has been a long tradition. As President Washington put it, 'Europe has a set of primary interests, which to us have none or a very remote relation'.

That may have been true two centuries ago, but that view was swept away in the violence of two world wars. It became clear that there was no sensible alternative to an active policy of collective security if the democratic nations of the West were to survive.

So long as the sense of common heritage and interests remains vigorous in the West, and so long as the world remains the dangerous and challenging place that it is today, then the Atlantic alliance must be strong and vibrant. On the occasion of the signing of the North Atlantic Treaty, President Harry Truman stated: 'If there is anything certain today, if there is anything inevitable in the future, it is the will of the people of the world for freedom and for peace'. I share President Truman's optimism. Looking ahead on this anniversary, I am confident that our peoples will be celebrating many more anniversaries of this wonderful enterprise.

BUILDING ON THE NEW REALISM

Margaret Thatcher
BRITISH PRIME MINISTER

The late 1970s was a period of illusion and self-deception. Domestically Western governments pretended their economies could live with the inflationary fever which wracked them: internationally they pretended that détente had ushered in a new and co-operative period in East–West relations. Overheated economies and overheated imaginations weakened resistance at home and abroad.

In the 1980s we have brought the temperature down. The treatment has been difficult. It is much easier to pretend that things are all right than to put them right. Responsible economic management has replaced inflationary *laissez-faire*. Sound money is back in fashion. A hard-headed assessment of Western security has replaced a world of East–West make-believe. Secure defences have been restored. We have broken decisively with a period of intellectual laziness when the seductive charms of self-deception were leading us towards self-destruction. We are stronger and fitter and better able to deal with the issues that face us at home and abroad.

Events in the past four years leave no doubt that a reassessment of East–West relations, and a rebuilding of Western defences, was overdue. At the end of 1979 the Red Army invaded Afghanistan, the first time since the Second World War that it had been used outside the Warsaw Pact. It is still there. In 1980–81, we watched a drama of towering courage and terrible disappointment much closer to home, in Poland. Anyone still deluding himself about the true nature of communist power had only to watch the ruthless suppression of the Polish people's efforts to secure some of those civil and political freedoms which we take for granted. And all the time, despite their peaceful protestations, the Russians continued to deploy SS-20 missiles targeted against West European cities.

Those events reinforced the new mood of Western realism. But a realistic assessment of the nature of East–West relations was only the first step: the second was to act on that assessment. That is what Britain and the other members of the alliance have been doing. In the past four years we have increased our defence spending, and we have implemented our decision to deploy cruise and Pershing-II missiles and so prevent the Soviet Union from establishing a monopoly of medium-range missiles in Europe. No Western government has taken pleasure in having to do either of these things. But the Soviet military build-up, and Soviet refusal to negotiate seriously in Geneva and Vienna about nuclear and conventional arms reductions, gave us no choice if we wished to ensure the continued strength and credibility of the Western alliance. By showing that we are ready to meet the Soviet military challenge we have reduced the risk that the Russians will mistake our resolve. By doing that, we have reduced the risk of war.

For it was not just the West that was deluding itself in the late 1970s. The Russians, to judge from their international conduct, had concluded that the Western attachment to détente was so great that we would turn a blind eye to Soviet behaviour that did not affect us directly; and even to some Soviet behaviour that did. They were wrong. Western governments have spent more on defence despite the recession. Western publics have held firm on INF deployment despite a Soviet propaganda campaign designed to frighten and confuse them. We must hope that the Russians have re-learnt the lesson that the West will not allow its interests to go by default. If so, with illusions shed on both sides, we can now pursue a realistic dialogue with the aim of negotiating agreements which are in the interests of East and West.

That is what the Western alliance has been saying to the Russians in recent months. It was the message of a number of speeches which I made in the last few months of 1983. President Reagan signalled it loud and clear in his speech on 16 January. It was central to what I told Hungarian leaders when I visited Budapest in February, and the new Soviet leaders when I went to Moscow for the funeral of President Andropov. It is what the NATO allies said at the meetings of Foreign and Defence Ministers in December, and what they have been saying since at the CDE negotiations in Stockholm. We want an East–West dialogue that leads not to declaratory texts of little substance, but to concrete steps of practical value.

We are not just looking for progress in Stockholm, where the agenda is confidence-building measures. We want agreements on conventional and chemical weapons. Above all we want agreements in the nuclear field. The Americans are ready to resume START and INF talks in Geneva at any time. The Russians must show an equal willingness. They will not be understood or forgiven if they stay sulking in their tent. The Americans, supported by the allies, are looking for major reductions in the nuclear arsenals of both sides. They have put forward radical proposals. They are prepared to be flexible. But at present all they can see is an empty chair.

The West will persevere. That is the way forward. But we must do so by settling patiently to the task of constructing a stable East–West relationship built on the rock of mutual understanding and respect, not on the sand of high-flown rhetoric and dramatic initiatives. This means building up our contacts with the Russians so that we can discuss the whole range of questions which concern us, not just arms control. For without a broad framework, and the understanding and confidence which comes from multiple and substantial contact, progress towards arms control agreements will be much more difficult. We must also expand and strengthen our links with the East European countries, remembering that each of them has a distinct history and tradition and a particular contribution to make. This is the stuff of steady, unspectacular diplomacy, not political theatre. There will be a place for summits between the leaders of East and West but they must not be seen as a substitute for daily, undramatic contact; nor are they an end in themselves. East–West relations require time and patience if they are to be soundly built. Summits are usually the key-stone, not the foundation.

It is only sixteen years until the year 2000. There is much to do if we are to begin the new century and the new millennium with hope and confidence.

We in Western Europe believe passionately in our democratic way of life; and we are determined to defend it. But we also believe in working to reduce the artificial barriers that divide the two halves of our continent. European stability must not for ever rest uneasily on the frozen postures of confrontation. That is why arms control is a Western priority. We want to reduce the number of weapons and the money spent on them. The question is whether the Russians want to do so too. There are some grounds for optimism. The determined way in which the allies have reasserted themselves in the past four years will have done much to persuade the Soviet leaders that they cannot hope to secure unilateral political and military advantages by refusing to negotiate seriously with us. They know now that we will meet the challenge in whatever form it comes. That provides a strong incentive to talk.

A further incentive is provided by the facts of economic life. The Soviet economy is growing much more slowly than it was and may slow even more. New weapons cost huge sums to design and produce, sums which could be spent with much greater benefit on civilian development. As the Soviet leaders reflect on the high proportion of the national budget which is absorbed by military spending they may well be attracted by arms control agreements which promise to check these spiralling costs.

This does not mean that agreements will be easy to reach. Nor does it mean that the West will conclude agreements unless they are balanced and fair. No agreement is better than a bad agreement. Political factors also counsel realism. The prospects for progress may well be affected this year by the fact that there is a Presidential election in the United States, and a new leadership in Moscow. But if both sides display imagination, flexibility and political will, the second half of the 1980s might prove as fertile a time for genuine arms control agreements as the early 1980s was fallow. Certainly the British government will be doing what it can to make it so.

The events of the past four years have not only led us to review the management of East–West relations. They have prompted us to think hard about the management of the Western alliance too. Its enduring success is a monument to those who founded it 35 years ago. Their shared experience of one war determined them to band together to try to prevent another. That remains our overriding priority. Their chosen instrument was an alliance in which all were committed to the defence of each. Our commitment remains the same. Indeed, as defence technology becomes steadily more complex and more expensive, the concept of common defence enshrined in the North Atlantic Treaty is as relevant as it has ever been.

The value of the alliance does not change but the world around it does. The challenge confronting us is to ensure that the alliance adapts successfully to those changes. Some are integral to the defence debate itself: we must look hard at the resources the members of the alliance allocate to defence. Are we getting good value for money? How can we tackle the difficulties over weapons standardisation? Secondly, we must consider the role of conventional weapons in NATO's strategy. Will technological developments make it possible to rely more on them and less on nuclear weapons? What would be the financial implications of any shift in emphasis? Thirdly, we must think now about the implications of weapons in space. The concepts and the weapons themselves may still seem largely theoretical, but the speed of technological development means that they could soon be with us. Finally, we must also insist on the effective verification of arms control agreements. More declarations of intent are not enough. Success in the current negotiations for a total ban on chemical weapons, a high priority for the government, would be an important demonstration of this principle.

The alliance must adapt to a changing political landscape too. We must agree on a political, as well as a military, strategy towards the Soviet Union. If East–West relations are to improve and develop, the members of the alliance must be united in their aims and coordinated in their actions. As part of this political strategy we must decide how best to handle East–West economic relations. This is a particularly difficult issue. Somehow we must agree on where to draw the line between strategic and non-strategic goods. Further, in the next few years many of the problems for Western interests are likely to arise outside the NATO area. We must be ready to respond to these together. Close consultation is essential. Lastly, we must remember that we ourselves are changing and not to take each other for granted. We must work at our friendship, reinforcing old links and forging new.

These are some of the issues confronting NATO which its new

Secretary General and my old friend and colleague Lord Carrington will be tackling in the months and years ahead. It is a formidable agenda. But the alliance will rise to it, just as it has risen to meet the challenges of the last 35 years. We shall not always agree on everything; we never have. That is inevitable in an association of free nations and no cause for shame or recrimination. But where there is and will be no dispute is over our enduring commitment to shared democratic values, and to their common defence. We know they are a priceless asset; and we know that NATO is the guarantee that we shall be able to pass them on to those who follow us.

BRIDGING THE BARRIER

Helmut Kohl
CHANCELLOR OF THE FEDERAL REPUBLIC OF GERMANY

The Federal Republic of Germany has been a member of the Atlantic alliance since 1955. Together with the European Community, the alliance constitutes the foundation of my country's foreign and security policy. As a grouping of free democracies, it represents a defensive community founded on shared values and convictions. Its commitment to the 'principles of democracy, individual liberty and the rule of law' are of particular importance for the Federal Republic as part of a divided nation. Nowhere else has the alliance's commitment to these values been more clearly visible than with regard to the situation in Germany and Berlin. From these common values the alliance derives its dynamism and the strength to meet external and internal challenges.

The alliance unites sixteen countries of Europe and North America for the purpose of safeguarding the freedom, common heritage and civilization of their peoples. It has fulfilled this demanding task in the three and a half decades since its inception. In that period, during which other regions of the world suffered war and armed conflicts, the alliance proved its ability to preserve peace and demonstrated its nature as a defensive organization that threatens no one. Spain's accession in 1982 reaffirmed the alliance's appeal.

NATO has acquitted itself well as a forum in which the allies can continuously discuss and coordinate wide areas of their foreign policies, for instance arms control and CSCE policy. The successful prevention of war in Europe is the product of responsible action, of reason and statesmanship, which must be maintained and enhanced.

After more than twelve years in office, Secretary General Joseph Luns has handed over his responsible post to Lord Carrington. I should like to pay tribute to Dr Luns for his services and express the conviction that Lord Carrington will perform as new Secretary General with the same efficiency and expertise as he displayed when he was British Foreign Secretary.

Last year was a testing year for the alliance. The start of missile deployment in accordance with the twin-track (deploy-and-negotiate) decision of 1979 showed that the other members of the alliance can rely on the Federal Republic of Germany, just as we can rely on them. Essentially it was a question of whether or not the alliance can, on the basis of the trust and friendly relations linking Western Europe, the United States of America and Canada, continue to fulfil its task of safeguarding peace and freedom. For my country the question was whether it is willing and able to counter, together with its allies, the Soviet Union's claim to hegemony. Like the other members of the allinace, we stood the test.

The start of the deployment of new American intermediate-range missiles brings home to the Soviet Union that it stands no chance of acquiring, with its build-up of SS-20 missiles, a tool for exercising political hegemony in Europe or for decoupling Western Europe from the United States. This is where the great significance of our steadfast-ness lies for the development of European security and East–West relations in Europe. We have kept our word.

This decision, specifically reflecting the reliability and continuity of German policy, will not fail to make an impression on the Soviet Union. Implementation of the twin-track decision shows that the Western alliance remains capable of action. It affirms that the alliance's cohesion has been strengthened by the unprecedentedly close consultations between the European members and the United States. It is essential that the alliance should display unity in the face of the Soviet Union's attempts to split it. This requires that full use be made of the existing consultative mechanisms.

Even after the start of the deployment of American intermediate-range missiles in response to the SS-20 build-up, the alliance's concept remains steadfast and clear-cut: military security and a policy of détente, which – as stated as early as 1967 in the Harmel Report – are mutually complementary. According to that report, the Atlantic alliance has two main functions: firstly, to maintain adequate military strength and political solidarity, and secondly, to pursue the search for progress towards lasting and constructive relations between East and West, which can also serve as a basis for solving controversial political issues wherever possible.

The Federal Republic of Germany will continue to contribute to Western collective security by helping to maintain a defensive capability. Now as ever, our goal is, in concert with out allies, to prevent war, in order that both peace and freedom can be preserved.

NATO's strategy of flexible response serves this goal. We want to prevent any war, be it nuclear or conventional. In the current debate on the risk of nuclear war, the fact is frequently ignored that conventional weapons now have more devastating effects than ever before. In view of the Warsaw Pact's vast superiority in conventional forces, we remain dependent on a deterrent that effectively counters both this threat and the East's nuclear arsenal. To this end, we need a balanced triad of strategic nuclear, tactical nuclear and conventional weapons. In order to eliminate its dependence on the early use of nuclear arms, the alliance must give priority to strengthening the conventional element of this triad.

Unilateral disarmament or renunciation of the war-preventing concept of deterrence would not promote peace, but endanger it. Peace and freedom are our most valuable assets. They must not be placed at risk by hazardous experiments. On this subject I said the following in my policy statement of May 4, 1983: 'We cannot overnight eliminate nuclear weapons from the face of the earth. Unilateral renunciation of such weapons would not reduce the nuclear threat directed towards us, but only increase the danger of war. There is only one way out of this dilemma: we must drastically reduce the number of nuclear weapons on both sides, those which threaten our existence and those which we are now forced to maintain in the interest of our security'. These ideas remain fully valid.

Until such a time when comprehensive, verifiable disarmament renders military means of safeguarding peace superfluous, we shall remain dependent on the alliance's tried and true strategy of deterrence and defence founded on equilibrium. Over the decades, my fellow-countrymen have backed this strategy; this backing must be preserved in the future, too. For this reason I call attention to NATO's Bonn Declaration of June 10, 1982, in which the members of the alliance stated once again that none of their weapons will ever be used except in response to attack.

At its ministerial meeting in Brussels last December NATO renewed its extensive offer of co-operation with the East and sent a clear signal for the continuation of the dialogue on arms control. The alliance's unequivocal re-affirmation of its security policy must be accompanied by new efforts for disarmament talks.

In the field of nuclear disarmament, particularly the West has tabled proposals aimed at deep cuts in nuclear arsenals and hence at reversing the existing trend in this domain of vast importance to global security and peace. At the Strategic Arms Reduction Talks (START), the United States suggested that Soviet and American warheads be decreased by a third. And at the INF talks in Geneva the Americans proposed a complete, worldwide renunciation by the United States and the Soviet Union of long-range, land-based INF, but they also stand ready to accept, on the basis of equality, any agreement reducing these weapons to as low a level as possible.

The alliance has responded to the Soviet walk-out on these two sets of talks with level-headedness and with a readiness to resume the dialogue. We have stressed that the start of deployment does not establish an irreversible situation. We have also made it clear that any change in the deployment schedule can only come about as a result of a mutually acceptable agreement reached at the talks. The Soviet Union, too, has of necessity an interest in a continued dialogue on arms control and in tangible results that limit nuclear potentials and afford both sides greater security. Reason demands negotiations.

At the MBFR talks in Vienna the allies concerned have submitted a draft treaty envisaging a verifiable reduction of the land and air forces of both alliances to 900,000 on each side in the area involved. Progress is possible in Vienna once the Eastern negotiators are ready to deal seriously with the unresolved issues.

At the Geneva Conference on Disarmament the West is striving for a treaty that reliably prohibits the production and stockpiling of all chemical weapons.

The Conference on Confidence and Security-building Measures and Disarmament in Europe, which came about as a result of a Western initiative, enables the 35 participating countries to negotiate for the first time ever the question of security in the whole of Europe from the Atlantic to the Urals. This conference in Stockholm must be exploited as a new means of expanding the dialogue between East and West, negotiating confidence-building measures and promoting stability and security throughout Europe. Success in these endeavours would at the same time open up new prospects for conventional arms control in Europe. In addition, with this conference we want to enhance the CSCE process so that the political and military aspects of co-operation for peace in Europe suitably supplement each other. We regard the conference as part of our efforts to obtain ultimately a broad-based, stable East–West relationship. That is its political significance.

However, above and beyond security policy, we must consider the shape that relations between NATO and the Warsaw Pact are to take in the future. We must show the leaders of Eastern Europe that after the start of missile deployment, their assertions still lack foundation: it does not involve a question of war or peace, nor does it constitute a step towards destabilization instead of the restoration of equilibrium, or the pursuit of a Western strategy of confrontation. Especially as a country in which the missiles are being deployed, we advocate a policy of moderation and understanding on the basis of equality, equilibrium and mutuality. Both sides, East and West alike, can but benefit by co-operation for a shared future founded on the manifold ties and experiences of a shared past.

The genuine results of the policy of détente pursued in the 1970s, must be consolidated and improved. The East–West dialogue is still under strain because Western Europeans' vital security interests are being impaired by the Soviet policy of stockpiling more and more weapons and seeking to decouple Europe from the United States. On NATO's 30th anniversary, five years ago, the then Secretary General, Dr Joseph Luns, said that détente had a different meaning for the West than for the East. Whilst the West construes it as the dismantling of bureaucratic barriers in the wide field of human contacts as well as economic and commercial relations, the East interprets it in the narrow sense of 'peaceful co-existence', permitting an unbridled ideological offensive. The Soviet Union and its allies must abandon this attitude: détente can be achieved in the long run only if neither side views it as an instrument for obtaining security advantages to the detriment of the other.

It is in our mutual interest to foster East–West relations. To this end a modicum of stability and steadfastness is required in the relationship between the two superpowers. This should indeed be attainable in view of their parallel interests in essential areas: to prevent armed conflicts that could result in nuclear escalation, to achieve tangible results in disarmament negotiations, and to reap mutual benefits from economic co-operation.

Considerable importance attaches to intensifying the direct political dialogue between the superpowers. I would, therefore, welcome an early meeting between President Reagan and President Chernenko.

In the eyes of a German head of government, the German and European aspects of the foregoing considerations are of special significance.

The two German states – the Federal Republic and the GDR – must, particularly at difficult junctures, contribute towards the preservation of peace in Europe by engaging in constructive co-operation. One of the principle aims of the latter is to ease the situation of the people in our divided nation. The Federal Republic and the GDR have a shared responsibility for ensuring that peace must emanate from German soil. Our policy on Germany, which is backed by the alliance, is therefore in fact a policy for peace in Europe. This backing gives us reason to hope that the division of Germany and Europe can ultimately be overcome and that we can attain a state of peace in Europe, in which the German nation regains its unity through free self-determination. For this reason, too, my country sets great store by European unification.

Only if my country is firmly integrated in the Western alliance and the European Community will it be respected by the East. Thoughts of neutralism and going it alone are downright illusory. Whenever the European countries demand that they be accorded greater weight in the alliance, they must bear in mind that this requires making greater efforts and shouldering more responsibility for implementing the joint security policy. The United States' contribution to the alliance is indispensable, but Europe's efforts are equally important. Only a strong and united Europe can contribute towards a strong and united alliance. Transatlantic co-operation and European unification must be strengthened and advanced simultaneously.

In its relationship with the Soviet Union the alliance must speak plainly. We must make it clear to Moscow that the hope of decoupling Western Europe from the United States will not materialize, just as the

168

members of the alliance will never accept Soviet military superiority. Proceeding from this firm foundation we are able to work for a policy of accommodation. Without neglecting its security interests, the alliance is seeking equitable and long-term co-operation with the countries of Eastern Europe to our mutual benefit. This was expressly re-affirmed by the 16 Foreign Ministers of NATO in their Declaration of Brussels of December 9, 1983, and at the meeting in Washington, DC, in May, 1984.

PART SEVEN

Is Western civilization an obsolete concept?

AT THE MORAL CROSSROADS

David M. Abshire
US AMBASSADOR TO NATO

The Times' superb series on the 35th anniversary of the Atlantic alliance is striking for its recurrent emphasis on sustaining public support as the key to NATO's future. Critical to that ongoing public support is the continued perception of the legitimacy – political, military and moral – of the alliance and its strategy.

The question of the morality of alliance stategy has now fired debate, especially within the churches, educational institutions and among the young. The ethics of nuclear warfare has become one of the most vibrant public policy issues of our day. The outcome of that debate touches the future of the alliance, for the public must be convinced of its moral legitimacy if NATO's support is to be sustained.

The maturation of a new generation unscarred by the tragedies of two world wars, the emergence of new currents of thought and opinion are bringing NATO to a moral crossroads. With such a critical inter-section in sight, it is essential that we within NATO enter this debate.

There is, however, confusion over the term 'moral' that has made NATO advocates hesitant to enter the fray. On one side stand many political activists, some in the peace movements, who proclaim certain absolute moral positions and insist on their morality to the exclusion of all other factors. On the other side are active men of affairs who also view moral values as absolute but impractical – something postulated by priests, preachers, rabbis or educators, but not applicable to their daily affairs or real world choices.

I say a plague on both their houses. Absolutism of either kind is not appropriate. Those who would take one issue – such as INF deployment – and look at it out of context are too simplistic in their analysis. Those who would moralize about absolute peace without ever studying the complex problems of achieving real peace, or considering the threats to peace, or the conduct of a potential adversary, are doing little to actually advance the cause of peace. Equally, those who believe moral considera-tions have no place in their decisions will not take long to discover that their cynicism is not shared and their policies not supported.

The great theologians have known that absolutism doesn't work and that in the lives of nations, as distinguished from the lives of men, clear moral choice is more difficult because it is so much more ambiguous. This dilemma was identified by the great Protestant theologian Reinhold Niebuhr in the very title of his classic book, *Moral Man and Immoral*

Society. St Augustine of Hippo argued that until the City of God appeared, it was one's duty to further the City of Man. US Catholic Bishop John Roach, president of the US Bishops Conference, has made the point in saying that 'ambiguity is a legitimate and treasured part of our moral tradition'.

In foreign and security policy, only partial solutions are possible; one must constantly strike unsatisfactory balances – between compromise and security, between order and progress. That is the challenge NATO faces.

The two world wars and the immediate post-war experience that fostered NATO's birth also conjured four new horsemen of the Apocalypse: fears of nuclear war, of a world-wide conventional war, of blackmail and coercion, and of human tyranny and bondage. Hiroshima, the Somme, Munich and Auschwitz embodied these spectres. The moral imperative became the prevention of their happening again. For that reason, NATO was formed. NATO must confront not just one of these evils but all four.

Each of these phantoms threatens the Judaeo-Christian, multi-faceted concept of peace which, unfortunately, has largely gone un-addressed by many in the 'peace' movements and others in the debate. This notion of 'peace' is an integrated balance of two traditional concepts – one reflected in the Hebrew word '*shalom*' and the other in the Latin word '*pax*'. Shalom implies a sense of peace that relates to an individual's wholeness and health, security and prosperity in their fullest sense. 'Pax', on the other hand, connotes the peace of the ordered political community that makes living together possible. It has to do with order and stability.

This classical concept of peace, then, implies much more than the absence of war and the avoidance of war more than a determination simply not to fight. It focuses on the creation of conditions in which individuals and societies can flourish and in which there are recognized limitations on the use of force.

A strong sense of human justice, embodied in civic freedom and a political order that safeguards the individual is a vital component of what we mean by peace. St Augustine described peace as the 'tranquillity of order'. For true peace, that order must be moral as well as physical. We would be deluding ourselves if we believed there is peace today in a country like Poland just because there is quiet in the streets. As long as courageous men and women are herded to the Gulag, there is no peace.

Peace is a dynamic process in which we must be constantly and positively engaged. It is a multi-faceted concept, encompassing both the individual and society. The only legitimate peace policy is one that neither sacrifices freedom of the individual for the order of the state, nor ignores the threat to the state because it is consumed by the personal comfort of the people.

Because the threat to peace is multi-faceted, absolute solutions won't work. They only address one dimension of the threat; they only secure one facet of the peace. Some people, for example, have suggested unilateral disarmament as the absolute solution. Such a policy may achieve our relief from the threat of nuclear or conventional war, but would it really relieve us from the threat of tyranny?

Our problem in securing a just defence – and the basic moral ambiguity we must confront – is that all of our options are unattractive; there is no good choice. All involve some element of moral risk and the possibility of pain and suffering.

The issue facing NATO today, then, is the problem of providing a just defence against this multi-dimensional threat. If moral absolutes are inappropriate, what does a just defence mean? St Augustine defined one criteria as proportionality – that particular means must be in proper relation to desired ends. A second element is proper motivitation. Just defence must also be adaptable to the world's constantly changing conditions that might generate new threats or re-configure old ones. Therefore, just defence must be flexible.

I believe that the current NATO strategy of deterrence meets the criteria. Reinforcing deterrence is the best path for ensuring the peace.

On the military side, reinforcing deterrence requires reducing the nuclear risk by improving NATO's conventional capabilities, thereby making flexible response truly flexible. The problem is not that the allies have stopped their common defence efforts, but that the Warsaw Pact has so markedly stepped up its efforts in the last dozen years that serious gaps have developed.

Flexible response remains a good strategy – one of proportionality and legitimacy. It must be made to work. By making flexible response work we will achieve stability in Europe. In its turn, stability will foster effective deterrence, NATO's ultimate goal.

NATO's role, however, goes beyond the purely military. When NATO, in 1979, committed itself to the two-track approach, it recognized that arms control efforts must parallel military ones.

The Soviet walkout from the negotiations on intermediate nuclear forces and their enforced delay in beginning the next round of the strategic arms negotiations have not dissuaded NATO from aggressively pursuing meaningful arms control agreements. In January 1984, for example, as a result of Western initiatives at the Madrid CSCE follow-up talks, the Conference on Disarmament in Europe opened in Stockholm, and the allies were quick to table a package of pragmatic confidence and security-building measures. Shortly thereafter, NATO allies participating in the MBFR talks in Vienna concluded agreement on a new Western proposal and placed that on the table. Then, with President Reagan's personal involvement, the United States, after close consultation with its allies, offered a draft treaty at the Conference on Disarmament in Geneva calling for a global ban on chemical weapons.

In addition to arms control considerations, NATO has been fully cognizant of the economic dimension of security. The NATO Charter stresses that economic progress and economic co-operation are essential to achieve the individual and national well-being inherent in our concept of peace, and it warns of the potential problems inherent in economic nationalism and protectionism.

Until now we've been talking about *pax* and just defence. Let us turn to *shalom*. Part of *shalom* relates to the dignity of the inividual. NATO is a unique alliance of democracies. Since its creation, four states have joined the Atlantic alliance. They did so not just because it was a way to enhance their security, but because they recognized and wanted to be associated with the values for which NATO stands. They wanted it to be known that their people, too, enjoy the freedom and justice that NATO secures.

Few people realize the role of the alliance as the coordinating centre for the Western position on the Helsinki Accords and the problems of human rights. The West's achievements at Madrid and its efforts at the follow-up meeting in Stockholm have only been possible because of individual member nations' commitment to NATO's shared values and their steadfast cohesion during negotiations.

Finally, NATO has been unrelenting in its efforts to develop a constructive relationship with its potential adversaries. The legitimate pursuit of peace demands positive engagement, and NATO members have recognized that a posture of unremitting hostility toward the Soviet Union and its allies will not be productive in the long run. Through the report mandated by Belgian Foreign Minister Tindemans, the alliance is currently exploring how best to define a long-term realistic approach to the East that avoids the ups and downs of false détente but that also diminishes tensions and mutual suspicions.

As a result of this study and the Washington Declaration highlighting its conclusions, the United States and its allies will now be more attentive than we were a decade ago to the concept of reciprocity, and the importance of holding the Soviets accountable for aggressiveness, lack of restraint and recurrent violations of solemn obligations taken, for example, in the UN Charter and the Helsinki Final Act. The alliance is also agreed on a programme for improving East–West relations. Both of these elements are parts of what we mean by a 'more constructive dialogue' with the Kremlin and its allies.

NATO's goal is the deterrence of any war whether nuclear or conventional. The Atlantic alliance was created in the wake of the excesses of a world at war and gave hope that conflict would no longer be the final arbiter in the settlement of disputes among nations. The alliance may not be perfect, but it is unparalleled in its values and in its dedication to peace. Indeed, it has legitimacy and a strong moral basis. It surely provides the best possible basis for sustaining the public consensus and securing a true peace.

PLURALISTIC SOCIETIES
AT STAKE

Sidney Hook
SENIOR RESEARCH FELLOW, HOOVER INSTITUTION OF WAR,
REVOLUTION AND PEACE, STANFORD UNIVERSITY

The nature of the NATO alliance guarantees that there will always be differences of opinion and points of friction among its members. Were this not so we would have no alliance but a hegemonic structure in which one dominant power controls its satellites. This is the system among the nations of the Warsaw Pact. When differences and frictions emerge among the members of NATO there must be a realization of the underlying rationale of their alliance if their association is to endure and be effective. In its absence the genuine burdens and hardships that result from specific decisions tend to erode the bonds of unity.

What is the rationale of NATO? Why does it exist? Some answer that it is the defender of European civilization, its values and institutions against the expansion of communism. I cannot accept this formulation because if we use the phrase 'European civilization' *descriptively*, then communism, like Nazism and other kindred forms of totalitarianism, is part of European civilization. It is not European civilization which is at stake but only a certain expression of it that has painfully developed over the centuries. NATO exists to defend the open, pluralistic societies of the West against the military encroachments of communism. I choose the phrase 'pluralistic society' because it encompasses the substantial differences that exist in the internal structures of the NATO nations. A pluralistic society is one that recognizes the legitimacy of different centres of power, not only political but social and cultural. Above all, it respects the relative autonomy of the private sphere of human experience, and therefore denies and rejects the omnipotence of the state.

Although most pluralistic societies in Western Europe accept political democracy or some form of popular sovereignty this has not always been true. However, the very fact of their plural structure (the existence of islands of culture, religion, economic behaviour and other non-political forms of association) has facilitated the transformation of political dictatorship into viable democracies. Spain, Portugal and Greece are cases in point. On the other hand, there is no instance of a communist society peacefully reverting or transforming itself into a democracy. Were the attempt seriously to be made, the Kremlin, under the Brezhnev doctrine, openly threatens to prevent it.

What is at stake, then, in the conflict between Western Europe, of which North America is an extension, and the Soviet world is not the clash of doctrines but ways of life. NATO exists not to combat ideology but to resist the forcible imposition of a way of life on a people or nation averse to it. The evidence is incontestable that the communist way of life has never been freely chosen by any people living under a communist regime. Just as manifest is the fact that no communist regime, whether the Soviet Union after almost 70 years, mainland China after 35 years, Cuba after 25 years, would dare risk today permitting its subjects a free choice between the existing system and a genuine alternative.

Although sympathetic to the plight of the unfortunate human beings that live in the shadow of the Gulag Archipelago, NATO harbours no aggressive designs against the communist world. It is purely defensive. Despite its rhetoric the Kremlin knows it. If it had any doubts the behaviour of NATO during the communist butcheries in East Germany, Hungary, Czechoslovakia should have allayed them. The same cannot be said about the Soviet Union. Although the very existence of the open pluralistic societies of the West constitute a source of potential dissatisfaction among the Soviet people, afflicted by their economies of scarcity and regimes of terror, the Soviet Union is in a state of permanent military mobilization. A comparison of the maps of the world in 1945 and 1984 reveal a striking increase in the global power of the communist world. In almost every area it is armed far beyond its defensive needs. Only NATO's nuclear deterrent has preserved the peace in Western Europe.

More alarming than the Soviet arsenal of weapons in recent years has been the erosion in the awareness of many groups in the West, especially the young, of the values that divide the monistic totalitarian culture of the communist world from the pluralistic culture of their own countries. The fear of a nuclear holocaust has demoralized large sections of the young into the belief that the differences between the communist and the open societies of the West are relatively unimportant, and that whatever differences exist, nothing is worse than the continued threat of a nuclear war, not even the universal domination of communist tyranny. This is the basic premise of unilateralism, and accounts for the growth of neutralism and anti-Americanism.

Such an attitude reflects a profound failure to understand the nature of the Kremlin's strategy and its mode of thought. What may be just as fateful is the failure to gauge the influence of such European sentiment on American political behaviour.

What the European peace movements in all their nuanced expressions, including the dominant faction of West Germany's Social Democratic Party, do not understand is that barring an invasion of its space, the Soviet Union will not initiate a war against Western Europe, unless it is sure to win it. So long as the Western nuclear deterrent is in place, the Kremlin can never be sure.

There are many reasons for this conclusion. First, the communists worship at the altar of history. No value is more imperative to them than survival. It makes no sense for them to go down in defeat on behalf of a cause. Second, they are hard-headed realists. Even Hitler, who was a madman, did not resort to the use of poison gas during the Second World War, because he knew what the inevitable consequences would be. The members of the Politburo, who alone make the decisions in the USSR, are far from being madmen. They are shrewd and tough. There is something comical about the view, sedulously calculated by some 'experts' on communism, that their feelings are hurt by President Reagan's reference to the Soviet Union as an evil empire. The Soviet leaders have themselves exhausted the vocabulary of the vilest expletives in characterizing capitalist powers, especially the United States. They must read with amused contempt the statement of an influential American Kremlinologist that President Reagan's reference to the Soviet Union as an evil empire, 'has badly shaken the self-esteem and patriotic pride of the Soviet political élites'. How short human memory is! No-one has matched Hitler's furious denunciations of the Soviet Union and everything it stood for. Yet the Soviet leaders embraced him with open arms when it served their purposes. Third, why should the communist leaders risk a world war for, at best, a Pyhrric victory, when they believe they are winning the world piecemeal without war? The 'correlation of world forces', they boast, has turned in their favour and a good case can be made for that view. Fourth, they still believe that the West is beset by 'internal contradictions', which sooner or later will result in widespread economic distress, the loss of confidence and of nerve in Western ruling circles and the weakening of their will and capacity for external adventure. The growth of pacifism in the West, which they encourage by material aid and intensified campaigns about the horrors of nuclear war, they regard, as Lenin did before them, as an expression of Western decadence. Genuine pacifists in the Soviet Union are either sentenced to concentration camps or committed to insane asylums.

Why, then, if NATO's nuclear deterrent is in place and the United States is prepared to defend the freedom of the West should the USSR go to war? However, if that deterrent is not in place or if the citizens of the United States conclude that it is not possible to defend the freedom of peoples unwilling to defend their own freedom, there will be no war. All that will be required is for the Soviet Union to make a threat of war to precipitate a rush to capitulation. With no fear of nuclear retaliation from the United States, Europe will not be Finlandized; it will be Sovietized. Even Sweden, which has contributed so much to the victory of the Vietnamese communists, may end up as a Soviet province.

It is not only European peace activists and unilaterlists who are unaware of the effects of their propaganda on American public opinion.

Some of the chancellories of Western Europe too seem to be oblivious to the growing manifestations of neo-isolationism in America. The relative unconcern of NATO nations in Europe with developments in the Persian Gulf, on whose oil their economies depend, and their indifference, if not outright hostility, to American interests in Central America, have fuelled among conservative voters latent isolationist tendencies to withdraw to an antiquated conception of 'Fortress America'. Among liberal American voters there is a rising resentment against the costs of military involvement in world affairs and the consequent restriction of social services. More and more questions are being asked not only about the advisability of stationing token forces in Lebanon but about the wisdom of keeping American troops in a Europe unwilling to defend itself, and which vents its frustrations at its own helplessness by a rabid anti-Americanism. On the agenda of discussion groups, and among articles of the popular press, are questions no-one would have seriously raised twenty years ago or even ten years ago: 'Should the United States Defend Europe?' 'NATO and the Fire Next Time'.

There are some historical events that are irreversible. If American troops are ever withdrawn from Europe, they will not return again.

Responsibility for the current state of affairs must not be laid at the doors of Europe alone. Some American administrations, misled by their advisers on Soviet affairs, have discounted the influence of communism on Soviet foreign policy as so much theology, and interpreted Russian behaviour as merely the pursuit of nation-state interest in the age-old Tsarist tradition. Tsarist Russia, however, never had a global strategy that extended to intervention in African and Central European affairs. To be sure, it would be absurd to explain Soviet thought and behaviour in terms of ideology alone. Not even wars of religion were purely ideological. But to dismiss any significant influence of Marxism-Leninism on Soviet thought and behaviour is just as absurd. Incredible as it may appear, there is some reason to believe that this ideology is not always understood. Marshall D. Shulman, head of the prestigious Institute of Russian Studies at Columbia University and adviser on Soviet affairs to the Secretary of State, at a time when Carter proclaimed that the American people were suffering from 'inordinate fear of communism', has recently asserted: 'In truth there is as much variance in the Soviet interpretation of Marxism-Leninism today as there is in American Protestantism'. Ignorance about the varieties of doctrine in American Protestantism from Anglican and Calvinist orthodoxy to God-is-Dead existentialism is forgivable in a Kremlinologist, but hardly ignorance of the central features of Marxism-Leninism. This doctrine goes far beyond the prediction of the ultimate triumph of world communism. Central to its teachings is the insistence that wherever and whatever degree of communism exists, it must be administered by the absolute dictatorship of the Communist Party, operating through the dictatorship of its Political Committee. Public disagreement with this cardinal principle of Leninism (it is not Marxist), will only be heard among inmates of concentration camps and insane asylumns in the USSR.

In the final analysis, the destiny of Western Europe rests on the public opinion of its own peoples. There is a risk and burden in defending the imperfect freedoms they now enjoy. Once lost, they will appear all the more precious, but they will not be recovered. The willingness to defend these freedoms may make it unnecessary to fight for them. In time this willingness to accept the risks of the defence of freedom may inspire the suffering masses in communist countries to exercise the pressure that may moderate the political terror under which they live.

Winston Churchill was right when he characterized the Second World War as a needless war. There will be no Third World War so long as the West is prepared to avoid the errors and illusions that brought on the Second. The United States will never desert its NATO allies if they remain faithful to the common cause which brought it into being. European freedom cannot survive without American support. The converse is not as certain.

PART EIGHT

Appendices

APPENDIX A

The North Atlantic Treaty
WASHINGTON, DC, 4 APRIL, 1949*

The Parties to this Treaty reaffirm their faith in the purposes and principles of the Charter of the United Nations and their desire to live in peace with all peoples and all Governments.

They are determined to safeguard the freedom, common heritage and civilization of their peoples, founded on the principles of democracy, individual liberty and the rule of law.

They seek to promote stability and well-being in the North Atlantic area.

They are resolved to unite their efforts for collective defence and for the preservation of peace and security.

They therefore agree to this North Atlantic Treaty:

ARTICLE 1

The Parties undertake, as set forth in the Charter of the United Nations, to settle any international dispute in which they may be involved by peaceful means in such a manner that international peace and security and justice are not endangered, and to refrain in their international relations from the threat or use of force in any manner inconsistent with the purposes of the United Nations.

ARTICLE 2

The Parties will contribute toward the further development of peaceful and friendly international relations by strengthening their free institutions, by bringing about a better understanding of the principles upon which these institutions are founded, and by promoting conditions of stability and well-being. They will seek to eliminate conflict in their international economic policies and will encourage economic collaboration between any or all of them.

ARTICLE 3

In order more effectively to achieve the objectives of this Treaty, the Parties, separately and jointly, by means of continuous and effective self-help and mutual aid, will maintain and develop their individual and collective capacity to resist armed attack.

ARTICLE 4

The Parties will consult together whenever, in the opinion of any of them, the territorial integrity, political independence or security of any of the Parties is threatened.

* The Treaty came into force on 24 August, 1949, after the deposition of the ratifications of all signatory states.

ARTICLE 5

The Parties agree that an armed attack against one or more of them in Europe or North America shall be considered an attack against them all, and consequently they agree that, if such an armed attack occurs, each of them, in exercise of the right of individual or collective self-defence recognized by Article 51 of the Charter of the United Nations, will assist the Party or Parties so attacked by taking forthwith, individually, and in concert with the other Parties, such action as it deems necessary, including the use of armed force, to restore and maintain the security of the North Atlantic area.

Any such armed attack and all measures taken as a result thereof shall immediately be reported to the Security Council. Such measures shall be terminated when the Security Council has taken the measures necessary to restore and maintain international peace and security.

ARTICLE 6†

For the purpose of Article 5, an armed attack on one or more of the Parties is deemed to include an armed attack

- on the territory of any of the Parties in Europe or North America, on the Algerian Departments of France‡, on the territory of Turkey or on the islands under the jurisdiction of any of the Parties in the North Atlantic area north of the Tropic of Cancer;
- on the forces, vessels, or aircraft of any of the Parties, when in or over these territories or any area in Europe in which occupation forces of any of the Parties were stationed on the date when the Treaty entered into force or the Mediterranean Sea or the North Atlantic area north of the Tropic of Cancer.

ARTICLE 7

This Treaty does not effect, and shall not be interpreted as affecting, in any way the rights and obligations under the Charter of the Parties which are members of the United Nations, or the primary responsibility of the Security Council for the maintenance of international peace and security.

† As amended by Article 2 of the Protocol to the North Atlantic Treaty on the accession of Greece and Turkey.
‡ On the 16th January, 1963, the French Representative made a statement to the North Atlantic Council on the effects of the independence of Algeria on certain aspects of the North Atlantic Treaty. The Council noted that insofar as the former Algerian Departments of France were concerned the relevant clauses of this Treaty had become inapplicable as from 3rd July, 1962.

ARTICLE 8

Each Party declares that none of the international engagements now in force between it and any other of the Parties or any third State is in conflict with the provisions of this Treaty, and undertakes not to enter into any international engagement in conflict with this Treaty.

ARTICLE 9

The Parties hereby establish a Council, on which each of them shall be represented to consider matters concerning the implementation of this Treaty. The Council shall be so organized as to be able to meet promptly at any time. The Council shall set up such subsidiary bodies as may be necessary; in particular it shall establish immediately a defence committee which shall recommend measures for the implementation of Articles 3 and 5.

ARTICLE 10

The Parties may, by unanimous agreement, invite any other European State in a position to further the principles of this Treaty and to contribute to the security of the North Atlantic area to accede to this Treaty. Any State so invited may become a party to the Treaty by depositing its instrument of accession with the Government of the United States of America. The Government of the United States of America will inform each of the Parties of the deposit of each such instrument of accession.

ARTICLE 11

This Treaty shall be ratified and its provisions carried out by the Parties in accordance with their respective constitutional processes. The instruments of ratification shall be deposited as soon as possible with the Government of the United States of America, which will notify all the other signatories of each deposit. The Treaty shall enter into force between the States which have ratified it as soon as the ratifications of the majority of the signatories, including the ratification of Belgium, Canada, France, Luxembourg, the Netherlands, the United Kingdom and the United States, have been deposited and shall come into effect with respect to other States on the date of the deposit of their ratifications.

ARTICLE 12

After the Treaty has been in force for ten years, or at any time thereafter, the Parties shall, if any of them so requests, consult together for the purpose of reviewing the Treaty, having regard for the factors then affecting peace and security in the North Atlantic area including the development of universal as well as regional arrangements under the Charter of the United Nations for the maintenance of international peace and security.

ARTICLE 13

After the Treaty has been in force for twenty years, any Party may cease to be a Party one year after its notice of denunciation has been given to the Government of the United States of America, which will inform the Governments of the other Parties of the deposit of each notice of denunciation.

ARTICLE 14

This Treaty, of which the English and French texts are equally authentic, shall be deposited in the archives of the Government of the United States of America. Duly certified copies will be transmitted by that Government to the Governments of the other signatories.

APPENDIX B

A chronology of 35 years of NATO

Following is a chronology of major events in the 35-year history of the North Atlantic Treaty Organisation (NATO):

APRIL 4, 1949

The North Atlantic Treaty Organisation – also known as the Atlantic alliance – is formed with the signing in Washington, DC, of a Treaty for collective defence by 12 countries: Belgium, Canada, Denmark, France, Iceland, Italy, Luxembourg, the Netherlands, Norway, Portugal, the United Kingdom and the United States.

The preamble to the 14 articles of the North Atlantic Treaty emphasises that the alliance is created within the framework of the United Nations Charter. It also outlines NATO's main objectives:

– to live in peace with all peoples and all governments;

– to safeguard the freedom, common heritage and civilisation of their peoples, founded on the principles of democracy, individual liberty and the rule of law;

– to promote stability and well-being in the North Atlantic area;

– and to unite their efforts for collective defence and for the preservation of peace and security.

The Treaty is the framework for a military alliance designed to deter, or if necessary repel, aggression. It also provides for continuous co-operation and consultation in political, economic and other non-military fields.

Article 5 is the core of the Treaty: an armed attack against one member is to be treated as an attack against all.

AUGUST 24, 1949

The North Atlantic Treaty enters into force following ratification by all signatories.

SEPTEMBER 17, 1949

The North Atlantic Council (NAC) – NATO's highest decision-making body and forum for consultations – holds first session in Washington.

JANUARY 27, 1950

President Truman approves plan for the integrated defence of the North Atlantic area. Releasing 900,000,000 dollars in military aid funds.

AUGUST 1, 1950

Turkey announces decision to apply for membership of NATO.

OCTOBER 2, 1950

Turkey accepts NAC invitation to be associated with NATO military agencies in Mediterranean defence planning.

OCTOBER 5, 1950

Greece accepts NAC invitation to be associated with Mediterranean Defence Planning.

DECEMBER 19, 1950

US General Dwight Eisenhower becomes Supreme Allied Commander Europe (SACEUR).

DECEMBER 20, 1950

The Western Union Defence Organisation – created in September 1948 by Belgium, France, Luxembourg, the Netherlands and the United Kingdom – merges into NATO.

APRIL 2, 1951

Allied Command Europe (ACE) becomes operational with Supreme Headquarters Allied Powers Europe (SHAPE) located near Paris.

JULY 24, 1951

A conference convened by the French government in Paris (February 15), approves an interim report to NATO governments recommending the creation of a European army.

JANUARY 30, 1952

US Vice-Admiral Lynde McCormick becomes first Supreme Allied Commander Atlantic (SACLANT).

FEBRUARY 18, 1952

Greece and Turkey join NATO.

FEBRUARY 20-25, 1952

NAC meeting in Lisbon reorganises the structure of the alliance and NATO becomes a permanent organisation with headquarters in Paris.

FEBRUARY 21, 1952

UK Admiral Sir Arthur Power becomes first Commander-in-Chief of the NATO Channel Command (CINCHAN).

APRIL 4, 1952

Lord Ismay takes office as Secretary General of NATO.

APRIL 10, 1952

Supreme Allied Command Atlantic (SACLANT) becomes operational, with headquarters in Norfolk, Virginia, USA.

APRIL 28, 1952

North Atlantic Council meets for first time in permanent session in Paris.

MAY 27, 1952

Belgium, France, Italy, Luxembourg, the Netherlands and the Federal Republic of Germany sign a Treaty in Paris setting up the European Defence Community (EDC). NATO governments give guarantees to EDC members.

MAY 7, 1954

In reply to Soviet note of March 31, France, the UK and the US reject Soviet Union's request to join NATO.

MAY 5, 1955

The Federal Republic of Germany becomes a member of NATO.

JULY 18, 1955

First conference of NATO parliamentarians (becoming the North Atlantic Assembly in November 1966) meets in Paris. The conference, independent of NATO, is formed to encourage Atlantic solidarity in national parliaments.

DECEMBER 15-16, 1955

Ministerial meeting of the North Atlantic Council decides to equip NATO forces with atomic weapons. It also decides to strengthen air defences by closer co-operation between European NATO countries in this field.

MAY 4-5, 1956

NAC ministerial instructs Gaetano Martino of Italy, Halvard Lange of Norway and Lester Pearson of Canada (the 'Three Wise Men') to draw up a report with recommendations on how to improve and extend co-operation between the NATO countries in non-military fields and develop greater unity within the Atlantic community.

DECEMBER 13, 1956

NAC approves report of the 'Three Wise Men' and adopts resolutions on the peaceful settlement of disputes between member countries and on non-military co-operation in NATO.

MAY 16, 1957

Paul-Henri Spaak of Belgium succeeds Lord Ismay as Secretary General of NATO.

DECEMBER 16-19, 1957

Heads of Government meeting in Paris reaffirm principles and purposes of NATO. NAC decides to promote closer co-operation in the political and economic fields and to increase scientific and non-military co-operation.

DECEMBER, 1957

NATO sets up the Science Committee to strengthen the scientific and technological capabilities of the alliance.

APRIL 15-17, 1958

NATO defence ministers meeting in Paris reaffirm defensive character of NATO strategy.

MAY 5-7, 1958

NAC ministerial meeting in Copenhagen says it favours negotiations with East providing they offer prospects of settlement of outstanding problems.

DECEMBER 16, 1958

In response to November 10 Soviet plan to terminate the Four-Power Agreement on the status of Berlin, NAC ministerial declares right of Western powers to remain in Berlin.

DECEMBER 16-18, 1960
NAC ministerial confirms its declaration of December, 1958, on Berlin.

APRIL 21, 1961
Dirk Stikker of the Netherlands succeeds Spaak as Secretary General of NATO.

DECEMBER 13-15, 1961
NAC ministerial in Paris reaffirms its position on Berlin and condemns erection of the Berlin Wall in August. It also approves renewal of diplomatic contacts with Soviet Union to seek basis for negotiation.
    NATO establishes a mobile Task Force.

MAY 4-6, 1962
NAC meeting of foreign and defence ministers in Athens establishes guidelines for alliance use of nuclear weapons.

DECEMBER 18-20, 1962
At a meeting in the Bahamas, President John F. Kennedy and Prime Minister Harold Macmillan agree to contribute part of the US and UK strategic forces to NATO.

MAY 22-24, 1963
NAC ministerial meeting in Ottawa assigns the British V-Bomber Forces and 3 American Polaris submarines to SACEUR, who is to appoint a deputy responsible to him for nuclear matters.

JUNE 25, 1963
On a visit to Europe, President Kennedy reaffirms America's guarantee to defend Europe. He also reaffirms the principle of equal partnership within NATO.

DECEMBER 16-17, 1963
President Lyndon Johnson renews US pledges of 'steadfast resolve' concerning NATO in message to NAC ministerial meeting in Paris.

AUGUST 1, 1964
Manlio Brosio of Italy succeeds Dirk Stikker as Secretary General of NATO.

NOVEMBER 27, 1965
Special Committee of NATO defence ministers initiates study to explore ways of improving allied participation in nuclear planning.

MARCH 29, 1966
French government announces that France will withdraw from NATO integrated military commands July 1, 1966, and that all NATO military forces and facilities are to be removed from France by April 1, 1967.

JULY 25, 1966
NATO defence ministers meeting in Paris adopt a NATO force plan for the period up to and including 1970.

DECEMBER 5, 1966
The Defence Planning Committee (DPC) approves IBERLANT, the first NATO command in Portugal.

DECEMBER 14, 1966

The DPC establishes the Nuclear Defence Affairs Committee and the Nuclear Planning Group (NPG).

MARCH 31, 1967

Official opening ceremony marking transfer of SHAPE to Mons, Belgium.

APRIL 6-7, 1967

First meeting of the Nuclear Planning Group held in Washington.

JUNE 5, 1967

NATO sets up NAVSOUTH in Malta as a principal subordinate command under the Commander-in-Chief Allied Forces, Southern Europe.

OCTOBER 16, 1967

New NATO headquarters officially opens in Brussels.

DECEMBER 13-14, 1967

NAC ministerial meeting approves the Harmel Report on the future tasks of the alliance.

NATO adopts new strategic concept of a flexible and balanced range of appropriate responses, conventional and nuclear, to all levels of aggression or threats of aggression.

NATO establishes a Standing Naval Force Atlantic (STANAVFOR-LANT).

MAY 10, 1968

Ministerial session of the Defence Planning Committee in Brussels:

(1) Reaffirms need for a balance of forces between NATO and the Warsaw Pact.

(2) States that present circumstances do not justify the development of an anti-ballistic missile system in Europe.

JUNE 24-25, 1968

At NAC ministerial meeting in Reykjavik, Iceland, NATO proposes negotiations with the Warsaw Pact on Mutual and Balanced Force Reductions (MBFR) in Central Europe.

NOVEMBER 13-14, 1968

The Eurogroup is set up within the framework of NATO as an informal association of defence ministers of European member governments. It seeks to:

(1) Improve the effectiveness of the European contribution to the alliance through closer coordination and the best possible use of resources.

(2) Provide a forum for defence ministers to exchange views on major political and strategic questions affecting the common defence.

NOVEMBER 21, 1968

MARAIRMED is activated at Naples to improve NATO surveillance of the Mediterranean area.

NOVEMBER 6, 1969

NATO sets up the Committee on the Challenges of Modern Society (CCMS) to promote international action on problems of the human environment.

DECEMBER 3-5, 1969

NAC ministerial meeting in Brussels issues declaration on East-West relations.

MARCH 20, 1970

NATO launches its first communications satellite from Cape Kennedy in the US.

MAY 26-27, 1970

At NAC meeting in Rome, NATO elaborates its MBFR proposal of December 1968.

DECEMBER 2-4, 1970

US pledges to maintain and improve its forces in Europe if the other NATO allies will do the same. The US promises that reductions will only be made in the context of reciprocal East-West reductions.

The Defence Planning Committee adopts study on 'Alliance Defence in the '70s'.

AUGUST 20, 1971

DPC orders transfer of NAVSOUTH from Malta to Naples.

OCTOBER 1, 1971

Joseph Luns of the Netherlands succeeds Manlio Brosio as NATO Secretary General.

MAY 30-31, 1972

At NATO ministerial meeting in Bonn, NATO agrees to begin multinational preparatory talks in Helsinki for a Conference on Security and Co-operation in Europe (CSCE). NATO also proposes multilateral explorations on Mutual and Balanced Force Reductions (MBFR).

DECEMBER 7-8, 1972

NAC ministerial in Brussels resolves to maintain NATO defences in face of expanding Warsaw Pact forces.

JULY 3-7, 1973

First phase of the 35-nation Conference on Security and Co-operation in Europe (CSCE) begins in Helsinki.

OCTOBER 30, 1973

Mutual and Balanced Force Reduction talks between NATO and the Warsaw Pact open in Vienna.

DECEMBER 10-11, 1973

At NAC ministerial in Brussels, members of NATO's integrated military structure recognise that a common alliance effort is needed to maintain US forces in Europe at current levels.

JUNE 14, 1974

NATO Defence Planning Committee reaffirms importance of standardisation and specialisation of defence tasks.

JUNE 18-19, 1974

Observing 25th anniversary of NATO, NAC ministerial in Ottawa adopts and publishes a Declaration on Atlantic Relations.

AUGUST 14, 1974

Greek forces withdraw from NATO's integrated military structure.

JULY 31 – AUGUST 1, 1975

Final phase of CSCE in Helsinki. The United States, Canada and all European countries except Albania, sign the Helsinki Final Act.

DECEMBER 9-10, 1975

Defence Planning Committee ministerial in Brussels notes continued increase in Warsaw Pact strength and capabilities, reaffirms importance of maintaining and strengthening NATO forces and reviews efforts to improve standardisation and compatibility of military equipment within the alliance.

DECEMBER 9-10, 1976

NAC ministerial expresses determination to enhance allied cohesion and strength and, in light of the Helsinki Final Act's provisions, rejects Warsaw Pact proposals to renounce first use of nuclear weapons and to restrict alliance membership.

MAY 17-18, 1977

Defence Planning Committee ministerial agrees to a long-term defence programme for NATO.

JUNE 8-9, 1977

NATO Nuclear Planning Group meeting in Ottawa notes continuing improvements in Soviet nuclear forces, including mobile intermediate-range systems.

OCTOBER 4, 1977

First CSCE follow-up meeting opens in Belgrade to review compliance with the Helsinki Final Act.

OCTOBER 11-12, 1977

Nuclear Planning Group ministerial meeting in Bari, Italy, establishes a high-level group on theatre nuclear force modernization within the context of the long-term defence programme.

MARCH 9, 1978

CSCE follow-up meeting in Belgrade ends without agreement.

APRIL 18-19, 1978

Nuclear Planning Group meeting in Denmark notes with concern increased Soviet capability in longer-range theatre nuclear weapons, including the triple-warhead SS-20 mobile missiles, and endorses the importance of modernizing NATO's theatre nuclear forces.

NOVEMBER 18, 1978

NATO launches its third communications satellite from Cape Canaveral, USA.

DECEMBER 5-6, 1978
NATO approves an Airborne Early Warning and Control System (AWACS) programme.
APRIL 11, 1979
NATO sets up a special group to study the arms control aspects of theatre nuclear systems.
DECEMBER 12, 1979
Following intensive NATO consultations, a special meeting of NATO foreign and defence ministers adopts a 'dual-track' strategy to redress the Soviet build-up of intermediate-range nuclear forces (INF) through arms control negotiations with the Soviet Union if possible but, if necessary, through modernization of its own INF forces:
  – arms control track: NATO offers US-Soviet arms control negotiations to limit or eliminate LRINF missiles.
  – modernization track: NATO decides to deploy 572 US single-warhead Pershing-II and ground-launched cruise missiles (GLCM) in Western Europe beginning at the end of 1983 if no arms control agreement had been reached by that time. NATO also decides to withdraw 1,000 nuclear warheads. In addition, NATO pledges to withdraw one older nuclear weapon for each Pershing-II and GLCM deployed.
DECEMBER 29, 1979
Special NAC session discusses December 21 Soviet invasion of Afghanistan.
JANUARY 24, 1980
NATO establishes the Special Consultative Group (SCG) to serve as forum for consultations on INF arms control matters.
OCTOBER 20, 1980
Greek forces are reintegrated into NATO's military structure.
NOVEMBER 11, 1980
The second CSCE follow-up meeting opens in Madrid.
NOVEMBER 20, 1981
NATO's Special Consultative Group welcomes President Reagan's 'zero/zero' proposal of November 18 to eliminate the entire class of US and Soviet land-based, longer-range INF missiles.
NOVEMBER 30, 1981
The United States and the Soviet Union open Geneva negotiations on intermediate-range nuclear forces.
DECEMBER 2, 1981
Spain formally applies to join NATO.
DECEMBER 10, 1981
NATO issues declaration condemning all acts of terrorism.
JANUARY 11, 1982
Special NAC ministerial issues declaration on Poland following General

Jaruzelski's imposition of martial law December 13, 1981.
MAY 30, 1982
Spain becomes NATO's 16th member.
JUNE 10, 1982
NAC summit meeting issues the Bonn declaration setting out NATO's programme for 'Peace in Freedom'.
MARCH 31, 1983
NAC issues statement supporting US INF initiative of March 30, 1983, to break the stalemate by proposing an 'Interim Agreement' at the Geneva INF negotiations.
SEPTEMBER 9, 1983
CSCE follow-up meeting ends in Madrid with the signing of a concluding document by all 35 participating nations.
OCTOBER 27, 1983
The Nuclear Planning Group meeting in Montebello, Canada, announces that NATO will remove about 1,400 warheads from Europe over the next 5-6 years and thus reduce its nuclear stockpile to the lowest level in 20 years. These unilateral reductions are in addition to the 1,000 tactical nuclear weapons already withdrawn in 1980 in accordance with the December 1979 dual-track decision.
DECEMBER 7, 1983
In final communique of NATO's Defence Planning Committee ministers:
- emphasise determination to move ahead with dual-track approach of LRINF modernization and arms control to redress the military imbalance with the Soviet Union;
- regret Soviet suspension of INF talks November 23, 1983, and emphasise desire for resumption as soon as possible;
- reaffirm that NATO is prepared, in accordance with the terms of any INF agreement which may be reached, to halt, modify or reverse its current missile deployments in conformity with the 1979 decision;
- reaffirm need to strive for a mutually acceptable solution to the issues still barring progress at the mutual and balanced force reduction talks in Vienna;
- stress importance they attach to the conference on confidence – and security-building measures and disarmament in Europe (CDE) as an opportunity to negotiate politically binding, militarily signifcant and verifiable measures to reduce the risk of surprise attack.
DECEMBER 8, 1983
The SCG releases a report in Brussels listing NATO's efforts to secure an INF agreement. The SCG report concludes that:
- despite intense, sustained alliance effort over last two years, Soviet insistence on retaining a monopoly on LRINF has prevented agreement;

– continued alliance implementation of the 1979 decision remains essential to the prospects for arms control, to ensure the security of the alliance, and to provide the foundation for a more stable and co-operative relationship with the East.

JANUARY 17, 1984

The Conference on Disarmament in Europe (CDE) opens in Stockholm. Its mandate, adopted by the 35 CSCE nations in Madrid, is to negotiate confidence and security-building measures to reduce the risk of a military confrontation in Europe.

JANUARY 24, 1984

The 16 NATO nations table the first package of proposals at the Stockholm CDE.

APPENDIX C

Statement on East-West relations
Issued by NATO Foreign Ministers
in Washington, DC, May 31, 1984.

1. At their meeting in December 1983 the Ministers of Foreign Affairs of the member countries of the Alliance, on the initiative of the Foreign Minister of Belgium, decided that the Council should undertake an appraisal of East-West relations with a view to achieving a more constructive East-West dialogue.

2. The appraisal has confirmed the continuing validity of the balanced approach contained in the Harmel Report of 1967. To ensure the security of members of the Alliance, the most appropriate long-term policies are the maintenance of adequate military strength and political solidarity and, on that basis, the pursuit of a more stable relationship between the countries of East and West through dialogue and co-operation. These elements are complementary: dialogue can only be fruitful if each party is confident of its security and is prepared to respect the legitimate interests of others: military strength alone cannot guarantee a peaceful future. Experience points to the continuing need for full, consistent and realistic implementation of the two tasks of the Alliance set out in the Harmel Report.

3. In pursuit of this approach the Allies sought to alleviate sources of tension and to create a propitious climate for expanded co-operation. Steps such as the Berlin Quadripartite Agreement, improvements in relations between the two German states with positive results for individuals, the Strategic Arms Limitation Talks (SALT 1) accords including the Anti-Ballistic Missile Treaty, and the Final Act of the Conference on Security and Co-operation in Europe (CSCE) were the fruits of this policy. However, progress towards the expansion of human contacts and human freedoms remains unsatisfactory.

Individuals have nonetheless benefitted from increased opportunities for contacts and communication.

4. At the same time, the Soviet Union engaged in a massive military build-up. This poses a continuing threat to Alliance security and vital Western interests. The Soviet Union has sought to exploit any apparent weakness which it has perceived on the part of the Alliance. Further, Allied restraint has not been met with reciprocal restraint by the Soviets. Instead they have pursued a relentless campaign to breach the solidarity of the Alliance. Soviet willingness to threaten or use military power for political ends has been exemplified most notably in the invasion of Afghanistan and pressure on Poland.*

    * Greece and Spain reserve their positions on this paragraph.

5. Notwithstanding continuing fundamental differences between countries in East and West, the Allies remain convinced that there exist areas where common interests should prevail. These include the need to safeguard peace, to build confidence, to increase security, to improve mechanisms for dealing with crises, and to promote prosperity.

To this end, the Allies remain determined to build upon these and other areas of common interest in pursuing their efforts to promote more constructive dialogue and co-operation with the members of the Warsaw Pact with a view to achieving genuine détente.

6. The Allies support the continuation and strengthening of the CSCE process which represents an important means of promoting stable and constructive East-West relations on a long-term basis. They insist on the implementation of the Helsinki Final Act and the Madrid concluding document in all their parts. While important agreements have been reached within the CSCE framework, much remains to be done. Any improvement in East-West relations would be incomplete if individuals were not able to benefit from greater respect for human rights and increased human contacts.

7. The Allies will continue to be guided by the awareness of a common history and traditions of all European peoples. Given the continuing division in Europe and particularly Germany, the Alliance continues to support the political aim of the Federal Republic of Germany to work toward a state of peace in Europe in which the German people regains its unity through free self-determination.

8. Neither side must seek unilateral advantage, military superiority or dominance over other states. Mutual respect for each other's security on the basis of equality of rights, non-use of force as called for in the United Nations Charter and other current international agreements, restraint, and respect for international rules of conduct are essential for strengthening confidence and co-operation.

9. The Allies respect the sovereignty and independence of states everywhere and genuine nonalignment. This is reflected in their political, economic and aid relations with other countries. Responsible Soviet behaviour worldwide would be an important contribution to a durable improvement in East-West relations.

10. The Allies recognise that, as members of the Alliance, their vital security interests can be affected by developments outside the Treaty area. They will engage in timely consultations on such developments. They underline the responsibility of all states to prevent the transfer of East-West differences to the regions of the Third World. They would like to see the benefits of peace, stability, human rights and freedom from interference which they themselves have enjoyed for over 35 years secured in other areas of the world as well.

11. On the basis of unity of purpose and assured security, the Allies

reaffirm their offers to improve East-West relations, made most recently in the Declaration of Brussels of 9th December 1983. They propose that particular efforts be devoted to the following:

(a) dialogue, co-operation and contacts at all levels on the full range of questions between East and West – including political and security problems, human rights and bilateral matters – aimed at increasing mutual understanding, identifying common interests, clarifying objectives, expanding areas of agreement and resolving or isolating areas of disagreement;

(b) mutually advantageous trade and economic co-operation with Warsaw Pact members on commercially sound terms which are consistent with Allies' broad security concerns, which include avoidance of contributing to Soviet military strength;

(c) achieving security at the lowest possible level of forces through balanced, equitable and verifiable agreements on concrete arms control, disarmament and confidence-building measures.

To these ends, the Allies concerned will continue in particular:

(i) to emphasize the readiness of the United States to resume bilateral negotiations on Intermediate-Range Nuclear Forces (INF) and Strategic Arms Reductions (START) with the Soviet Union at any time without preconditions and to call on the Soviet Union to return to the negotiating table;*

    * Greece reserves its position on this sub-paragraph.

(ii) to work for progress at the Mutual and Balanced Force Reductions (MBFR) negotiations where they have recently made new proposals to break the impasse on conventional force reductions;

(iii) to urge the worldwide elimination of chemical weapons which is the objective of the United States draft treaty tabled at the Conference on Disarmament;

(iv) to press at the Stockholm Conference (CDE) for agreement on concrete measures, as proposed by the Allies, designed to build confidence and ensure the openness of military activities in the whole of Europe, thus reducing the risk of surprise attack and the threat of war. In order to give further effect and expression to the existing duty of all participating states to refrain from the threat or use of force in their mutual relations, agreement would be necessary on the above concrete measures in accordance with the Madrid mandate.

12. The purpose of the Alliance is exclusively defensive: none of its weapons will ever be used except in response to attack. The Alliance does not aspire to superiority, but seeks a stable balance of forces. Defence and arms control are integral parts of the security policy of the Alliance. The legitimate security interests of all countries must be respected on a reciprocal basis. The cohesion and security of the Alliance, based on a firm linkage between its European and North American members, and

reinforced by close consultations, remain the foundation for the protection of their common interests and values. In the course of carrying out their appraisal, the Allies have confirmed their consensus on the conduct of East-West relations and their commitment to a constructive East-West dialogue.

13. Peace and stability require a united effort: the allies look to the Soviet Union and the other Warsaw Pact countries to join in an endeavour which would be of benefit to the world at large. The allies are prepared to do their part and are ready to examine any reasonable proposal. A long-term, constructive and realistic relationship can then be brought about.

APPENDIX D

Notes on the contributors

DAVID M. ABSHIRE is presently the US Ambassador to NATO. Until July 1983, he served for more than a decade as President of Georgetown University's Center for Strategic and International Studies. Between 1970 and 1973 he was US Assistant Secretary of State for Congressional Relations and between 1974 and 1977 served as first chairman of the US Board for International Broadcasting.

His publications include *International Broadcasting: A New Dimension of Western Diplomacy* (1976) and *President vs. Congress* (1979). He is also co-editor of *The Growing Power of Congress*.

HANS E. APEL, Social Democratic member of the Bundestag since 1965. He is a former Minister of Finance (1974-78) and of Defence (1978-82). Earlier (1958-61) he was secretary of the Socialist group in the European Parliament.

His publications include *Europas nene Grenzen* (1964); *Der Deutsche Parlamentarismus* (1968); *Bonn, den...*, *Tagebuch eines Bundestagsalegeordneten* (1972).

BETTINO CRAXI has been the Italian Prime Minister since August, 1983. He is the first socialist to head a government in the 37-year history of the Italian republic. He has been leader of the Socialist Party (PSI) since 1976.

Among his publications are: *Socialism and Reality*; *Pluralism and Leninism*; and *One Hundred Years Later*.

EMILIO COLOMBO is a former Italian Minister of Foreign Affairs (1980-83); Prime Minister (1970-72); Minister of State for UN Affairs (1972-73); Minister of Finance (1973-74); President of the European Parliament (1977-79). Formerly Vice-President of Italian Catholic Youth Association.

CHARLES DOUGLAS-HOME has been Editor of *The Times* since 1982; Deputy Editor (1981-82); Foreign Editor (1978-81); and Home Editor (1973-78). Earlier he also served as defence correspondent and Features Editor.

Among his publications are: *The Arabs and Israel* (1968); *Britain's Reserve Forces* (1969); *Rommel* (1973) and *Evelyn Baring: the last Proconsul* (1978).

ABBA EBAN has held a wide range of positions in international politics, diplomacy and academic life, including those of Israel's Ambassador to the United States, Chief Delegate to the United Nations and Minister of Foreign Affairs.

He is the author among others of *Tide of Nationalism*; *My Country*; *My People*; and *The New Diplomacy – International Affairs in the Modern Age*.

BÜLENT ECEVIT is a former Turkish Prime Minister (January – November, 1974 and January – November, 1979). He also served as a Minister of Labour between 1961 and 1965.

He is also a former journalist and among his works are: *The Left of Centre* (1963); *This Order Must Change* (1967); and *Ataturk and Reformism* (1970).

LAWRENCE FREEDMAN has been Professor and Head of the Department of War Studies, King's College, London at the University of London since April 1982. He held research positions at Nuffield College, Oxford and at the International Institute for Strategic Studies and then became Head of Policy Studies at the Royal Institute of International Affairs.

In addition to many articles on defence and foreign policy, Professor Freedman is the author of *US Intelligence and the Soviet Strategic Threat* (1977); *Britain and Nuclear Weapons* (1980); *The Evolution of Nuclear Strategy* (1981); *Nuclear War and Nuclear Peace*, (with others, 1983) and *The Troubled Alliance* (editor, 1983).

JOSEPH GODSON is European Coordinator of the Center for Strategic and International Studies, Georgetown University, and Joint Editor of the Labour and Trades Union Press Service. He was, for twenty-one years, a senior Foreign Service Officer with the US State Department.

He is the editor of *Transatlantic Crisis: Europe and America in the 70s*; and co-editor of *The Soviet Worker: From Lenin to Andropov*.

ALEXANDER M. HAIG, Jr. is a former US Secretary of State (1981-82); Chief of White House Staff (1973-74); Supreme Allied Commander in Europe (1974-79); President and Chief Operating Officer, United Technologies (1979-81); with the Hudson Institute for Policy Research since 1982.

Author of *Caveat: Realism, Reagan and Foreign Policy* (1984)

JOHAN JØRGEN HOLST, Director of the Norwegian Institute of International Affairs since 1981. Beforehand he served as State Secretary in the Royal Norwegian Ministry of Foreign Affairs (1979-81) and State

Secretary in the Ministry of Defence (1976-79). He is currently also President of the European Movement in Norway and a member of the Foreign Policy Council of the Norwegian Labour Party.

LORD HOME OF THE HIRSEL is a former British Prime Minister (1963-64); Secretary of State for Foreign Affairs (1960-63); Secretary of State for Foreign and Commonwealth Affairs (1970-74).

His publications include *The Way the Wind Blows* (1976) and *Border Reflections* (1979).

SIDNEY HOOK is a philosopher and educator. Head of all-university Department of Philosophy at New York University 1948-69; currently a senior research fellow at Hoover Institution of War, Revolution & Peace, Stanford, California.

His publications include *The Ambiguous Legacy; Marx and the Marxists* (1955); *Common Sense and the Fifth Amendment* (1957); *The Paradoxes of Freedom* (1962); *Education and the Taming of Power* (1973); and *Philosophy and Public Policy* (1980).

ROBERT D. HORMATS is a former US Assistant Secretary of State for Economic and Business Affairs and senior staff member for international economic affairs at the National Security Council. He is currently vice-president, Goldman Sachs and Co., and director, Goldman Sachs International Corporation.

MICHAEL HOWARD has been Regius Professor of Modern History and Fellow of Oriel College, Oxford, since 1980; Chichele Professor of History of War, University of Oxford, 1977-80; Trevelyan Lecturer, Cambridge, 1977; and Vice-President and co-founder, International Institute for Strategic Studies.

Among his publications are: *Disengagement in Europe* (1958); *The Franco-Prussian War* (1961); *The Theory and Practice of War* (1965); *Studies in War and Peace* (1970); *The Continental Commitment* (1972); *Clausewitz on War* (with P. Paret, 1977); and *Restraints on War* (editor, 1979).

WILLIAM G. HYLAND is the editor of *Foreign Affairs* and author of *The Fall of Khrushchev*. He is a former Director (Assistant Secretary), Bureau of Intelligence & Research, Department of State (1973-75); Deputy Assistant to the President for National Security Affairs (1975-77); Senior Fellow, Georgetown Center for Strategic & International Studies (1977-81); and Adjunct Professor, Georgetown University, School of Foreign Service (1982-84).

ROY JENKINS is the Member of Parliament for Glasgow, Hillhead. He is one of the four original leaders of the Social Democratic Party (SDP) which was formed in 1981, and was leader of the SDP from 1982 to 1983. Between 1977 and 1981 he was President of the EEC Commission. Formerly he was deputy leader of the Parliamentary Labour Party from 1970 to 1972, and served in a number of Labour governments, notably as Chancellor of the Exchequer (1967-1970) and was twice Home Secretary (1965-1967, and 1974-1976).

AMOS A. JORDAN has been President of the Georgetown University's Center for Strategic and International Studies since July 1983. He is a former Professor of Social Sciences at West Point and served among others as Director of the Near East-South Asia Region in the office of the US Secretary of Defence; Deputy Under Secretary of State and Acting Under Secretary for Security Assistance (1976-77); and Principal Deputy Assistant Secretary for Defence for International Security Affairs (1974-76) before he joined CSIS in 1977.

He published *American National Security: Policy and Process* (with William J. Taylor, Jr.) in 1981.

KARL KAISER has been, since 1973, Director of the Research Institute of the German Society for Foreign Affairs in Bonn and since 1974 Professor of Political Science at the University of Cologne. He has been a member of the German Social Democratic Party for 20 years.

Among his published works are: *Die Internationale Politik* (1968-69); *Jahrbuch für Friedens u. Konfliktforschung*, 1st vol., (1971).

LANE KIRKLAND, President of the American Federation of Labor–Congress of Industrial Organizations (AFL-CIO) since 1979; for ten years before that he was Secretary-Treasurer of the organisation. He has served on numerous Presidential boards and commissions, the latest as a member of the National Bipartisan Commission on Central America headed by Henry Kissinger.

HENRY A. KISSINGER is a former US Secretary of State (1973-77); Assistant to the President for National Security Affairs (1969-74) and Professor of Government at Harvard University. Since 1977 he has been on the faculty of Georgetown University School of Foreign Service and a counsellor to CSIS.

Among his books are *Nuclear Weapons and Foreign Policy* (1957); *The Troubled Partnership: A Reappraisal of the Atlantic Alliance* (1965); *The White House Years* (1979); *For the Record* (1981) and *Years of Upheaval* (1982).

HELMUT KOHL, Chancellor of the Federal Republic of Germany since 1982; Chairman of the Christian Democratic Union (CDU) of Western Germany since 1973; Minister-President for Rheinland-Pfalz (1969-76); Leader of the Opposition, Bundestag (1976-82).

His publications include *Hausputz hinter den Fassaden* (1971); and *Zwischen Ideologie und Pragmatismus* (1973).

THIERRY DE MONTBRIAL, Director of the French Institute for International Relations since 1979 and Professor and Chairman of the Department of Economic Sciences at Ecole Polytechnique since 1974.

Among his publications are: *Economie théorique* (1971); *Le désordre économique mondial* (1974); and *Energie: le compte á rebours* (1978).

NORMAN PODHORETZ has been Editor-in-Chief of *Commentary* magazine in New York since 1960. He is author of *Doings and Undoings, The Fifties and After in American Writing* (1964); *Making It* (1968); *Breaking Ranks* (1979); and *The Present Danger* (1980).

RONALD REAGAN has been President of the United States of America since 1981. Governor of the State of California (1967-74); businessman, rancher and commentator on public policy (1975-80). Served as captain in the USA Air Force (1942-45) and co-founder of the Screen Actors Guild and its president (1947-52, 1959).

JOHN E. RIELLY has been President of the Chicago Council on Foreign Relations since 1974. He served with the alliance for Progress Programme in the Department of State (1961-62); as foreign policy assistant to Senator and Vice-President Hubert H. Humphrey (1963-69); and as consultant to the National Security Council in the White House from 1979-80.

Among his publications are: *American Public Opinion and US Foreign Policy* (editor, 1979); *American Public Opinion and US Foreign Policy* (editor, 1975); and *Development Today: A New Look at US Relations with the Poor Countries* (1972).

JAMES R. SCHLESINGER is a former US Secretary of Defence (1973-75), and Secretary of Energy (1977-79). Earlier he served as Chairman of the US Atomic Energy Commission and Director of the Office of Management and Budget. Since 1979 he has been senior adviser to the CSIS, Georgetown University, and Lehman Bros. Kuhn Loeb, Inc.

FRANZ-JOSEPH SCHULZE (ret.) was General Commander in Chief of Allied Forces Central Europe from 1977 to 1979 and Deputy Chief of

Staff, Plans and Operations, Allied Command Europe, from 1973 to 1976.

HENRI SIMONET was Foreign Minister of Belgium (1977-80); Minister of Economic Affairs (1972); Vice-President of the Commission of the European Communities (1973-77); and Mayor of Anderlecht (1966-84).

His publications include various books and articles on economics, and financial and political subjects.

MARIO SOARES has been Prime Minister since the Portuguese general election in April 1983. He was Minister for Foreign Affairs in the first, second and third provisional governments after the revolution of 1974. He also served as Prime Minister of the first and second constitutional governments until 1978. He has been a vice-president of the Socialist International since 1976.

FRANZ JOSEF STRAUSS has been Minister President of Bavaria and Chairman of the Christian Social Union (CSU) since 1961. He is a former Minister of Nuclear Energy (1955-56), Minister of Defence (1952-62) and Minister of Finance (1966-69). In 1979 he was nominated by the CDU/CSU factions as candidate for the Chancellorship but lost to Helmut Schmidt.

ROBERT S. STRAUSS is former Chairman of the Democratic Party's National Committee (1972-77); special US representative for trade negotiations with rank of Ambassador in the office of the President (1977-79); President Carter's personal representative for Middle East negotiations (1979-81), and currently practises law in Washington, DC.

SHUNJI TAOKA is senior defence correspondent for *Asahi Shimbun* in Tokyo. He is a graduate of Waseda University, Tokyo School of Political Science, and in 1974-75 was a Fulbright visiting lecturer at the School of Foreign Service, Georgetown University.

MICHEL TATU has been editorial writer for *Le Monde* in Paris since 1980. Earlier he was the paper's correspondent in Moscow (1957-64), in Eastern Europe (1966-69), and then Foreign Editor (1971-77) and correspondent in Washington.

Among his published books are: *Power in the Kremlin* (1969) and *La Bataille des Euromissiles* (1983).

MARGARET THATCHER, the first British female Prime Minister, took office on May 4, 1979. She was elected as Leader of the Conservative Party and Leader of the Opposition in February 1975. Prior to that

(1970-74) she was Secretary of State for Education & Science and (1961-64) Parliamentary Secretary, Ministry of Pensions & National Insurance.

BUNROKU YOSHINO was Ambassador Extraordinary and Plenipotentiary, Permanent Delegation of Japan to the OECD; Deputy Minister of Foreign Affairs; Japanese Representative at the GATT ministerial meeting in Geneva in 1982, and since 1982 has been President of the Japanese Institute for International Economic Studies.